ng

on

ities

chers

. Flynn

HEINEMANN
Portsmouth, NH

Heinemann
A division of Reed Elsevier Inc.
361 Hanover Street
Portsmouth, NH 03801–3912
www.heinemanndrama.com

Offices and agents throughout the world

The authors and publisher wish to thank those who have generously given permission to reprint borrowed material.

Excerpts from *Freedom Train: The Story of Harriet Tubman* by Dorothy Sterling. Published by Scholastic, Inc. Copyright by Dorothy Sterling. Reprinted by permission of the author.

Excerpts from "Shakespearean Slide Shows" by Rosalind Flynn. From English Journal (Vol. 92, No. 1, September 2002). Copyright © 2002 by the National Council of Teachers of English. Reprinted by permission.

Library of Congress Cataloging-in-Publication Data
Kelner, Lenore Blank.
  A dramatic approach to reading comprehension : strategies and activities
for classroom teachers / Lenore Blank Kelner and Rosalind M. Flynn.
    p. cm.
  Includes bibliographical references.
  ISBN 0-325-00794-2 (alk. paper)
  1. Reading comprehension—Study and teaching (Elementary)—United States.
2. Reading comprehension—Study and teaching (Elementary)—Activity
programs—United States. 3. Drama in education—United States. I. Flynn,
Rosalind M. II. Title.
LB1573.7.K45 2006
372.47—dc22   2006001417

Editor: Lisa A. Barnett
Production: Elizabeth Valway
Typesetter: Argosy Publishing
Cover design: Night & Day Design
Manufacturing: Steve Bernier

Printed in the United States of America on acid-free paper
10 09 08 07 06 VP 1 2 3 4 5

This book is dedicated to the memory of
Dr. John C. Carr
1929–1999

The connections you cultivated created the possibility
of this book. You lifted the veil and allowed us to see.
Jack, we are forever grateful.

CONTENTS

FOREWORD

Drama is a significant reading intervention. If you were to perfect just one drama technique from this book, it could change your literacy time by cracking open the words of a text and letting children live inside the book. That is the essence of why we all work so hard to help every student become a good reader—so that students can taste how delicious it is to really know and love a book. This book is inviting you to take a delightful journey.

Teachers see immediate classroom results when using drama. Students eagerly anticipate drama, showing us their motivation to be actively involved in text. During drama, they begin to demonstrate surprising insights that observers may have not seen before. After drama the class discussions become more engaging and to the point. Weeks later, students still make references to the characters and the book, and the important ideas and new words carry over into new conversations. Drama makes a significant impact on students.

Observers of drama often want to see the benefits of this reading tool in their own reading workshops but wonder how to do it all without a theatre background or a resident drama specialist. And so readers of this book will love that everything they need to know is right here. This is critical because the role of the teacher is so essential to coaching students in building meaning as they work with a text. The influence of a good teacher with a wide repertoire of strategies for meeting the needs of a diverse group of students can change a child's reading life forever.

We know that there are a variety of barriers that prevent students from making meaning from text. Teachers and reading specialists, administrators and parents puzzle over each child and look for interventions that will help each one break down the barriers and become a strong reader. There are many good books that help us understand more about teaching word recognition, building reading fluency, introducing vocabulary, and catching students with weak phonemic awareness. This book will add to your teaching repertoire significant drama techniques that can be used to build the underlying strengths of attention, focus, memory, and motivation, so that students can truly engage in books and learn to think more deeply. Then each chapter will help you investigate a drama technique in ways that will teach children how to think. Students will be immersed in drama methods that scaffold the reading lesson for them so that they can begin to ask more questions, visualize the story, make inferences about the characters, and synthesize to find the most important ideas.

Those who work in the field of reading and want to open new doors of understanding for students will find the support they have been hoping for in this book.

The authors are offering you a wonderful gift for you and your students. Give yourself the chance to delve into a new way of working and enjoy it.

—Roberta Mantione

FOREWORD

Arts integration. It's the biggest trend in the field of arts education. Some say it is the future of the arts in American schools; some say the quality of learning it sparks makes it the future of schooling in general. The trend is driven by a belief that two separate but equal learning domains, art and another subject area, can be brought together in ways that synergistically advance the learning of both further than either could go alone.

Given the scarce commodity of time in our schools, arts integration is a bit of a gamble—can teachers afford to take time to open up a subject area through the arts? Will the gamble pay off in greater learning? Will connecting the arts to another subject matter dilute the arts learning? Good educators across the country are taking the gamble, in increasing numbers. In my travels, I see so much experimentation that we seem to have a laboratory of future schooling under way.

Arts integration doesn't always work. I have seen the arts used as a handmaiden to curricular material—the subject matter gets priority, and the arts are used to pep up a dull curriculum. I have seen the inverse as well, when the subject connection is really just an excuse for having a great art project.

A Dramatic Approach to Reading Comprehension, however, is a powerful and important contribution to our national experiment. Indeed, Lenore Blank Kelner and Rosalind M. Flynn erase the gamble of arts integration with a step-by-step process that ensures the quality of arts learning, and the literacy payoffs make integration more than worth the time involved. The next time you hear a doubter question the efficacy of arts-integrated learning, tell that traditionalist to shut up, and hand over a copy of this book.

The authors have created an extraordinarily complete example of arts-integrated learning that works for everyone. They have included all the pieces any educator needs. They based their process in the key that I find most essential too: engage young minds and hearts in the dynamic relevance of theatre work, and then guide that organic enthusiasm into literacy development in the natural flow of the invested learning.

Kelner and Flynn are deeply grounded in theatre art; not only are their activities authentic yet accessible, but even their prose has the bounce and vitality of a good actor. They are deeply aware of the spontaneous connections that spark between theatre work and literacy skills—sparks that lead to research verifying increased language arts test scores for students who experience theatre work like this.

Like the great teaching artists they are, Kelner and Flynn write for every educator, at any level of teaching experience or theatrical background. A novice can pick up this book and be running fast right away. Because the authors have distilled deep practices of the art to such inviting and unthreatening step-by-step activities, any teacher can guide students in authentic dramatic work in no time. Their activities are so inviting—I was glad to read the book alone in my house, so I could indulge in the fun of enacting a frustrated orchestra conductor and finding the words for how I appeared and felt. The activities catch the innately joyful, fun energy of theatre, and I found myself engaged in language learning without even knowing it. (By the way, a panicked bodybuilder is a very amusing sight.)

This comprehensive book even guides the reader to assess the learning that explodes in these adventures. This book takes the gamble out of arts-integrated learning, replacing it with joy, creative engagement, and learning that will play out in the short and long terms in the lives of teachers and students.

—Eric Booth

ACKNOWLEDGMENTS

We are grateful for the roles played by the many people in our lives and work whose efforts and ideas contributed to the contents of this book. We would especially like to recognize the inspiration and support of our editor, Lisa Barnett, who passed away recently. Lisa was a staunch advocate for drama in education. Often a lone voice of support for writers like us, her impact will continue to be profoundly felt by educators and students worldwide. Without her support, this and many other educational drama books would not have been published.

For years of support in shaping and sharing our work, thanks to Amy Duma, Barbara Shepherd, Lynne Silverstein, Jeanette Spencer McCune, and Darryl Ayers in The John F. Kennedy Center for the Performing Arts Education Department. And for their continuing support, thanks also to Mimi Flaherty and the Wolf Trap Institute for Early Learning Through the Arts. For the many ways in which hundreds of students locally and nationally taught us, we thank them and their teachers and principals, especially Sharon Avery, Keegan Callanan, Richard Chinn, Dr. Carol Dahlberg, Kiersten Drumm, Bessie Forrester, Jeffrey Peang-Meth, Arlene Permisohn, and Margaret O'Neill. For photographs and holding down the fort, thanks to Barbara Holden and Ali Oliver.

We express deep gratitude to Susan Denvir for her enthusiastic willingness to review our writing with the trained eye of a reading expert and for her helpful advice. In dual roles as colleagues and companions, there's no better supporting cast than the Gonks—Sean, Judy, Cynthia, Stacey, and Marcia. And finally, for best performances as patient, positive, fun, and fabulous family members, we thank (in order of appearance) Paul, Mal, Audra, Justine, Timmy, and Dennis.

1 Drama and Reading Comprehension
Merging Purposes

Background

The idea for this book grew out of work that began in the fall of 2003. The senior program director of the Professional Development Opportunities for Teachers at the John F. Kennedy Center for the Performing Arts in Washington, D.C., was inspired by the book *Weaving Through Words: Using the Arts to Teach Reading Comprehension Strategies* (Mantione and Smead 2003). To focus teacher training on the arts activities that support reading comprehension described in the book, she assembled a team of specialists in drama, music, dance, visual art, and reading. Each arts specialist teamed with the reading specialist and led a one-day session of a multipart course for classroom teachers. Each session focused on a different arts strategy recommended in *Weaving Through Words*. The educational drama specialists were this book's authors. Lenore Blank Kelner's focus was the role-drama technique called character interview. Rosalind Flynn's focus was tableau.

The authors of *Weaving Through Words* urge teachers to employ the drama techniques tableau, character interview, and process drama. They are absolutely right that drama is a powerful teaching and learning tool, especially when it is merged with reading comprehension objectives.

Weaving Through Words provides excellent advocacy for integrating the arts with reading comprehension, but as drama specialists who work regularly with teachers and students, we recognized a need to go beyond the brief descriptions of drama activities in that book. For meaningful and successful applications of the drama techniques, teachers need thorough descriptions of all the layers of an effective drama lesson. For drama to enhance reading comprehension, students need skill building in the art form and a specific focus on its relationship to and support of reading comprehension.

This book grew out of the work we each did to prepare for daylong sessions focused on the planning and implementing of just one drama strategy. That work was preceded by years of drama work in classrooms and teacher workshops around the United States. Focusing classroom drama on reading comprehension strategies, however, honed and sharpened our work, increasing its relevance for teachers.

The six reading comprehension strategies detailed in *Weaving Through Words* and drawn from *Mosaic of Thought: Teaching Comprehension in a Reader's Workshop* (Keene and Zimmerman 1997) and *Strategies That Work: Teaching Comprehension to Enhance Understanding* (Harvey and Goudvis 2000) are:

- developing sensory images
- building and activating schema
- questioning
- determining importance
- inferring
- synthesis

Since those fall 2003 presentations, we have continued to develop our dramatic approaches to reading comprehension in classrooms and teacher workshops around the country. We hope that this book increases teachers' understanding of how to integrate drama and reading comprehension effectively.

Arts Integration

Integration occurs when separate parts or elements are combined into a unified whole. In education, arts integration refers to the equal incorporation of an art form and another content area into lessons so that objectives in both subjects are addressed. To integrate an art form with another area of curriculum, authentic connections must exist between the two subjects.

The teaching and learning methods may be unique to drama, for example, but the material explored within a dramatic context is often shared with other disciplines (Somers 2001). These authentic connections make what the Chicago Arts Partnerships in Education (CAPE) call an "elegant fit"—uniting separate pieces of the curriculum to create a new and more satisfying whole (Burnaford, Aprill, and Weiss 2001).

Drama and reading comprehension share a multitude of natural links; fluency, expressive oral interpretation, connecting new with prior knowledge, insight into character values and motives, and reader response are just a few (Catterall and Wagner 2002). Simply stated, students demonstrate with voice and body (drama) that they understand the text (reading comprehension).

The goal of this book, therefore, is arts integration—equally incorporating skills in drama and reading comprehension into all lessons. Each lesson's drama objectives are just as important as its reading comprehension objectives. Where reading comprehension is enhanced by drama, it does not occur at the expense of superficial learning in the art form (Perkins 2001).

Project Zero is an educational research group at the Graduate School of Education at Harvard University. Part of its mission is to understand and enhance learning, thinking, and creativity in the arts. One of its projects, REAP (Reviewing Education and the Arts Project), stresses that the arts in education must not be justified solely or primarily by how well they transfer learning to academic areas of the curriculum (Somers 2001). The strong learning in both drama and reading comprehension advocated in this book supports this belief. The classroom use of drama is not justified because it transfers learning to reading comprehension. Each subject complements the other, leading, ideally, to increased abilities in drama and reading comprehension. Both subjects are equally important.

Drama and Reading Comprehension

Scores of books, articles, and reports endorse the use of drama in conjunction with reading comprehension. Theoretical and empirical support for the belief that drama can improve reading comprehension is also plentiful (Catterall 2002; Podlozny 2001; Rose et al. 2000; DuPont 1992).

As anyone who has ever read and staged a play for performance knows, drama requires the same skills that are fundamental for reading comprehension (McMaster 1998). Actors and directors examine a script, picturing the characters, scenery, and reactions to imaginary sights, sounds, smells, tastes, and textures. They read the lines of dialogue to discover important information and make inferences based on both the playwright's words and their personal experiences and prior knowledge. Everyone involved works toward a synthesis of the text—the performance of the play.

Theatre professionals concentrate, for example, on the importance of character study (which begins with reading comprehension) in order to perform genuinely on the stage or in film, writes Catterall (2002). They continually return to the script and ask questions about why characters behave in certain ways, how characters should move or react, where they should be positioned in relation to other characters, and how a line should be delivered. These thorough theatrical reading habits are noted by writers who advocate integrating drama with reading comprehension: "In drama's highest form, professional actors are lauded for their ability to understand the motivations and emotions that their characters experience" (Rose et al. 2000).

Researchers also confirm that the mental requirements for understanding drama are similar to those for reading (Sun 2003). Visualization, or mental imaging, for example, is a vital component of both drama and reading comprehension. To create a meaningful story, actors must read and then envision a scene and all its elements. They need a clear image of the scene's contents, characters, sequence, and timing (Rose et al. 2000). If students engage in this same process of creating mental images, reading becomes less dependent on memory of text and more focused on the visual images described. Readers, then, are more likely to store, retain, and recall more about what they read (Rose et al. 2000). McMaster (1998) agrees that mental imaging is a comprehension strategy that aids readers in storing information for retrieval. When students act out material they have read, they gain valuable practice in this strategy.

"Research shows consistent positive associations between dramatic enactment and reading comprehension, oral story understanding, and written story understanding," writes Catterall (2002) in *Critical Links: Learning in the Arts and Student Academic and Social Development*. Some researchers go even further and assert that drama-based reading instruction can improve students' reading skills more than traditional reading instruction (Rose et al. 2000). Perhaps this is because theatre is a language-rich environment that actively engages students with issues of language (Catterall, Chapleau, and Iwanaga 2000). Maybe it is because drama activities can easily be structured to focus students directly on print and expand their receptive written language skills (McMaster 1998).

Like actors who re-create scenes, students engaged in the reading process must learn to segment the pieces of a story. They must also learn to understand the meaningful relationships between the segments that create the whole of a story (Rose et al. 2000). Several key ingredients of story understanding, in fact, are better conveyed through drama: main idea, character identification, and character motivation. These ingredients are essential elements of comprehension (Catterall and Wagner 2002).

Perhaps the most persuasive support for merging drama with reading comprehension comes from the work of Project Zero's REAP (Reviewing Education and the Arts Project). This project examined an enormous number of studies on the effects of arts instruction on cognition and learning in nonarts areas. The relationship of classroom drama and verbal skills was one of only three areas in which REAP found reliable causal links.

REAP's examination of eighty studies investigating the relationship between drama instruction and achievement in verbal areas such as reading comprehension, oral language ability, and writing showed that classroom drama had a strong positive effect on six of seven verbal areas. The researcher concluded that participation in drama increases students' vocabulary, oral language, and writing skills, whether applied to the stories enacted or to entirely new stories. It also increases their reading ability for new texts (Podlozny 2001).

The Theatrical Roots of Classroom Drama

Classroom drama activities have their roots in the art form of theatre. Yet, in a survey of educational drama research studies in *Critical Links*, Catterall (2002) finds no studies containing an explicit identification of drama as an art form and practically no references to theatre as being fundamental to drama. The studies use drama as a teaching methodology, but mention of its relationship to the conventions and practices of theatre is minimal at best. This omission is also prevalent in books and articles about the use of drama as a learning method.

Additionally, in published materials describing drama used in classrooms, it is rare to find references to instances in which drama experiences did not go as smoothly as anticipated. Also rare is advice on how to work with students to achieve beneficial drama learning experiences. Drama, when effectively implemented, draws heavily from excellence in elements of the art form of theatre.

This book, therefore, stresses classroom drama's theatrical roots, such as examining a text for meaning, comprehension, and interpretation. It also emphasizes the importance of the imagination/mind, voice, and body; the willing suspension of disbelief; concentration and ensemble; creation of dialogue; vocal expression and projection; rehearsal and revision; and the role of the audience. Strengthening these theatrical elements contributes to more effective lessons involving reading comprehension or any content area explored via drama. The art form of theatre, from which educational drama springs, is integral to all the classroom drama activities described in this book. A discussion of these ideas continues in greater depth in Chapter 2.

Drama Methods: Providing Clarity for Teachers

"Drama is an invaluable tool for educators because it is one of the few vehicles of instruction that can support every aspect of literacy development" (McMaster 1998, 574). True as that statement may be and despite the enormous demonstrated value of drama for student learning, there still exists a gap between teachers' understanding of drama's worth and their actual use of it in the classroom. Overwhelmingly, teachers remain unfamiliar with how to facilitate dramatic activities (Sun 2003). Catterall (2002) agrees, noting that while teachers may be supportive of drama as a learning method, many do not use it in their classrooms. Most do not know what to do, how to do it successfully, or even where to begin to incorporate drama.

Teachers' lack of familiarity with drama methods is not a new discovery. In 1976, Betty Jane Wagner, an internationally recognized authority on the educational uses of drama, expressed these same sentiments. In her book about British educational drama expert Dorothy Heathcote, Wagner writes, "Heathcote feels that for too long we have been concentrating on training drama specialists, a process that has widened the gap between what these specially trained persons do with groups of children and what ordinary teachers do. The time has come to show all teachers— ordinary day-in and day-out classroom teachers—how they can use drama at times to achieve something that cannot be attained as effectively in any other way" (Wagner 1976, 15). To see how basic arts learning outcomes are integral to the comprehensive K–12 education of every American student, see the National Standards for Theatre on page 220.

How do we take children to a fictional world? What benefits do we expect for the child in entering the fictional? These questions are posed by Somers (2001), who identifies them as priorities in educational drama research. One reason for the sparseness in the educational uses of drama may lie in assumptions authors make about teachers' grasp of drama methods. In the many articles and books about successful classroom dramatizations, for example, the drama instructions to teachers are overwhelmingly minimal:

"Have students act out . . ."

"Create a skit to illustrate . . ."

"Place the students in roles . . ."

"Cast the students as the characters . . ."

"Create tableaux or frozen scenes of . . ."

"Have students pantomime . . ."

"Instruct students to enact the scene . . ."

"Have students take turns portraying a character . . ."

Effective use of drama in the classroom requires skill building in the art form. Drama methods can be incredibly powerful, but more so with careful planning, scaffolding of drama activities, and the coaching of students toward proficiency in elements of drama and theatre. Successful use of these processes requires more than a one-sentence instruction. This book, therefore, seeks to provide teachers with a greater understanding of all the facets that contribute to their students' successful classroom dramatizations and increased reading comprehension. Its goal is to make what is implicit to educational drama specialists explicit for classroom teachers.

Teachers who identify with any of the following statements will find their concerns addressed in the upcoming chapters:

- "I tried to have students 'act something out' and it failed miserably."

- "While acting, my students kept dissolving in laughter, and their drama was not very good."

- "I had high hopes for what I could accomplish using drama, but in reality, things didn't go so well."

- "My students really respond to hands-on, kinesthetic, active learning experiences like drama, but I have never done any acting."

- "When I think of drama, I think of unproductive chaos in the classroom."

- "I have no idea where to start in the planning of a dramatization."

- "How can I do drama? I have no theatre background whatsoever."

- "Drama is too time-consuming."

The presentation of each drama strategy and activity in this book seeks to share with teachers the thinking, planning, and implementing that experienced educational drama specialists bring to their lessons. The basic skills and procedures that teachers may use to introduce and integrate four drama strategies (story dramatization, character interviews, tableau, and human slide show) with six reading comprehension strategies (developing sensory images, building and activating schema, questioning, determining importance, inferring, and synthesis) constitute the content of this book.

The Format of This Book

This book is written as a guidebook for the teacher with little to no experience in drama or theatre. It contains information, advice, directions, steps, tips, charts, lists, photos, and ideas all addressed to teachers for use with students in grades 1 through 8. Chapter 2 provides definitions, supplies background information, and identifies the learning objectives in drama and reading comprehension that anchor all the applications of classroom drama detailed in later chapters.

Chapter 3 focuses on preparing students for participation in drama and offers a selection of acting tool- and skill-building activities intended to increase students' abilities to achieve the drama objectives. Chapter 4 examines the topic of assessment in drama and reading comprehension, offering a variety of assessment tasks, checklists, and definitions of terms.

Chapters 5 through 8 are each devoted to a specific drama strategy—story dramatization, character interviews, tableau, and human slide show. Each chapter begins with a definition of the drama strategy, the roles of the teacher and students, the rationale for the strategy's use in relation to reading comprehension, and its drama and theatre connections. A step-by-step process for classroom implementation of the drama strategy follows, including:

1. preparation for using the drama strategy, including teacher planning and student preparation
2. conducting the drama strategy
3. reflecting on the drama strategy, including assessment from both drama and reading comprehension perspectives

Interspersed throughout these drama strategy chapters are boxed sections—titled "Teaching Tip," "Dramatic Detail," or "Dealing with Difficulties"—intended to help teachers successfully implement the drama strategies.

These chapters are followed by a collection of supplemental materials to further support teachers who wish to increase their experience with drama in the classroom. They include a bibliography of works and literature cited, recommended reading, suggested books for story dramatization and character interviews, the National Standards for Theatre, and a glossary of drama and theatre terms.

2 *Drama and Reading Comprehension*
Background and Objectives

Effective integration of drama with reading comprehension requires clear objectives in each of these content areas. This chapter defines and provides background information on drama and reading comprehension, and lists the objectives in each area that ground the content of this book. Each chapter that follows refers back to the objectives stated here.

Drama

The term *drama* is used to describe the classroom activities and strategies presented throughout this book. Other names for drama in educational settings include *creative drama*, *creative dramatics*, *educational drama*, *dramatic play*, *classroom drama*, *educational drama*, *playmaking*, and *improvisation*.

Drama, especially as it is used in classrooms for learning purposes, exists for the benefit of the participants. Although it uses many theatre terms and conventions, its focus is on the process of the experience for students and teachers, not on a product created for others. Theatre, on the other hand, is a disciplined artistic experience in which artists work and rework the same material with the goal of performing it perfectly for an audience.

The word *drama* comes from the Greek word *dran*, meaning "to do or to act." Students and teachers do, act, and create in the moment—improvisationally. What they create is not meant for anyone else's eyes. Their acting and dialogue are generated spontaneously for their own self-expression and learning. Using no sets and few, if any, costumes and props, drama does not result in a polished production. Drama revolves around the creative process.

The participants are simultaneously the playwrights, directors, actors, audience, and critics. As playwrights, they decide what story to tell and what words to speak. As directors, they decide what drama strategies to use and which actors play which roles. As actors, they play the characters in the drama. As audience members, they observe the acting of others. As critics, they assess the dramatic experience and reflect on how to improve future presentations.

Drama activities in the classroom have evolved from many sources: theatre games, acting exercises, actors' characterization work, staging techniques, theatre conventions, children's theatre, and understandings of children's play and the creative process. In the United States, many state and local school systems have adopted standards for the teaching of drama and theatre based on the National Standards for Theatre Education (see page 220 for a description of these standards).

In drama, participants *live in the moment* of the action. By using their imaginations, participants play roles and experience what others think and feel. Drama allows them to experience empathy for other people, comprehend complex situations, consider varying viewpoints and opinions, and feel the consequences of choices and behaviors. All of these dramatic experiences may cause participants to change their personal feelings or attitudes, thus impacting their real-life choices.

Drama Strategies

A drama strategy is a specific way of involving participants in a dramatization. The drama strategies included in this text involve students and teachers in thinking and working like actors, directors, playwrights, audience members, and critics. These strategies invite students and teachers to take text on the *page* and use it on the *stage*. The stage for drama is the classroom.

This book focuses on four drama strategies:

- *Story Dramatization*—Student actors enact scenes or a single scene from a story using their own words.

- *Character Interviews*—Role dramas in which student actors portray characters from a book and answer a series of interview questions.

- *Tableau*—A silent frozen picture made by student actors striking poses to represent a significant moment in a story.

- *Human Slide Show*—A sequence of tableaux presented in chronological order.

Some of the strategies require students to create their own dialogue based on information from the text. Students do so by reading and exploring the text, subtext, character traits, and character motivations.

Other strategies rely on visual images. Students create stage pictures based on information from the text. Students do this by delving into the essence of a scene to uncover its implicit and explicit meanings.

Drama Mentors

Many practitioners and authors set the stage for the work that led to this book. Their contributions to the field of educational drama influenced the practices of this book's authors and thousands of drama teachers and specialists worldwide. Whether their goal for using drama in classrooms was to promote children's social, emotional, and physical well-being, to develop techniques to elicit creative expression from children, or to involve them in a creative process, these mentors understood that drama is deeply connected to what children do naturally—play.

One American writer about drama was Winifred Ward. At the start of her 1930 text *Creative Dramatics*, she claimed that creative drama allows children to "develop plays out of their own thoughts, imaginations, and emotions." (3) She felt that dramatizing stories either from literature or original tales was an extremely "valuable avenue" leading to student growth.

British educator Brian Way was another important voice. His book *Development Through Drama* (1967) is filled with practical advice, ideas, and instructions for using drama in schools. Way's primary concern, however, remained not with the development of drama, but with the development of people. He wrote about the ways in which drama could be a valuable tool for teaching other subjects. Way's contribution to teachers was a wealth of concrete drama exercises to develop areas such as students' concentration, imagination, and improvisational skills. He provided definite direction for educators who wanted to add drama to the curriculum.

Nellie McCaslin was a tireless writer about creative drama and children's theatre. She constantly updated her work to reflect the latest trends in the fields. She and author-educator Geraldine Brain Siks articulated the shared objectives of drama and education. They clearly described how drama promotes creativity, social, emotional, and physical development, communication skills, character building (morals, values), and self-esteem.

Learning through drama, specifically using drama teaching methods to enable students to reach a greater understanding of themselves and their world, is an approach popularized by British educator Dorothy Heathcote (Wright 1985). Heathcote's work went beyond the drama objectives of personal development and social adjustment. Beginning in the early 1960s, Heathcote used drama not to reinforce facts, but to explore issues, principles, consequences, and social responsibilities (Bolton 1985).

Her drama work incorporated children's existing personal knowledge about human behavior with the subject matter being studied. Heathcote believed that when you put yourself into other people's shoes, using your own personal experience to understand their point of view, you discover more than you knew when you started (Johnson and O'Neill 1984).

Carole Tarlington's (1985) writings on tableau and Ruth B. Heinig's (1992) wealth of practical drama activities and techniques influenced the ideas in this book. The use of role drama as described by Cecily O'Neill and Alan Lambert (1987), Carole Tarlington and Patrick Verriour (1991), and Norah Morgan and Juliana Saxton (1987) also contributed to strengthening the practices detailed within these pages. Years of studying with and observing firsthand the educational drama work of the late John C. Carr were priceless in shaping the dramatic approaches to reading comprehension that follow.

Each strategy included in this text builds on the work of these and other individuals and adds an arts-integration dimension by combining the teaching of drama with the teaching of reading comprehension. There is a natural connection between the two subjects and both are enhanced when they become partners in students' learning.

Drama Objectives

In order to use drama in the classroom, students must think and behave primarily like actors. To do so, students need to understand the actors' basic tools and skills. Just as students use tools (paper, pencils, desks, etc.) and skills (reading, writing, listening, etc.) to perform at school, actors use tools and skills to perform on stage.

The three basic acting tools are *imagination/mind*, *voice*, and *body*. To be proficient, actors must use these tools well. In addition, there are a variety of complex skills that effective actors use. For classroom drama work, however, students need the basics. The two basic acting skills are *cooperation (working as an ensemble)* and *concentration*. To participate in classroom drama, it is essential that students develop these tools and skills.

The Basic Acting Tools

IMAGINATION/MIND

To participate meaningfully in the fictional world of a drama experience, students will use their imaginations and minds.

Imagination When they plan, enact, observe, and reflect upon their work, students will:

- agree to pretend (willingly suspend disbelief) to be characters and objects in different settings and situations

- interact with real and/or imagined characters and objects

- react to imaginary sights, sounds, smells, tastes, and textures

Mind When they plan, enact, observe, and reflect upon their work, students will:

- demonstrate comprehension of the basic acting tools and skills
  - identify the basic acting tools and skills
  - use drama vocabulary accurately
  - analyze when and how the basic acting tools and skills are used in the drama experience
- analyze a character's personality, traits, thoughts, and feelings
  - find personal connections with characters
- differentiate reality from fantasy
- recall and/or retell the predetermined story in correct sequence
- reflect upon dramatic work to improve its quality

VOICE

When they play roles, students will use aspects of voice to communicate information about their characters and the drama's circumstances. While acting, students will:

- vary vocal tone and pitch to create character voices and/or sound effects

- create and deliver dialogue that is *in character*—accurately communicates information about the character and the drama's circumstances

- speak with expression that reflects the personality, traits, thoughts, and feelings of characters

    - *project*—speak loudly enough to be heard

    - *articulate*—speak clearly enough to be understood

    - *modify Word Tempo*—speak slowly enough to be understood

BODY

When they play roles, students will use aspects of body to communicate information about their characters and the drama's circumstances. While acting, students will:

- modify posture, poses, gestures, movements, and/or walk

    - use energy when modifying body

- use facial expressions that communicate the thoughts and feelings of characters

The Basic Acting Skills

COOPERATION

Because drama is a collaborative art form, students will work as members of an ensemble. When they plan, enact, observe, and reflect upon their work, students will:

- create a community of actors who work together and support each other as members of a team

    - follow instructions

        - listen to peers and the teacher

        - remain silent when cued

        - remain frozen when cued

    - collaborate with peers and the teacher

        - alter actions and responses based on *side coaching*—suggestions and prompts provided by the teacher during the drama

        - demonstrate respect for ideas contributed by peers

When they play roles, students will use aspects of concentration to maintain the effectiveness of the drama experience. While acting, students will:

- focus intently on the given drama task
  - remain in character
    - speak only as the character
    - control inappropriate laughter
- attend and respond appropriately to the other characters
- disregard actions and noises unrelated to the drama

An Additional Vital Basic: The Audience

Participation in a drama experience often requires that students observe the work of others. When they are audience members, students will:

- differentiate reality from fantasy
  - agree to pretend (willingly suspend disbelief), that is, to accept the fictional world of the drama
- demonstrate respect for the work of the actors
  - watch quietly
  - listen carefully
  - refrain from distracting others
  - show appreciation

Reading Comprehension

Reading comprehension is the ability to read and understand text. It is more than decoding words, phrases, and sentences because comprehension means that readers get the message, get the picture, see the point of and grasp the meaning of the words on the page.

Reading Comprehension Strategies

A reading comprehension strategy is a specific way that readers engage with text in order to deepen their understanding of it. Reading comprehension strategies do not work in isolation. They are simultaneous processes that occur during and following reading.

This book focuses on six reading comprehension strategies:

- *Developing Sensory Images*—The use of some or all of the five senses to imagine what the text describes in words.

- *Building and Activating Schema*—The development and application of background knowledge to increase understanding of the text.

- *Questioning*—The use of questions to clarify and speculate about elements of the text.

- *Determining Importance*—The ability to distinguish significant text information from minor details.

- *Inferring*—The ability to interpret or draw conclusions about what is not directly stated in the text.

- *Synthesis*—The ability to create something new based on information in the text.

Reading Comprehension Mentors

Guiding students to unlock their abilities to truly make meaning of what they read has been the subject of countless articles, books, manuals, and dissertations. There are hundreds of theories, methods, and practices, each with its own terminology and strategies, intended to lead students to full comprehension of text.

The foundation for the aspects of reading comprehension in this book come from the work described in *Weaving Through Words*, by Roberta D. Mantione and Sabine Smead (2003), *Strategies That Work*, by Stephanie Harvey and Anne Goudvis (2000), and *Mosaic of Thought*, by Ellin Oliver Keene and Susan Zimmerman (1997).

The reading comprehension approach developed in these texts is fresh, exciting, simple, and yet broad based. It embraces fundamentals found in many other approaches, but instead of being skill driven, this approach is more global. Individual reading skills are still present, but they are embedded in larger reading comprehension strategies.

The approach is based on research done in the 1980s that investigated the reading strategies proficient readers use to understand a text. The authors of the aforementioned texts believe that teachers can strengthen students' reading comprehension with specific instruction in these reading comprehension strategies. When students are aware of how they can better understand a text, they become more thoughtful and capable readers. These authors advocate that students should understand both the content of what they read and the processes they use to make that understanding occur.

Reading Comprehension Objectives

In addition to the drama objectives established for each of the drama strategies in this text, there are reading comprehension objectives. Clarifying these objectives sets clear goals for students, helps students develop skills, and sets the stage for more accurate assessment.

Developing Sensory Images

To enhance their understanding of a text, students will use multiple senses to create mental images when they read. Students will:

- visualize the setting, characters, and action of the text (create a mental movie)
- imagine the sights, sounds, smells, tastes, and textures described in the text

Building and Activating Schema

To more deeply comprehend what they read, students will consider how their life and learning experiences are similar to those described in a text. Students will:

- make connections among various parts of the text
- make connections between the text and other texts they have read (text to text)
- make connections between the text and their personal experiences (text to self) and prior knowledge (text to world)

Questioning

To explore unresolved issues, concerns, and ideas raised during and after reading a text, students will engage in questioning. Students will ask or develop questions that:

- clarify evidence in the text
- probe for deeper meaning
- seek to discover new information
- promote wondering
- speculate on possibilities
- search for answers to problems

Determining Importance

To find the essentials in a text, students will distinguish between the main ideas and the details of what they read. Students will:

- demonstrate comprehension of the important elements of the text
  - identify setting, characters, conflict, obstacles, and resolution
  - list the sequence of key events
    - retell the plot (beginning, middle, and end)
- demonstrate an understanding of the author's intent
  - determine the text's primary message

Inferring

To extend and enrich the meaning of a text, students will draw conclusions and make interpretations based on information provided, but not specifically stated, in the text. Students will:

- make predictions
- discover the implied information within the text—read between the lines
- combine clues found in the text with prior knowledge to make logical guesses

Synthesis

To demonstrate their understanding of a text, students will take information from what they have read, combine it with prior knowledge, and create something new. Students will:

- summarize and paraphrase the main points of the text
- connect the text's main ideas with larger concepts and issues
- generalize and/or make judgments about the text
- extend and apply the information in the text to different contexts
- respond personally to the text
    - form new ideas, opinions, or beliefs
    - gain new perspectives

Integrating Drama and Reading Comprehension

There are strong, natural, and meaningful connections between reading comprehension and drama. Basic acting training and the very purposes of drama dovetail beautifully with the reading comprehension strategies. Each chapter of this book explores these connections in detail.

Combining drama with reading comprehension strengthens students' abilities in both subjects. Using reading comprehension strategies within a dramatic context gives students the skills and awareness of what they need when they approach a text. One teacher in Oklahoma compared integrating drama and reading comprehension to training for a marathon: "When my students use drama with these reading comprehension skills, it's like they are working out in the gym. They are training and developing their muscles so they can run the race . . . they can read and understand a text."

Another teacher in inner-city Washington, D.C., agreed: "Comprehension goes through the roof when I use drama with my students."

Qualities of an Integrated Lesson

An arts-integrated lesson is designed to address objectives in both the art form curriculum (drama) and the nonarts curriculum (reading comprehension). Students should be aware of both sets of objectives, all of which should be measurable and, therefore, assessable. Posting the objectives for the students helps guide them in meeting the lesson's objectives.

A high-quality arts-integrated drama and reading comprehension lesson includes:

- clearly stated and explained objectives in both drama and reading comprehension

- an acting tool- and/or skill-building activity or warm-up that teaches or reinforces one or more drama objective

- a drama strategy that encompasses both sets of stated objectives

- reflection on the effectiveness of the lesson based on the objectives

- revision of the drama to allow students to implement understandings gained during the reflection

- assessment from both drama and reading comprehension perspectives

An Arts-Integration Challenge

Teachers are generally familiar with a variety of theories and practices regarding reading comprehension. Only when teachers also know enough about an art form, however, can they implement fully arts-integrated lessons. A major goal of this book is to increase teachers' understanding of the art form of drama to promote its frequent, confident, and effective use. Teachers who strengthen their knowledge and skills in drama and combine them with existing reading comprehension knowledge and skills are more fully prepared to meet the challenge of successfully integrating these two subjects.

The next chapter concentrates on expanding teachers' proficiency with drama. Its focus is on ways and means of preparing students to use drama successfully and productively in the classroom.

3 *Preparing for Drama*

Setting the Stage for Successful Classroom Dramas

Establishing consistent procedures and guidelines for using drama in the classroom ensures that students understand expectations. Developing students' mastery of the basic acting tools and skills outlined in Chapter 2 helps them become more proficient actors. This groundwork also increases the likelihood that drama experiences will be effective and positive for all.

This chapter includes suggestions for establishing fundamental procedures that serve as a strong foundation for all drama experiences. It also includes a series of acting tool- and skill-building activities intended to strengthen students' abilities.

Secure the Students' Agreement to Pretend

A fundamental element necessary for any theatre experience is the willing suspension of disbelief. Audiences must willingly accept the illusions and conventions of a theatre performance in order for the experience to be of any value. Audiences agree to accept an artistic reality.

Agreeing to pretend simply states this implicit understanding between audiences and actors in a positive way. In the theatre, actors agree to pretend that they are characters in a different setting speaking their own words and moving in their own ways for the first time. In truth, the actors have rehearsed and memorized lines and blocking (movement on stage) that they repeatedly perform during the run of a play. To complete the theatrical experience, the audience must agree to pretend that the action on stage is real and is happening for the first time. To do otherwise diminishes the overall effect.

Emphasizing this concept to students prior to classroom drama work reinforces the connection of the learning activities to the art form of theatre and establishes *agreeing to pretend* as a necessary element of drama. Young students overwhelmingly approach drama with enthusiasm, so you do not need to spend much time and effort securing their agreement to pretend. With older students, however, acknowledging the element of pretense and connecting it to the work of stage and movie actors can help students invest in the drama. Classroom drama succeeds only when the participants—both actors and audience—agree to work together, pretend, and commit to the experience.

Define the Acting Area

Drama can take place in any size space—big or small, a narrow portable classroom or a cavernous all-purpose room. The key to using the space well is determining where the acting will occur and establishing clear procedures for how the students will arrange themselves in preparation for participation: Where will the students be when they act? Where will they be when they are the audience? How many students can the acting area accommodate? If classroom furniture needs to be moved to create the acting area, how will this be accomplished?

The ideal classroom setup for the acting tool- and skill-building activities in this chapter is a clear space that is big enough for all students to stand, move, and sit comfortably. Students may sit in chairs, at their desks, or on the floor. Student seating will vary based on the activity and the behavioral nature of the class.

Here are some recommendations for defining the acting area in your classroom:

- Decide where your acting area will be and keep it the same for each drama experience.

- Decide whether your students will need chairs when they are audience members or whether all or some of them may sit on the floor, at desks, or on desktops.

- Preplan where desks and chairs will be moved and in which order.

- Provide specific instructions to explain to students how moving the furniture will happen. The first time you explain and conduct this procedure with your students, keep the pace slow and methodical. Emphasize minimal noise and safety.

- Rehearse the setup procedure several times. Investing time to make this process run smoothly from the start saves time and frustration in the future.

- For young children or active classes, define the acting area with a tape line (see the next section).

[0] Teaching Tip

It is helpful if you plan your acting area as you set up your classroom room in the beginning of the school year. If a defined acting area is a part of your classroom design, the movement of furniture will be minimal.

A Taped Acting Area

A clearly defined acting area helps students know where to sit, stand, act, and observe. When you work with young children or an active class, taping off a large rectangular area on the floor with blue or orange painter's tape is an effective way to delineate the acting area. The taped space is the classroom stage. The acting occurs within that space. When students are outside of that space or seated on its perimeter, they are observers or audience members who are off stage. (See Figure 3–1.)

A taped-off acting area also serves as a classroom management tool. The rectangular taped space gives the students a home base. If students get overly excited, you can ask them to stand or sit on or behind the acting tape.

Once you have established the taped box as your defined acting area or "stage," instruct the students to return to the perimeter of the tape when their job as actors ends and their job as audience members begins. After repeated drama experiences in the same defined acting area, you and your students may not need to tape off the space anymore. The students will know what is expected of them.

[◊] Teaching Tip

Why use painter's tape instead of regular household masking tape to define the acting area? Painter's tape has a light adhesive that does not leave residue on carpets or floors, and it is easy to remove. If all you have is household masking tape, folding each end of the tape back upon itself to create a tab will make removal easier.

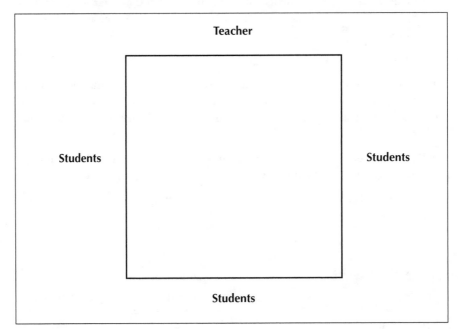

FIGURE 3–1 *Diagram of Taped Acting Area*

Each drama strategy detailed in Chapters 5 through 8 includes information about the acting area that works best with that strategy. As you prepare to use drama, consider what will work best for your classroom space and your students. A clear plan for defining your acting area and involving your students in setting it up provides a strong starting point for drama work.

Establish Personal Space

In addition to defining the physical space in the room, make students aware of personal boundaries between themselves, other people, and objects in the room. Clarifying the concept of personal space helps students understand how to work safely and respectfully in close proximity with others and reinforces the acting skill of cooperation.

Explain to students that personal space is the space directly around a person's body. It is the invisible boundary that they claim as their own even when they move about. To respect everyone's personal space, students need to be aware of how close they are to one another and keep their movements safely out of each other's personal space, unless invited. Respecting personal space means not touching any person or object in the room. It is making sure you are not on, by, leaning upon, or under any piece of furniture.

One way to establish the concept of personal space is to have the students draw an imaginary personal space bubble around their bodies.

Sample Language: Imagine that you have a piece of chalk in your pocket. Use your hand to get it out of your pocket. Now extend your hand and the chalk straight over your head and draw a circle that extends an arm's length in front of you. Continue drawing your circle between your feet, up behind your back, and then up over your head. Stop when you have returned to the spot where you began drawing.

Now do the same thing from side to side. Extend your arm over your head, but draw the circle from left to right. Draw the line under your feet and back up over your head. This is your personal space bubble. It is always with you. Take a walk around your bubble.

Ask the students to walk silently around the room, keeping the feeling of this large bubble around their bodies in all directions. Explain to the students that this imaginary bubble is always there—in everyday life and in drama—even if the bubble shrinks and is right next to the body. Have the students pull in the sides of their bubble and shrink it until it is only two inches from the edge of their bodies. Shrinking the bubble helps students understand that even when they are right next to another person, they must still honor personal boundaries. Now, ask the students to envision this smaller bubble surrounding them and again silently walk around the room, keeping the feeling of the bubble around them.

Sample Language: This is your personal space. No one is allowed in your space and you should not enter anyone else's unless invited. It is your personal space, and you will need to find it when we do drama.

Once you have established this procedure, you can use the term *personal space* to help students define boundaries and understand expectations for interacting with one another in close proximity.

Sample Language: Students, please find your personal space so that we can begin our drama.

Establish Drama Cues

Consistent cues in drama signal students when to begin, move, be still, speak, or be silent. Clear cues also help students know when they are playing roles and when they are themselves once again. Spoken aloud by the teacher, the following words serve well as cues.

Places This cue indicates to students that they should be standing in their correct places in the acting area, prepared to begin the drama. It also alerts the student audience to quietly focus in preparation for the drama. "Places" is the direction used by stage managers to alert actors backstage that the play or a scene is about to begin.

Action This cue signals students to begin acting. Upon hearing this word, students begin to move and/or speak as their characters. "Action" is a cue most commonly spoken by directors to movie actors. In theatre rehearsals, other cues for beginning the acting are "Curtain," "Curtain up," "Scene," and "Begin."

Freeze This cue indicates that the students should stop whatever they are doing and remain perfectly still and silent. This cue can be used to:

- signal the start of a frozen picture or tableau

- indicate the end of a scene

- stop the action and clarify a point the students may be missing in the drama

- stop the action to resolve an issue that is not a part of the drama, such as a behavioral issue, a knock on the door, an intercom announcement, or another interruption

Curtain This cue indicates the end of the scene or drama. Upon hearing this word, student actors discontinue playing their characters and the student audience knows that the acting has ended. Other commonly used theatre cues that signal the end of the drama are "Curtain down" and "Scene."

Introduce Other Drama Terms

POINT OF CONCENTRATION

Explain to students that the term *point of concentration* means a place where the actors focus their eyes and energy. It is a specific spot or small object (the numeral six on the clock, the light switch, a square on the calendar) in the room. The actors fix their gaze and full attention upon that point to help them maintain concentration.

SIDE COACHING

Explain to students that the term *side coaching* refers to comments that the teacher makes to the actors while they are acting. Side coaching prompts actors during a drama activity with ideas and suggestions to incorporate into their acting. The actors, like athletes who receive coaching while playing a game, continue acting as the teacher speaks and use the side coaching to advance or improve the drama.

Sample Language: Use your face to show how angry you are. Tell the other characters why you are angry. Use your voice to make them listen. Tell them what will happen if they do not listen.

Create a Chart of the Basic Acting Tools and Skills

A posted chart on which you have listed the basic acting tools and skills provides an effective classroom reference point. (See Figure 3–2.)

- Before a drama experience, use the chart to remind students of expectations and/or objectives.
- After a tool- or skill-building activity, refer to the chart to aid students' analysis of the acting tools and skills used in the activity.
- After a drama experience, use the chart to help guide reflection.
- The chart is a visual that reinforces drama vocabulary.

Review the Acting Tools and Skills

Reviewing the acting tools and skills before every drama experience increases students' familiarity with them. For young children, it helps to create a gesture and a

```
┌─────────────────────────────────────────────────────────────┐
│                                                             │
│              Basic Acting Tools                             │
│                  ■ Imagination/Mind                         │
│                  ■ Voice                                    │
│                  ■ Body                                     │
│              Basic Acting Skills                            │
│                  ■ Cooperation                              │
│                  ■ Concentration                            │
│                                                             │
└─────────────────────────────────────────────────────────────┘
```

FIGURE 3–2   *Basic Acting Tools and Skills Chart*

vocal quality when naming each tool and skill. The students can then move as they chant each acting tool and skill.

Sample Language: Actors, what acting tools will we need in order to act today? Let's say them all together.

Imagination. [*Hand flutters away from the side of the forehead*]

Mind. [*Index finger points to the front of the forehead*]

Voice. [*Fingers in the shape of a V move away from the neck. Voice ascends in pitch*]

Body. [*Hands touch shoulders, thighs, and toes, and voice descends in pitch*]

What acting skills will we need?

Cooperation. [*Arms come together with fingers fluttering and then interlocking in front of the body*]

Concentration. [*Index finger at the front of the forehead becomes a fist that is pounded in the opposite palm on each syllable of the word concentration*]

Acting Tool- and Skill-Building Activities

The following activities are designed to help students gain a level of proficiency with using the basic acting tools and skills. Each activity is connected with one or more of the drama objectives identified in Chapter 2. The activities are categorized according to the basic acting tools and skills they primarily address, but many of them provide practice in additional tools and skills. There is no prescribed sequence to these activities, so choose them according to the needs of your students.

Once the students become proficient with these tools and skills, you can use the same activities as warm-ups to refresh and reinforce selected acting tools and skills before conducting the drama strategies outlined in Chapters 5 through 8.

These activities, or variations of these activities, are widely used by theatre teachers. Many of the activities are similar to those described in *Improvisation for the Theater*

(1999) or *Theater Games for the Classroom* (1986), by Viola Spolin, a teacher and author who popularized and published her improvisational acting exercises. The authors of this book created some of the activities; others come from their experiences in acting classes and drama workshops and from their own teachers and students.

Imagination/Mind Activities

The following activities provide practice and develop students' abilities to use the basic acting tool imagination/mind. The drama objectives pertaining to this acting tool appear on page 11.

GROUP MIRROR

Students agree to pretend to be reflections in a mirror. They collaborate with peers and teachers to imitate the body movements of a leader, reflecting back what they see.

Procedure
1. Explain to students that they are to imagine that you are looking into a mirror. As you move, the students are to copy your movements as if they were your mirror reflection.
2. Remind students that mirrors do not make sounds. This is a silent activity.
3. Invite students to stand facing you in their personal space. Be sure everyone can see you.
4. Ask the students to make your eyes their point of concentration (a specific point of focus upon which actors fix their gaze and energy). Choose as your point of concentration a spot on the wall behind the students and above their heads. Identify this point for the students.
5. Explain to students that during the mirror activity, they are to focus on your eyes as they mirror all of your movements. Briefly demonstrate with students how they can mirror your actions by using peripheral vision.
6. Begin the activity by focusing on your point of concentration. Maintain an expressionless face and perform slow, fluid movements that all the students silently mirror. Standing in one place facing the students, begin some slow, silent movements. Start with your arms and hands, and then feel free to bend at the waist, move your head and shoulders, and move your legs and body.
7. Continue moving in silence for about thirty seconds and then end the activity by praising the students for agreeing to pretend.
8. Discuss with the students what other acting tools and skills they used in the activity.
9. After this discussion, emphasize the need in drama for agreeing to pretend, cooperation, and concentration, and then repeat the Group Mirror activity. To increase the concentration challenge, students can also lead the activity.

Group Mirror. Photo by Barbara S. Holden.

IMAGINARY DOOR

Students open an imaginary door and envision a setting in which they react to imaginary sights, sounds, and smells.

Procedure
1. Invite the students to sit on the tape in the defined acting area.
2. Invite the students to agree to pretend that they each have a piece of chalk in their real or imaginary pockets.
3. Guide the students to work together to draw a door. To promote cooperation and concentration, it is important that they draw it in unison.

Sample Language: Everyone take your imaginary chalk. Let's use cooperation to work together as we each draw an imaginary door. Let's start at the bottom and go up one side, now across the top, down the other side, and across the bottom. Don't forget to draw a doorknob so we can get inside.

4. Once the door is drawn, use descriptive language to prompt the students to envision what you want them to see and hear when they open the door.

Sample Language: When you open the door, see a thick, green rain forest. On the count of three we will open our doors together—one . . . two . . . three. . . . Now open our doors. Take a look around. Listen to the rain. See the beautiful trees and all the thick, lush, green plants. Do you see any rain? What kind of plants do you see? Do you see any tall trees or thick plants? Look for animals. Look to see where they are hiding and how they move. See if anything is camouflaged by all the plants. Now let's close our doors. Tell me, what animals did you see?

5. You can also have the students open the door to listen just to the sounds or notice the smells of a setting. You can incorporate the senses of sight and sound at the same time.
6. Repeat the process several times, each time keeping the door open for a few seconds and then closing it. When the door is closed, you may want to list on the board or on chart paper what the students saw or heard before you open the door again. (Note: Save the lists you generate to use for the activity Environment Orchestra on page 30.)
7. When you have repeated the activity four to five times, guide the students in finding an imaginary eraser next to them and erasing the door in the same step-by-step procedure that you used to draw it. Again, it is best if they mime this together in order to build cooperation and concentration.
8. When the door is erased, guide students in making the imaginary eraser and chalk disappear.

Sample Language: Put your chalk on top of your eraser. At the count of three, we are going to throw them up in the air, and if we use our imaginations, they will disappear—one . . . two . . . three. . . .

9. Discuss with the students how they used their imaginations in this activity.

Variations The activity does not need to be restricted to a door. It can be a window, a porthole, a tent flap—any entryway that fits the location you want the students to envision.

IMAGINARY MASK
To envision a character, students put on an imaginary mask and use facial expressions that communicate the thoughts and feelings of the character. Students also vary vocal tone and pitch to create character voices.

Procedure
1. Invite students to sit on the perimeter of the defined acting area. They can remain seated for this activity and use upper-body motions to embellish their masks, or after they are comfortable with the activity, they can stand and use the entire body.
2. Invite students to agree to pretend to find behind their ears or in their pockets a small mask. Ask the students to shake out the mask and hold it in front of them.

3. Then explain to the students that the mask can be any person or character. Identify the character you want all the students to portray.

4. Include details that will provide students with hints about what the character is thinking and feeling at this moment. Choosing a character facing a problem or in a highly emotional situation heightens the use of facial expression.

Sample Language: In your hand is a mask of the character the littlest Billy Goat Gruff when he first sees and hears the troll as he crosses the bridge.

5. Together with the students, put the mask on.

Sample Language: At the count of three, let's put on our masks. Let me see what that goat was thinking and feeling at this moment. One . . . two . . . three. . . .

6. Repeat the activity with a new character, this time observing the students rather than donning a mask with them. Ask the students to shake out the mask and have it transform into the next character. You can then repeat the process.

7. When the students are able to don the mask independently, you may comment upon the feelings you observe or briefly interview the characters and ask them what they are thinking and feeling at this moment. Stand in front of the student you are interviewing. Ask a question and allow the student to answer as the character.

Sample Language: Oh my, you look so frightened! What just happened to you? I see you just heard the scariest voice in the world. What are you thinking at this moment? You want your mommy. I totally understand.

8. After they have become the character, ask students to remove the mask.

9. To close the activity, ask the students to take off the mask, roll it into a small ball, and return it to the same location in which they first found it.

10. After the activity, discuss with the students how they used their imaginations in this activity, what they learned about the characters, and any personal connections they made with the characters.

11. Discuss with the students what other acting tools and skills they used in the activity.

Voice Activities

The following activities provide practice and develop students' abilities to use the basic acting tool voice. The drama objectives pertaining to this acting tool appear on page 12.

LIPS AND TEETH AND TONGUE

Using tongue twisters, students practice speaking clearly by overarticulating.

Procedure

1. Students can sit or stand at their desks or on the perimeter of the defined acting area.
2. Explain to students that clear articulation or enunciation of words requires the use of lips, teeth, and tongue. It is easier to understand what people say when they use their lips and teeth and tongues effectively. Actors, in particular, need good articulation.
3. Ask the students stretch out their lips and mouths first by making them wide and then stretching them lengthwise.
4. Ask the students to stretch out their tongues as far as they can reach in all directions.
5. Ask the students to say the words, "Lips and teeth and tongue," overexaggerating how they use their lips, stretching out their tongues, and baring their teeth. This process is called overarticulation. Have them say the words in rhythm.

Sample Language: When we say the word *lips,* extend your tongues and stretch your lips wide. Let's stretch our mouths wide when we say the word *and.* Now let's smile wide and show our teeth on the word *teeth.* Stretch wide again for *and,* and then stretch your mouths vertically, overusing your tongues on the word *tongue.*

6. Use this same process of exaggerated articulation for any tongue twister or poem. Following are some sample tongue twisters that work well for this exercise. You may want to print them on a chart so that students can read them as they speak. Once the students can clearly articulate the tongue twister, ask them to repeat it three to five times consecutively.

- He threw three free throws.

- Two tiny tigers take two taxis to town.

- Fat frogs flying past fast.

- The queen in green screamed.

- Blue glue gun. Green glue gun.

- Greek grapes.

- Mommy made me eat my M&Ms.

- Peter Piper picked a peck of pickled peppers.

- A big black bug bit a big black bear, and the big black bear bled blood.

7. After the activity, discuss the value of tongue twisters for warming up the voice.
8. Discuss with the students what other acting tools and skills they used in the activity to successfully repeat the tongue twisters.

ENVIRONMENT ORCHESTRA

To help them envision a setting, students vary their vocal tone and pitch to create sound effects for that setting.

Procedure

1. Invite students to sit on the perimeter of the defined acting area.
2. Identify a setting you want the students to explore—a rain forest, a city, a haunted house, an airport, a desert, a bakery, and so on. The setting can also be from a text the students are reading.
3. Ask the students to predict sounds that could be heard in this setting. Write their suggestions on the board. For young students, draw a picture beside each suggestion to help them remember the sound. Generate a list of three to five environment sounds. (Note: If you generated a list of sights and sounds in the Imaginary Door activity on page 26, use it now.)
4. Explain to the students that they will use their voices to create the sounds on their list.
5. Model for the students, using your voice, an example of a sound that might be heard in this setting. Add a gesture (motion) to go along with this sound.

Sample Language: You said in the rain forest we might hear the sounds of macaws. I am going to use my voice to create the sound of a macaw. I am going to use my arms as wings and go, "Caw . . . ccc . . . caw! Caw . . . ccc . . . caw!"

6. Guide the students in creating sounds and gestures to go with the sounds on their list. Urge the students to experiment with their voices, varying tone and pitch to create the sounds they identified.
7. Divide the students into groups, assigning each group a sound from the list. Choose a section leader for each group. It is ideal if the student who suggested the sound is the section leader for that sound and motion.
8. Explain to the students that they will now become the orchestra, playing the symphony of this particular setting. You will be the conductor. Communicate the conductor's signals—gestures for start, stop, louder, softer, faster, slower, and so on. As the conductor, you control the symphony with your gestures, not with words.
9. Rehearse the orchestra by having all the students make their assigned sounds, watch the conductor's gestures, and stop on cue.

Sample Language: When I go like this with my hands, stop making the sound. Please use cooperation and let's see if we can stop all at the same time. Good job!

10. Remind the students to use the other acting tools and skills as they create their orchestra.

Sample Language: We are ready to begin the rain forest environment orchestra. Please use cooperation to work with your groups in making your sound and motion. Please use concentration to watch me and the signals I give for when to stop and start and to stay focused. Please, no talking or laughing. If you cooperate and use your voices effectively, the environment orchestra will help us envision the rain forest setting.

11. Conduct the orchestra. Signal one group at a time to start and continue making the sound. Increase the volume. Decrease the volume. Signal each group individually to stop, or stop the entire orchestra at once.
12. After the activity, discuss how the sounds helped students envision the setting and which sounds were particularly effective and why.
13. Discuss with the students what other acting tools and skills they used in the activity.

Variation At first, this activity can be done with students seated in the acting area or at desks, allowing students to use just their upper bodies to create the motions. With experience, the students can do this same activity standing, involving the entire body in the activity.

FINDING THE CHARACTER'S VOICE

Students create and deliver dialogue that is in character—communicating information about the character and the drama's circumstances. They speak with expression that reflects the personality, traits, thoughts, and feelings of the character.

Procedure
1. Invite the students to stand on the perimeter of the defined acting area.
2. Describe to the students a problem a character is facing—a generic problem or one from a book. Ask the students to predict the first line of dialogue the character might say when faced with this problem.

Sample Language: Imagine that you are an adult—a teacher. Your alarm clock did not go off and you woke up late for work. You are in your pajamas, racing around trying to get ready for work. You go to open your closet door to get your clothes for the day, but the door is stuck. You cannot get it open. You tug at the doorknob but it won't budge. What do you think would be the first thing you would say? Let's hear some ideas, and remember, no bad language.

3. Take the first usable line offered by a student and rehearse how to deliver the line and an action or gesture that emphasizes the words. You can determine the final delivery of the line and have the students perform their own actions with the line or you can select one action that everyone will do in unison.

Sample Language: So our first line of dialogue is going to be "Oh, come on! Give me a break!" and we are going to hit the door with our fists while we say it. Let's rehearse. When I say, "Places," become an adult teacher with your hands on the doorknob. When I say, "Action," pull on the doorknob three times and try to get it open, and then slam your fists against the door and deliver the line. Places. . . . Action.

4. Together with the students, perform the line and actions.
5. Repeat the process using the same circumstance and adding one to two more lines of dialogue and accompanying actions. Rehearse the delivery of the lines and the actions.
6. After the students have practiced each line and action, have them present the lines and actions consecutively.

Sample Language: Now that we have our three lines and actions, let's put them all together. When I say, "Places," become an adult teacher with your hands on the doorknob. When I say, "Action," say all three lines and perform the actions. Places. . . . Action.

Example:
[*Pull on the doorknob three times*]
Oh, come on! Give me a break! [*Hit the door with fists*]
I cannot believe this! [*Put hands on hips*]
I have got to get to work! [*Grab forehead with one hand*]

7. After the activity, discuss how the lines of dialogue reflected the character's circumstance and what made the line deliveries effective.
8. Discuss with the students what other acting tools and skills they used in the activity.

REPEAT AFTER ME

Students practice projecting and articulating so that they speak loudly, slowly, and clearly enough to be understood across the classroom.

Procedure

1. Divide the students into two groups. Have each group stand shoulder-to-shoulder in a line facing one another on opposite sides of the classroom.
2. Assign each student in each line a number, beginning with the number one for each group. This will result in two students having number one, two students having number two, and so on. Pairs of students sharing the same number are partners.
3. Explain that the students are each to create a three- to five-word sentence or *line* to speak aloud to their partners standing on the opposite side of the room.

Sample Language: Think of a simple sentence or line (as it is called in the theatre) to speak to your partner. For example, your line might be "I like vanilla ice cream." Don't share your lines yet. Just think of one in your head.

4. Tell students that the main acting tool they will use is voice. Explain that, individually, the students will speak their lines to their partners. The partner is to listen carefully and repeat the line exactly as it was spoken.
5. Emphasize that success in this activity occurs when the partner can perfectly repeat the spoken line because it was delivered loudly and clearly.
6. Cue each student to speak and each partner to repeat.
7. Encourage soft speakers to redeliver their lines using greater projection. If necessary, model a louder delivery and emphasize that projection does not mean yelling. In classroom drama, projection is simply stronger volume aided by speaking more slowly and pronouncing words more carefully. (See "Lips and Teeth and Tongue" on page 29.)
8. Encourage students who speak too quickly to repeat their lines more slowly. Help students whose words and syllables merge to enunciate more precisely. When necessary, model effective tempo and articulation.
9. Continue the activity, pausing to help students improve their projection until everyone in both groups has delivered a line and heard it repeated.
10. After the activity, discuss with students why projection is important in the theatre and in classroom drama.
11. Discuss with the students what other acting tools and skills they used in the activity.

Body Activities

The following activities provide practice and develop students' abilities to use the basic acting tool body. The drama objectives pertaining to this acting tool appear on page 12.

CONTRASTS

Students modify posture and body positions to create characters or objects that contrast in size, shape, personality, age, or some other aspect.

Procedure

1. Invite the students to stand in their personal space.
2. Explain to the students that they will use only their bodies to create characters and objects that contrast (are different in some way).
3. Explain that they will create these characters or objects by moving and then freezing in a position. They will not be moving around the acting area.
4. Lead the students in creating these contrasts.

Sample Language: When I say, "Places," become a huge bear. I don't want to hear his voice. I just want to see his body—his big, round, hairy body and his huge claws. Places. Great . . . and freeze. Now when I say, "Places," again, become a tiny mouse. This mouse has tiny ears and short little legs. Places. Good job . . . and freeze. Now when I say, "Places," let me see . . .

5. Lead the students in creating four to five sets of contrasting characters and/or objects, such as these:

    - bird and snake
    - giant and baby
    - triangle and curve
    - elephant and mosquito
    - tree and flower
    - solid and liquid
    - evil witch and angel
    - door and ball
    - lion and puppy

6. After the activity, invite the students to sit and discuss the differences in how they used their bodies in each set of contrasts.
7. Discuss with the students what other acting tools and skills they used in the activity.

Variation Once the students have explored contrasts using only their bodies, you may want to add voice. Have them make noises that accompany each contrasting object or character in the previous list, for example, the growl of the bear and the squeak of the mouse.

Bits 'n' Pieces: Bringing a Setting to Life

Students envision a setting and the objects found in this location. They then modify their body positions to become those objects. Other students interact with the objects.

Procedure

1. Invite students to stand on the perimeter of the defined acting area.
2. Invite the students to agree to pretend. Explain to the students that in this activity they will use their bodies to create objects that can be found in a particular setting. Examples include trees, brooms, doors, refrigerators, tables, lamps, televisions, and so forth.
3. Identify the setting for the students.
4. To clarify expectations, use student volunteers to model using their bodies to become objects.

Sample Language: The setting for this drama activity is a bakery. One thing we would find in this bakery is a big oven that bakes the bread. Could two students come up and create with their bodies a large oven? Great. I like the curved opening for the oven. Now we need someone to attach to them and be the oven door. Who would like to do this? Be sure you have a handle so you can be opened and closed easily. Let's hear the oven door squeak when I open it. Now, what else might we find in the bakery?

5. Guide the students to continue building the setting with objects. Encourage the students to add a sound effect for each object. Create three to five objects (oven, bowl, beater, pan, timer, etc.) for the setting.
6. Because it is difficult for them to hold the poses of their objects for a long period of time, encourage the participating students to relax while all the other objects in the setting are demonstrated.
7. Once the setting is complete and the objects are in position, invite one or two students to enter the setting and use each object as they do a particular task.
8. Remind the students who are playing objects to use concentration.

Sample Language: Is everyone ready to begin? Objects, don't forget to find a point of concentration so that you can hold your positions. Places. Good. Everyone is ready. Action.

9. You may want to narrate the scene to guide the action.

Sample Language: And so the bakers mixed all the ingredients for the special birthday cake in a big *bowl*. They turned on the *beater* so they could mix it faster and faster. Then they put the cake in a big *pan* and put it in the *oven*. They set the *timer*. . . .

10. Signal the end of the acting by calling, "Freeze and curtain."
11. Repeat the activity by using a different setting, perhaps the setting from a familiar story. Some setting suggestions:

- grocery store
- computer lab
- bedroom
- laundry room
- museum
- airport
- desert
- beauty parlor
- playground

12. After the activity, discuss with the students how they used their bodies.
13. Discuss with the students what other acting tools and skills they used in the activity.

Variation Students can work in small groups to create different objects found in various settings. Then, each group can share its objects and setting with the rest of the class.

SHOW-ME CHARACTERS

Students modify posture and body positions to communicate information about a character type. This is a silent activity that requires students to adjust poses, gestures, movements, or walks.

Procedure

1. Invite students to stand in their personal space.
2. Explain that you are going to name a particular type of character. The students' acting task is to use their bodies to show you how they would play that character.
3. Tell students that the main acting tool they will use is the body, not the voice. This is a silent activity.

Sample Language: I will name a character type and then cue you by saying, "Action!" For example, I will say, "Show me a friendly old lady—action!" When I say, "Action," show me by posing [*or gesturing or moving, or walking—choose whichever instruction you want students to practice*] like a friendly old lady.

4. Instruct students to remain in character until you name a new character type.

Sample Language: Remain in character until I say, "Curtain." Then listen for the next character type that you will show me using your bodies.

5. Encourage students to use energy in their portrayals.

Sample Language: Show me energy in your bodies when you play your character types. Energy means that you are powerful, active, and animated.

6. Begin and continue the activity.

Sample Language: Show me [*choose a character type from the following list*]. Action! Curtain.

7. Repeat with new character types as desired.

Character Types

- a cool teenager
- an army sergeant
- a cranky old man
- a scolding teacher
- an enthusiastic fan
- a supermodel
- a body builder
- a lottery winner
- a shy child

- a basketball player
- a proud parent
- an orchestra conductor
- a famous movie star
- a bratty child
- a powerful king
- a sad princess
- an angry goddess
- a strong soldier

7. After the activity, discuss with students the ways that they used their bodies and modified posture, positions, poses, gestures, movements, and walks.
8. Invite individual students to share their character portrayals with the class. Discuss effective examples of uses of body and energy.
9. Discuss with the students what other acting tools and skills they used in the activity.

SHOW-ME FACIAL EXPRESSIONS

Students use facial expressions to silently communicate various feelings.

Procedure

1. You may conduct this activity by having students remain seated at their desks or you may invite students to stand in their personal space.
2. Explain that you are going to name a particular emotion. The students' acting task is to use their faces to show you how they would play a character feeling that emotion.
3. Tell students that the main acting tool they will use is body—specifically the face—not voice. This is a silent activity.

Sample Language: I will name an emotion and then cue you by saying, "Action!" For example, I will say, "Show me angry—action!" When I say, "Action," show me with your facial expression how a character who is angry would look.

4. Instruct students to remain in character until you name a new emotion.

Sample Language: Remain in character until I say, "Curtain." Then listen for the next emotion that you will show me using your faces.

5. Encourage students to use energy in their portrayals.

Sample Language: Show me energy in your faces when you create the character experiencing this emotion. Energy means that you are powerful, active, and animated.

6. Begin and continue the activity.

Sample Language: Show me [choose an emotion from the following list]. Action! Curtain.

7. Repeat with new emotions as desired.

Emotions

- annoyed
- bored
- brave
- cheerful
- confused
- disgusted
- enthusiastic
- exasperated
- excited
- fascinated

- fearful
- frustrated
- gloomy
- grateful
- happy
- hopeful
- horrified
- hurt
- impressed
- infuriated
- jealous
- jolly
- joyful
- miserable
- nervous
- panicked
- peaceful
- proud
- refreshed
- sad
- scared
- shy
- shocked
- stressed
- weary
- worried

7. Discuss with students the ways that they used their faces to communicate various emotions. Invite individual students to share their character facial emotions with the class. Discuss effective examples of uses of facial expressions and energy.

8. Discuss with the students what other acting tools and skills they used in the activity.

Cooperation Activities

The following activities provide practice and develop students' abilities to use the basic acting skill cooperation. The drama objectives pertaining to this acting skill appear on page 12.

MIRROR PAIRS

Students collaborate with peers, working together in teams of two to create the movements of a person and his or her mirrored reflection.

Procedure

1. Explain to students that Mirror Pairs is an acting exercise in which two actors stand face-to-face. One actor is the person who leads, and the other is the mirror image (reflection) of the person. While the actors maintain eye contact, the person moves slowly, and the mirror imitates the person's motions. The pair's goal is to move so slowly and carefully that it is difficult for an observer to distinguish between the person and the mirror.

2. Invite students to find a partner with whom they can work effectively to build cooperation and strengthen concentration. Emphasize that picking a best friend as a partner may not be a good choice in the beginning stages of building cooperation and concentration.

3. Ask students to stand at arm's length facing their partners and decide which one will be the leader and which will be the mirror.

Sample Language: Discuss with your partner who wants to lead first. Do not declare yourself as the leader because that does not build cooperation skills. A community (ensemble) of actors makes decisions together. No one is more important than anyone else. Take twenty seconds to decide together who is going to lead first.

4. Ask the students to make the eyes of their partner their point of concentration.

5. Signal the start of the activity by calling, "Places," and "Action." Side coach the students by reminding them to move slowly. Remind them that their point of concentration is the eyes of the person they are facing. If looking into a partner's eyes causes a lot of giggling or talking, ask students to choose a different point of concentration—the forehead or a point right above the partner's head.

6. Move around the room, complimenting partners who move together and remain focused. Remind them that their goal is to work together so that it is difficult to tell who is leading and who is mirroring.

7. Call, "Curtain," to end the activity. Invite three or four pairs who cooperated well to demonstrate their mirrors for the class.

8. Repeat the activity by having the other partner lead.

9. Discuss strategies that students used to cooperate and concentrate while mirroring one another.

10. Discuss with the students what other acting tools and skills they used in the activity.

MIRRORS—SWITCH THE LEADER

Students collaborate with peers, working together in teams of two to share and switch leadership roles as they create the movements of a person and his or her mirrored reflection.

Procedure

1. Explain to students that a higher level of cooperation between mirror pairs occurs when the partners collaborate so well that they can switch leadership without any prompting from you. The idea is for the switch to be seamless. They are to give up leadership to their partner once the partner takes initiative to change or adapt the motion. The new leader picks up on his partner's movements and slightly transforms them. The process

continues as the leadership smoothly transfers back and forth. The idea is that the change is so subtle, so smooth, that an observer may not be able to detect who is leading and who is mirroring.

2. Choose a student volunteer to work with you to model this switching of leadership between a mirror pair.

3. After students have partners, begin conducting the Mirror Pairs activity as described previously. Then, side coach students to cooperate by becoming both leaders and followers.

4. Call, "Curtain," to end the activity. Invite three or four successful pairs to demonstrate their switching of leadership during Mirror Pairs for the class.

5. Discuss strategies that students used to cooperate and concentrate while mirroring one another.

6. Discuss with the students what other acting tools and skills they used in the activity.

Concentration Activities

The following activities provide practice and develop students' abilities to use the basic acting skill concentration. The drama objectives pertaining to this acting tool appear on page 13.

SHAKE AND FREEZE/POINT OF CONCENTRATION

Students hone their concentration skills by fixing their eyes and energy on one particular focal point. They focus intently on the drama task, control inappropriate laughter, and disregard actions and noises unrelated to the drama.

Procedure

1. Invite students to stand in their personal space.

2. Provide for the students a specific spot or object to focus on, for example, the letter *b* on the alphabet chart, the doorknob, or the purple magnet on the board. Explain to the students that this spot is called their point of concentration.

3. Tell students that when you say, "Freeze," they are to remain perfectly still and fix their eyes and energy on that point. When you say, "Shake," they are to shake their arms, legs, heads, and shoulders, and silently walk around the acting area until they hear you say, "Freeze."

4. Begin by calling, "Shake!" Allow students to shake and walk about, and then call, "Freeze!" so that the students silently focus their eyes on the point of concentration.

5. Have students maintain the focus for about ten seconds and then call, "Shake." Repeat the process as necessary to give them practice in improving their ability to focus.

6. Once the students have mastered the silent, still focus on the point of concentration, ask them to stay focused on that point as you walk around the room and look at each of them. Side coach the students as you walk.

Sample Language: I am walking around the room and looking at each one of you. If your eyes are focused on that purple magnet, you won't move or make a noise or blink when I go by because you have a point of concentration—a place where your eyes and energy are focused—and you are thinking of nothing else. Let me see who can stay focused as I walk by. I know it is hard. Let's see how well you can do.

7. As the students improve in their concentration, increase the challenge of this activity by having them do the following:

   ■ Choose their own points of concentration—spots that do not move and are not on a person. If they are facing another student when they freeze, their chosen point of concentration should be over that student's head.

   ■ Choose a point of concentration located in a different direction—behind them, beside them—from the direction that their bodies face when you say, "Freeze."

   ■ Remain focused when a peer, rather than the teacher, is the leader who walks around the room and looks at them.

8. End the activity by praising the students who maintained concentration and asking them to discuss any strategies they used to keep focused.
9. After this discussion, emphasize the need for concentration in drama. Set class goals of complete silence, concentration, and cooperation, and repeat any version of the activity as needed.
10. Discuss with the students what other acting tools and skills they used in the activity.

"WON'T YOU PLEASE SMILE?"

Students practice the acting skill of concentration with an emphasis on controlling inappropriate laughter while attending and responding appropriately to another character.

Procedure
1. Invite students to stand in a circle around you.
2. Explain to them that, from where they stand, they are to find and focus on a point of concentration.
3. Tell them that in this activity, the goal of the person in the center of the circle is to break their concentration by making them smile or laugh. Their goal is to remain focused and expressionless.
4. Explain that there are two lines of dialogue to learn for this activity. The person in the center approaches someone in the circle and says, "Won't you please smile?" The person approached responds with "No, I just can't smile."

5. Emphasize that the person in the center may deliver the line playing any type of character and using a variety of vocal tones, dialect, gestures, or movements, but she may *not* touch the person she is approaching.

6. Hold a few practices in which you are the person in the center who delivers the first line. Select various students to approach and try different characters or line deliveries (southern drawl, deep baritone, military officer, for example).

7. Begin and continue repeating the activity. The person in the center of the circle switches places with any student who does not maintain concentration before, during, or just after delivering the responding line ("No, I just can't smile.").

8. After several repetitions of the activity, discuss strategies that students used to maintain their concentration and avoid laughing. Repeat the activity so that all students have the opportunity to participate.

9. After the activity, emphasize the need for the acting skill of concentration in drama.

10. Discuss what other acting tools and skills they used in the activity.

These acting tool- and skill-building activities may be used repeatedly to build proficiency, to warm up, and to focus students for their work with the drama strategies detailed in Chapters 5 through 8. Once they are familiar with the activities, students enthusiastically participate in them, and you can conduct the activities in brief amounts of time. For books containing additional activities, consult the "Recommended Reading" section on page 217.

4

Assessment

ssessment is a process designed to help teachers and students understand and improve student learning. It involves setting clear expectations or objectives that are achievable yet challenging for students, and then gathering, analyzing, and interpreting evidence to determine if students have met those expectations. Assessment usually occurs by examining a student product or performance that provides appropriate evidence of student understanding or proficiency (McTighe and Wiggins 1999). The results of an assessment may document, explain, and improve student performance as well as provide information to teachers on how to modify instruction.

Because of the emphasis on accountability in instruction, assessment has become increasingly important in the field of arts education. Teaching artists, arts educators, and arts specialists are responsible for going beyond the delivery of a compelling artistic experience. More and more, they are required to define, describe, and communicate how students and teachers can recognize and achieve proficiency in the elements of their art forms. This chapter's intent is to clarify ways and means of assessment, especially in the art form of drama since that field may be less familiar to teachers, but also in the reading comprehension that fuses with this text's drama experiences.

The assessment expectations for each of the four drama strategies in this text are stated in the form of objectives. Since this text emphasizes arts integration, assessment focuses on objectives for both drama and reading comprehension.

The assessments, found at the end of each chapter, range from informal to written assessments. The assessment methods included are:

- observational assessments

- reflective discussions

- written assessments

- assessment checklists

Through these assessments, teachers and students gain valuable knowledge about each student's proficiency in using the acting tools and skills and in understanding and applying information from a text. Assessments also inform teachers, administrators, and parents with evidence of learning that justifies time spent in the classroom integrating drama with reading comprehension.

What follows is a description of each assessment method recommended in this text.

Observational Assessment

Teachers use observational assessment all the time. They continually and informally assess students as they watch and note students' level of engagement, attentiveness, and ability to respond on task.

The effectiveness of this informal assessment can be increased with a consistent procedure for observational assessment. One effective method is to observe the same three to five students over the course of four to five lessons and record notes about what each did during each lesson. The students selected for this assessment should be at varying levels of academic ability and self-control.

After each arts-integrated lesson (or each drama activity), record factual notes about each student's responses during the lesson. Avoid drawing conclusions about the student's progress until the end of the designated observation period. Observe students during the planning, enacting, observing, and reflecting components of the lesson.

A set of suggested questions or ideas to guide effective observational assessment is included at the end of each drama strategy chapter. The observations you record allow you to document students' progress over time.

A brief form to fill out for each observed student at the completion of a lesson is an effective tool for recording observations. Teachers often duplicate the form, three-hole punch it, and keep it with other forms in an observation notebook. Figure 4–1 shows an example of an observational assessment note-taking form that has been filled out. Figure 4–2 contains a blank form to photocopy and use.

Drawing Conclusions

At the end of four to five lessons, look at each set of notes and draw conclusions about each observed student's ability to meet the key objectives using both the acting tools and skills and the reading comprehension strategies. Note also whether each student shows improvement over the course of the lessons.

Consider whether your notes also indicate class trends. If, for example, all five observed students laughed or whispered to their peers during the drama experiences, they and all your students may need more work developing cooperation and concentration. This observation may influence you to focus on skill-building activities that will help students improve in these areas.

Your notes might also reveal that even though the students giggle, the dialogue they create is in character and fits the drama's circumstance. This observation

Observational Assessment Note-Taking Form
For Integrated Drama Lesson

Student's Name: Justine Poulin

Date: 1-21-2006

Text: "The Monster Year," retold by Lenore Blank Kelner

Key Drama Objectives: Consider the lesson's targeted drama objectives and place a check mark next to the acting tools and/or skills you wish to observe the student use in this lesson. Record brief notes on student behavior(s) regarding each tool or skill.

_____ **Imagination/Mind:** _____

__X__ **Voice:** Started to change her voice at the start, but lost it.

__X__ **Body:** As the beggar—bent over throughout her interview.

__X__ **Cooperation:** Grabbed the paper out of the hands of the student assigned to read the questions. Turned her back on the group when her idea was not taken.

_____ **Concentration:** _____

Key Reading Comprehension Objectives: Consider the lesson's targeted reading comprehension objectives and place a check mark next to the strategies you wish to observe the student use in this lesson. Record brief notes on student behavior(s) regarding each strategy.

_____ **Developing Sensory Images:** _____

__X__ **Building and Activating Schema:** Her dialogue reflected prior knowledge of hunger. She added information from another text on Chinese New Year.

_____ **Questioning:** _____

_____ **Determining Importance:** _____

__X__ **Inferring:** She made a logical inference about the past life of the beggar.

__X__ **Synthesis:** She was able to articulate a lesson the beggar hoped the villagers had learned.

Miscellaneous Observations: (Include observations of behaviors as an audience member.)

She tied and untied her shoes while peers performed.

She prompted Timmy next to her to speak by poking him in the ribs.

FIGURE 4–1   *Observational Assessment Note-Taking Form (Sample)*

Observational Assessment Note-Taking Form
For Integrated Drama Lesson

Student's Name: _____

Date: _____

Text: _____

Key Drama Objectives: Consider the lesson's targeted drama objectives and place a check mark next to the acting tools and/or skills you wish to observe the student use in this lesson. Record brief notes on student behavior(s) regarding each tool or skill.

_____ **Imagination/Mind:** _____

_____

_____ **Voice:** _____

_____

_____ **Body:** _____

_____

_____ **Cooperation:** _____

_____

_____ **Concentration:** _____

_____

Key Reading Comprehension Objectives: Consider the lesson's targeted reading comprehension objectives and place a check mark next to the strategies you wish to observe the student use in this lesson. Record brief notes on student behavior(s) regarding each strategy.

_____ **Developing Sensory Images:** _____

_____

_____ **Building and Activating Schema:** _____

_____

_____ **Questioning:** _____

_____

_____ **Determining Importance:** _____

_____

_____ **Inferring:** _____

_____

_____ **Synthesis:** _____

_____

Miscellaneous Observations: (Include observations of behaviors as an audience member.)

_____

_____

FIGURE 4–2   *Observational Assessment Note-Taking Form (Blank)*

indicates that the students are making inferences. The observation notes, therefore, may help you see that several or most of your students are progressing in some of the reading comprehension skills but need additional work on some of their acting tools and skills.

Modifying Instruction

Examining and interpreting the observation notes can lead you to modify instruction to meet the needs of the observed students. The modifications, however, will likely benefit the entire group. To continue the process, observe and record notes on the behaviors of three to five different students. Working in this way, you will eventually collect observation notes on every student in the class. The repetitive process of observing, noting, drawing conclusions, and modifying instruction allows you to help your students continually improve in their efforts to meet the drama and reading comprehension objectives.

Reflective Discussions

Students' reflections after a lesson provide insight into the depth of their understanding. Conversations that focus on the drama and reading comprehension objectives help students self-assess the extent to which they achieved the key objectives and guide them in setting goals for the next lesson. To facilitate productive reflective discussions, create open-ended questions that:

- *Recall Elements of the Drama Experience*—These questions help remind students of what happened—what they saw, heard, and did—during the drama experience.

- *Encourage Praise*—These questions invite students to comment on and commend the drama work of their peers, analyze the effective use of the acting tools and skills, and consider and be aware of the use of the reading comprehension strategies.

- *Encourage Change*—These questions invite students to critique their own drama work, reflect on their reading comprehension needs, and identify goals for future drama work.

(Note: Reflective discussion questions specific to each drama strategy appear at the end of the chapter devoted to that strategy.)

Pose Questions That Recall Elements of the Drama Experience

After completing an integrated drama lesson, it is helpful to collectively review what the class saw, heard, and experienced. Phrase your questions to focus first on the lesson's drama and reading comprehension objectives. Then broaden the discussion to include other relevant acting tools and skills and reading comprehension elements. Following are several sample questions and discussion starters.

From a Drama Perspective

- Who used imagination to . . . ?

- Which student actor used voice effectively to . . . ?

- Who used dialogue that . . . ?

- What was an effective use of body to . . . ?

- Which student actors used body effectively throughout the drama?

- What examples of cooperation did you see when . . . ?

- Who maintained concentration during . . . ?

- How was the audience helpful during . . . ?

From a Reading Comprehension Perspective

- When could you tell by student actors' faces that they were reacting to sensory images? Remember to think about imaginary sights, sounds, smells, tastes, and textures.

- Which student actors' movements helped you visualize . . . ?

- Did this remind you of . . . ?

- What questions do you have about . . . ?

- What details from the text were included in the drama?

- What dialogue not found in the text was accurate based on what we know about this character?

- What reading comprehension skill was used to create that dialogue?

- What do you predict might . . . ?

- What might you infer by . . . ?

- What was your favorite . . . ?

- What did you learn . . . ?

- What surprised you about . . . ?

Pose Questions That Encourage Praise

Once students have a clear understanding of the acting tools and skills and the reading comprehension strategies, they can give positive feedback on the work of their peers. During reflective discussions, this type of praise builds a sense of community (ensemble). The students compliment peers who used the acting tools and skills and demonstrated reading comprehension strategies effectively. They state explicit reasons and examples that support their compliments. Sincere and specific praise from peers about a student's performance clarifies expectations for all students. They know what they need to include in their next drama in order to receive a similar compliment. The bar is raised and students become eager to meet the challenge.

To prepare students for this type of reflective discussion, it is helpful to model praising students, stating specific reasons and examples to support the praise.

Sample Language: William, I was so happy with your work today. You really used imagination and inference when you added the line "All right, I did it!" to every trick your character got away with in the story. That line fit this character perfectly because throughout the story he was always boasting.

Kara, I liked the high, sweet voice you created for the mouse in the story. It fit so well the gentle personality of the character.

SAMPLE QUESTIONS

From a Drama Perspective

- Who do you think used the acting tool _____ effectively today? Tell me what you heard and why it was effective for this character. Remember, we want to compliment others, not ourselves.

- Who did you see use concentration throughout the drama today? Was there anyone who never got distracted but stayed in character the entire time? How did that make the drama better?

- Who was an excellent audience member today and why?

Remember to phrase your questions to elicit praise and support from students. Remind students that the purpose of these questions is to compliment others, not themselves. Here are some reflective discussion question starters that encourage praise in drama work:

- What were some of the most imaginative . . . ?

- Who effectively used the acting tool/skill . . . ?

- Why was it effective when . . . ?

- Who was in character when . . . ?

- Who made an excellent choice when . . . ?

- Why was this choice so effective . . . ?

- What delighted you . . . ?

- What made it delightful . . . ?

- What moved you . . . ?

- What made it so moving . . . ?

From a Reading Comprehension Perspective

- Think about the dialogue you heard today. What student actor created dialogue that fit the character and used the reading comprehension strategy inference?

- When Paul said that the beggar in "The Monster Year" was like the beggar in the book *Everyone Knows What a Dragon Looks Like,* by Jay Williams, what reading comprehension strategy was he using? Why was that comparison effective?

- What dialogue not found in the text was accurate based on what we know about this character? What reading comprehension strategy was used to create that dialogue?

- How was the story we worked with today similar to the story we read last week?

- By comparing this story with another text, which reading comprehension objective are we meeting?

Here are some reflective discussion question starters that encourage praise in reading comprehension:

- Which student actor helped you visualize . . . ?

- Whose character portrayal reminded you of . . . ?

 Dramatic Detail—Reflective Discussion Questions

The same type of reflective discussion questions can be modified for younger students. If you simplify the vocabulary and limit the number of objectives in each lesson, young students can be reflective about their work. Following are a few sample questions.

From a Drama Perspective

- Who did you see keep concentration all through the lesson? Who didn't laugh or talk to a neighbor? Raise your hand if you can name some students who thought only about the drama and what they were supposed to do.

From a Reading Comprehension Perspective

- In our story dramatization today, Ernesto, as the baker, created the line "My sweet rolls are best in the land!" The baker did not say that in the book. Why was that a good line for the baker to say? What do we know about this character? We have been working with two reading comprehension strategies. Which one did Ernesto use when he created that line?

- What connections did you make when . . . ?

- What questions about the text were answered when . . . ?

- What character made you wonder more about . . . ?

- How was the author's purpose shown by . . . ?

- Who used inference effectively when . . . ?

- Whose dialogue helped you understand . . . ?

- How did the drama help you understand . . . ?

- What new thoughts occurred to you when . . . ?

Pose Questions That Encourage Change

To promote change, encourage improvement, and set goals for the next integrated drama lesson, ask students to examine their own work. While questions that promote praise focus students on celebrating the good work of others, questions that encourage change challenge students to self-assess. Students analyze the effectiveness of their own roles in the drama and set goals for future work.

Develop reflective questions that guide students in analyzing the effectiveness of their roles in the drama. For young students, you may need to simplify the language of these questions, but these students can consider and articulate how they want to improve in the next drama experience. Again, to clarify expectations, it is helpful if the teacher begins by modeling a response to a reflective question that encourages change.

Sample Language: As I think about how I portrayed my character today, I feel that I did not maintain the voice I created throughout the drama. Sometimes I sounded like a news reporter, and other times I just sounded like myself. I want to try to change my voice during the entire drama next time.

I thought I created questions for my character that would encourage you to make inferences, but I think some of my questions could have been better. Not all of them worked well. I need to review my questions more carefully for next time.

SAMPLE QUESTIONS

From a Drama Perspective

- How might you use the acting tool body more effectively in the next drama?

- One of our body drama objectives today was to adjust poses, gestures, movements, and walk for our characters. Think about the character you played and the movements and walk you used. In the next drama, how might you improve on your use of the acting tool body?

Here are some reflective discussion question starters that encourage change in drama work:

- When was it most difficult for you to . . . ?

- How might you use . . . ?

- How might you improve . . . ?

- What changes would you like to make in . . . ?

- What do you think might help you to . . . ?

- What goals might you set for . . . ?

- What do you need to remember when . . . ?

From a Reading Comprehension Perspective

- One of our reading comprehension objectives today was to use inference and make some logical guesses about the language and actions of the characters in our story. Think about the inferences you made. Did they make sense based on what we know about the character? If not, why not?

- What can we do to make deeper inferences in our next lesson?

- How did participating in the drama make you think differently about the text?

Here are some reflective discussion question starters that encourage change in reading comprehension:

- What would you change to better portray your vision of . . . ?

- How might making personal connections with a character improve . . . ?

- What questions can you ask yourself that will improve . . . ?

- If we did this drama again, what dialogue would you include to . . . ?

- What important points did you forget to . . . ?

- In what ways could your role better reflect the author's message about . . . ?

- What were some inferences you could have made about . . . ?

- How might you revise . . . ?

For the best results, you may want to record the students' answers to the questions that encourage change and post them before conducting the next integrated drama lesson. Remind students that these are the changes and improvements they identified for themselves.

Benefits of Reflective Discussions

The entire reflective discussion process provides an informal assessment of the students' understanding of the drama and reading comprehension objectives. Through these discussions, students analyze and evaluate their achievement in terms of these objectives. The goals students identify at the conclusion of the reflective discussion provide them with additional information they can apply, analyze, and evaluate in the next drama. This reflective process is a spiral that encourages students to continually improve and strive for excellence.

Written Assessments

Observing and participating in drama provide many ways for students to respond in writing about their drama and reading comprehension. Written assessments are more formal than observational assessments because they provide tangible information about individual students' growth and responses to the drama and the text.

Design writing prompts to elicit students' thinking based on their use of the acting tools and skills and the reading comprehension strategies. Reading response logs, letters, postcards, captions, lists, newspaper-style reports, and other written responses can all be fashioned to address the stated objectives. Journal entries in which students draw or write their responses to drama experiences provide insight into students' levels of comprehension. Journals may have themes—an author's intent journal, a question journal, a character journal, for example—and writing in them may become a regular component of reflecting on arts-integrated lessons. The amount of writing requested of students can vary according the to the age and ability level of the students and your curricular goals.

Brief and Extended Responses

Young students can write a brief response—a few lines or a paragraph in response to a prompt that focuses on the drama and reading comprehension objectives. Note that a prompt that requests a specific number of answers or examples is more quantifiable, that is, easier to assess.

Older students can write a more extended and detailed reaction to an integrated drama experience. Instead of one sentence or a paragraph, students write a more extensive response that includes a specific number of examples and or details.

SAMPLE WRITING PROMPTS

From a Drama Perspective

Brief Responses

- Draw a picture and/or describe in words how you envisioned your character.

- List three things you imagined in the setting of our drama.

- In your question journal, write one question you would like to ask a character in our story.

- List three adjectives that describe the voice of your character.

- If Sarah had said as Cinderella, "I don't care what you tell me to do; I am going to the ball anyway!" would that have been in character—would it have fit with what we know about the character and the drama's circumstance? Why or why not? Give three reasons.

- Write down a line you spoke in the drama. Then write an improved line that adds new words or sentences to your original line so that it communicates information you wish you had included about your character and the drama's circumstances.

- In your response log, recall an effective use of body by one student actor. Provide two reasons you thought this was effective for the character.

- List one good example of cooperation that you observed in today's drama work.

- Describe one moment in today's drama when it was difficult to keep concentration.

Extended Responses

- Describe two imaginary objects that were important to today's drama. Include in your description the colors and textures of these objects.

- In your character journal, write a brief biography of your character. Include the character's personality, traits, thoughts, and feelings.

- Compare your use of voice [or any of the acting tools and skills] in today's lesson with how you used your voice in the last drama experience. Did you improve? If so, how? If not, why not? Address each of the following points in your comparison.

  - Were you able to sustain the vocal tone and pitch you created for your character throughout the lessons? If not, when did you lose them?

  - How well did the dialogue you created fit the character and the drama's circumstance in the last lesson and in today's? Give an example for each lesson.

- Describe the body [or any of the acting tools and skills] you created for your character in today's lesson.

  - Why did you choose that body for your character?

  - What are two aspects of body that worked well for your character?

  - Name at least one aspect of body that did not work as well as you had hoped.

  - What are two body goals you want to set for the next lesson?

- State three ways actors worked as members of an ensemble in today's lesson.

- Describe two examples of how the use of concentration improved in today's lesson.

- Write one thing you felt you did well in today's drama and explain why you feel this way. Set one personal goal for improvement in the next drama and explain your choice.

- Describe four supportive audience member behaviors.

From a Reading Comprehension Perspective

Brief Responses

- Cite two differences between the mental movie you made while you read the text and the drama that you and your classmates created.

- Yesterday we dramatized _____ and today we dramatized _____ . List two ways the characters you played were the same and two ways they were different.

- In your question journal, write two questions the character you played would like to ask another character in the story.

- Write a letter to any character in today's drama and include two inferential questions. Your questions should ask the character to interpret or draw conclusions about events or other characters.

- Think about today's drama and complete this sentence: I wonder _____ .

- Draw the story in the correct sequence and write a caption under each picture.

- Name a character in the drama that you did *not* play. Write two lines you would speak if you had played that character. (These lines should not be ones we heard today.)

- In your author's intent journal, describe the author's message and create a new title for the book we dramatized today (and/or create a new book cover).

- Write a postcard to a classmate and describe your favorite moment in today's dramatized story.

Extended Responses

- Describe the setting you envisioned for today's drama. Include sights, sounds, and smells.

- How was the character you played in the drama similar to and different from you? Include age, appearance, personality, and attitudes.

- In your response journal, explain how your own feelings and experiences helped you create your character. Provide at least four examples that reveal how you built and activated schema—that is, made connections between the text and your personal experiences and prior knowledge.

- How did dramatizing the story help you understand the author's purpose? Cite three ways.

- List five questions posed during the group work in which you planned the drama. How was questioning valuable in helping you make decisions about the drama?

- Explain three ways in which the reading comprehension skill inferring helped you make decisions about how to pose, move, or speak in the drama.

- Cite three examples of inferences that you heard in other student actors' lines of dialogue.

- In a newspaper-article format, describe three new pieces of information about the characters or circumstances that you learned by participating in or viewing the drama.

Assessment Checklists

FROM A DRAMA PERSPECTIVE

At the end of each drama strategy chapter, you will find assessment checklists with indicators pertinent to that drama strategy. The indicators provide descriptions of evidence that teachers and students can look for when determining whether students effectively use the necessary acting tools and skills. Each indicator comes directly from this book's stated drama objectives outlined in Chapter 2. Figure 4–3 is an abbreviated example of an assessment checklist. Note that there is a category for each acting tool or skill followed by indicators that apply to that tool or skill. The acting tools and skills are in bold; the indicators that apply to that tool or skill are listed below.

The assessment checklists combine features of both simple checklists and rubrics. By limiting the text to the left-hand column, the assessment checklist allows for the quick visual scan and ease of reading typical of a checklist. Like rubrics, however, the assessment checklist allows for varying degrees of student performance—consistently, usually, rarely, or never. Figure 4–4 on page 59 contains definitions of those terms.

Another way to read each indicator is to insert one of the adverbs—consistently, usually, rarely, or never—into its sentence: "The student actor *consistently* agrees to pretend" or "The student actor *usually* agrees to pretend." Place a check mark in the box under the column that best describes the student's degree of proficiency.

Assessment checklists provide students with tools for self-assessment as well as the teacher's appraisal of various aspects of their dramatic work. They also give teachers and students collaborative tools for assessment.

ABBREVIATED EXAMPLE OF ASSESSMENT CHECKLIST

Student Actor's Name _____

DURING THE DRAMA STRATEGY, THE ACTOR . . .	CONSISTENTLY 3	USUALLY 2	RARELY 1	NEVER 0
Imagination/Mind				
. . . agrees to pretend.				
. . . interacts with real and/or imagined characters and objects.				
Voice				
. . . creates and delivers dialogue that is in character.				
. . . projects—speaks loudly enough to be heard.				
Body				
. . . modifies posture, poses, gestures, movements, and/or walk				
. . . uses facial expressions that communicate the thoughts and feelings of the character.				
Cooperation				
. . . works as a member of an ensemble/team.				
Concentration				
. . . focuses intently on the given drama task.				
. . . remains in character.				

FIGURE 4–3   *Abbreviated Example of Assessment Checklist*

The checklists also serve to clarify performance goals. As with all assessment models, students who are aware of a task's desired results and goals perform better (McTighe and Wiggins 1999). Familiarizing students with the criteria in each category of a checklist prior to conducting the drama experience generally enhances the quality of their work.

Using the checklists can also help you identify students' strengths and weaknesses. You may then modify instruction by focusing future lessons on the acting tools and skills that students need to improve.

To translate the conclusions of the checklist into grades, you may use the suggested points assigned to each indicator category. Point allotments range from three for a determination of "consistently" to zero for "never." Adding up the points per indicator will result in a total performance score. Each checklist also includes quality labels to help you interpret the overall score. For example:

ASSESSMENT CHECKLIST: DEFINITIONS OF DEGREES OF PERFORMANCE			
CONSISTENTLY 3	USUALLY 2	RARELY 1	NEVER 0
The student demonstrates the behavior described by the indicator precisely and reliably throughout the drama experience.	The student largely demonstrates the behavior described by the indicator. There is evidence of an occasional lack of skill, but overwhelmingly, the student shows proficiency in the behavior.	The student intermittently demonstrates aspects of the behavior described by the indicator.	The student demonstrates no evidence of the behavior described by the indicator.

FIGURE 4–4   *Assessment Checklist: Definitions of Degrees of Performance*

32–36   Standing Ovation

27–31   Round of Applause

22–26   Polite Clapping

0–21   Back to Rehearsal

Also at the bottom of each checklist is a space for students to identify a personal goal for improvement in an acting tool or skill. This is an opportunity for students to target an individual objective to strengthen in the next drama experience.

The chart in Figure 4–5 is designed to help deepen your understanding of the indicators of student proficiency in a given drama task. In the left-hand column are the indicators or separate traits of performance as they appear on the assessment checklists. In the right-hand column are detailed descriptions of some examples of evidence of proficiency. Please note that proficiency in relation to an indicator does not require that a student demonstrate evidence of every example listed in the corresponding right-hand column. Focus on examples that are appropriate for your objectives and students.

FROM A READING COMPREHENSION PERSPECTIVE

In addition to assessing the students' proficiency by using assessment checklists for drama strategies, you can also use the Reading Comprehension Strategies Assessment Checklist for an integrated drama lesson (see Figure 4–6). Its indicators provide descriptions of evidence of students' use of reading comprehension strategies during integrated drama lessons. Each indicator comes directly from this book's

EXAMPLES OF PROFICIENCY FOR ASSESSMENT CHECKLISTS

Student's Actor's Name _____

IMAGINATION/MIND	
Indicators	**The extent to which the student actor:**
. . . agrees to pretend.	■ suspends disbelief and commits to participating fully in the drama experience. ■ portrays characters and objects in different settings and situations.
. . . reacts to imaginary sights, sounds, smells, tastes, and textures.	■ responds as a character to imaginary dramatic experiences or settings with appropriate movements, gestures, words, facial expressions, and/or noises.
. . . interacts with real and/or imagined characters and objects.	■ mimes handling imagined objects believably. ■ uses real objects as if they are something else. ■ accepts the roles (humans, animals, or objects) played by their classmates and teachers and engages in acting with them. ■ reacts and responds to characters not physically present in the classroom.
. . . retells the predetermined story in the correct sequence.	■ recalls the story or series of events accurately and in chronological order. ■ applies the rehearsed sequence in a dramatic presentation.

VOICE	
Indicators	**The extent to which the student actor:**
. . . varies vocal tone and pitch to create character voices and/or sound effects.	■ changes personal vocal characteristics to speak as a character with different vocal qualities—high, low, deep, squeaky, accented, and so on. ■ uses the voice to create sound effects that enhance the dramatic experience—wind, rain, birds, animals, machinery, clocks ticking, phones ringing, and so on.
. . . creates and delivers dialogue that is in character.	■ invents and speaks lines that accurately communicate information about the character and the drama's circumstances. ■ speaks statements, questions, and expressions likely to be spoken by the particular character in the particular dramatic circumstance.
. . . projects—speaks loudly enough to be heard.	■ demonstrates appropriate volume when speaking in role—neither too soft nor too loud. ■ maintains appropriate volume; avoids diminishing vocal volume at the ends of phrases or sentences.
. . . speaks with expression that reflects the personality, traits, thoughts, and feelings of the character.	■ conveys the character's qualities, mood, and emotions by vocal intonation, emphasis, inflection, tempo, and so on. ■ uses an effective tone of voice for the character played—haughty, sarcastic, innocent, powerful, annoyed, stern, sweet, foolish, and so on. ■ uses, if appropriate, an accent, drawl, twang, dialect, and so on.
. . . articulates—speaks clearly enough to be understood.	■ pronounces words precisely. ■ uses the lips, teeth, and tongue to carefully speak words aloud. ■ refrains from mumbling and merging syllables and words together. ■ pronounces word endings.
. . . modifies word tempo—speaks slowly enough to be understood.	■ refrains from speaking too rapidly. ■ avoids speeding up word tempo at the ends of sentences or phrases.

FIGURE 4–5   *Examples of Proficiency for Assessment Checklists*

BODY	
Indicators	**The extent to which the student actor:**
. . . modifies posture, poses, gestures, movements, and/or walk.	▪ reveals the physical dimensions of characters or objects he or she is playing. ▪ stands or sits in a manner fitting the age, health, attitude, energy level, occupation, and so on, of the character. ▪ poses and/or moves appropriately when playing the role of an inanimate object. ▪ enhances a character portrayal by altering normal manner of posing or moving— struts, shuffles, sweeps, strolls, marches, saunters, creeps, waves, shrugs, beckons, bows, and so on. **For Tableau and Human Slide Shows:** ▪ modifies poses and/or positions with an audience's perspective in mind—works with others to ensure that each actor's pose and face (as appropriate) are visible to observers. ▪ modifies poses and/or positions to include a variety of levels—works with others to create interesting stage pictures that include actors posed in low, medium, and high positions. **For Human Slide Shows:** ▪ alters poses from one slide to the next—changes each pose to show a progression of action that heightens visual interest.
. . . uses energy when modifying or adjusting body.	▪ enhances a character portrayal by posing or moving with appropriate vitality and intensity.
. . . uses facial expressions that communicate the thoughts and feelings of the character.	▪ enhances a character portrayal by adjusting the face to convey emotions, ideas, and opinions—arrogance, disbelief, compassion, bitterness, fear, horror, anger, and so on.
COOPERATION	
Indicators	**The extent to which the student actor:**
. . . works as a member of an ensemble/team.	▪ listens to peers and the teacher. ▪ follows instructions. ▪ demonstrates respect for ideas contributed by peers. ▪ collaborates with peers and the teacher. ▪ alters actions and responses based on side coaching—suggestions and prompts provided by the teacher during the drama. ▪ refrains from disrupting the dramatic work of others. **For Human Slide Shows:** ▪ changes positions quickly, quietly, and efficiently.
. . . remains silent when cued.	▪ responds to signals requiring quiet.
. . . remains frozen when cued.	▪ works as a member of an ensemble when the drama task requires stillness.
CONCENTRATION	
Indicators	**The extent to which the student actor:**
. . . focuses intently on the given drama task.	▪ pays deliberate attention while acting. ▪ disregards actions and noises unrelated to the drama.
. . . remains in character.	▪ speaks only as the character. ▪ attends and responds appropriately to the other characters. ▪ controls inappropriate laughter and giggling. ▪ stays in the fictional world of the drama.

FIGURE 4–5   (continued)

READING COMPREHENSION STRATEGIES ASSESSMENT CHECKLIST

Student's Actor's Name _____

DURING PLANNING, ENACTING, AND REFLECTING ON THE DRAMA STRATEGY, THE ACTOR . . .	YES	NO
Developing Sensory Images		
____ demonstrates in rehearsal a vision of a character by experimenting with voice and body. ____ interacts with setting, characters, and objects (both real and imagined). ____ articulates the sights, sounds, smells, tastes, and/or textures envisioned during the drama.		
Building and Activating Schema		
____ brainstorms ways in which personal life and prior learning experiences correlate with the text and/or the characters to be portrayed. ____ creates actions and/or delivers dialogue that demonstrate connections to personal life and prior learning experiences. ____ articulates ways in which personal life and prior learning experiences are similar to and different from the drama's characters and circumstances.		
Questioning		
____ discusses, asks, answers, and develops questions that ____ explore unresolved issues, concerns, and ideas. ____ probe for deeper meaning. ____ seek to discover new information. ____ speculate on possibilities. ____ search for answers to problems. ____ articulate unresolved issues, concerns, and ideas raised during the drama.		
Determining Importance		
____ discusses the essential elements of the text in preparation for the drama. ____ incorporates key information about the text (e.g., setting, characters, conflict, obstacles, and/or resolution) into dialogue and action. ____ articulates an understanding of the author's intent and/or the text's primary message gained during the drama.		
Inferring		
____ draws conclusions and makes interpretations based on information not specifically stated in the text in preparation for drama. ____ creates actions and/or delivers dialogue that demonstrates reading between the lines and/or making logical guesses. ____ articulates new understandings of the text gained by participating in the drama.		
Synthesis		
____ combines information in the text with prior knowledge to plan a drama. ____ creates action and delivers dialogue that demonstrates an understanding of new perspectives. ____ uses information from other texts, and/or makes judgments about the text. ____ articulates personal responses to the text and new ideas, opinions, beliefs, and/or perspectives gained by participating in the drama.		

FIGURE 4–6 *Reading Comprehension Strategies Assessment Checklist for an Integrated Drama Lesson*

stated reading comprehension objectives outlined in Chapter 2. The indicators correlate with the planning, enacting, and reflecting phases of a drama lesson.

The checklist is designed to be used with any of the four drama strategies outlined in this text. You can introduce it to the students before beginning the drama lesson and/or include it in any other form of assessment previously discussed. You can duplicate the checklist for student and teacher use and/or enlarge and post it.

Concluding Remarks

When integrated drama experiences consistently include (1) clear and understandable objectives in both drama and reading comprehension, (2) a well-crafted and well-executed lesson that addresses the objectives, and (3) a variety of assessment tasks that correlate with the objectives, students will improve in developing skills in both drama and reading comprehension. Direct application of the types of assessment discussed in this chapter appear for each of the four drama strategies explored in this text.

5

Story Dramatization

What Does Effective Story Dramatization Look Like?

In story dramatization, students enact a scene described or implied in a text or an entire story. The students portray all the characters and significant objects in the scene or story. The dialogue the students speak is created extemporaneously. They synthesize their knowledge of the text as they improvise the story line in their own words.

Drama Strategy: Story Dramatization

Story dramatization is a type of planned improvisation—an unscripted scene that the actors plan before presenting. Students use their acting tools and skills to become the characters or the objects in the scene or story. The text is the foundation of the dramatization. It guides the sequence of the action and the dialogue. A rough outline of the story dramatization is preplanned, but the words and actions occur in the moment of the drama. Students use their own words and movements to convey the action and meaning of the scene or story.

Suggested Grade Levels

Story dramatization is a flexible strategy that can be modified for use with students in grades 1 and above.

The Teacher's Role in the Drama

Here is an overview of the teacher's responsibilities in implementing this strategy. The teacher will:

- select an appropriate text
- familiarize the students with the text

- determine drama and reading comprehension objectives

- prepare the students to take on roles (review the acting tools and skills)

- direct the action

- facilitate and/or narrate the drama

- lead the reflection and assessment of the drama experience from both a drama and a reading comprehension perspective

The Students' Role in the Drama

The students' main responsibility is to enact a scene or story by portraying its characters and objects. To do so effectively, students will:

- comprehend the basic plot of the text

- understand the characters' thoughts, feelings, and motivations

- apply the basic acting tools and skills

- demonstrate their understanding of the text by enacting the scene or story in their own words

- reflect on the drama experience in relation to the drama and reading comprehension objectives

The Rationale in Relation to Reading Comprehension

Story dramatization is a rich drama strategy that integrates drama with all of the reading comprehension strategies.

Developing Sensory Images For students to become characters and reenact events from a text, they must first envision the characters and the sequence of events. They must visualize the setting and the circumstances of the events. For students to take on the voices of the characters, they must be able to hear the characters in their imaginations.

Building and Activating Schema As students portray characters, they make conscious and unconscious personal connections with a character's thoughts, feelings, and circumstances. In addition, they apply knowledge they have gained about the character while reading the text. They demonstrate their understanding in the dialogue they create, the manner in which they express the dialogue, and the actions they execute.

Questioning To dramatize scenes that are implied but not specifically described in the text, students internally ask and answer questions about the characters' dialogue and actions. In addition, in their planning, students ask and ponder questions about the most effective way to dramatize characters, events, and circumstances in a scene or story.

Determining Importance Since the dialogue and actions in a story dramatization reflect the story line, students must distill the entire scene or story to its essential components. To convey the essence of a scene or story, students distinguish the main events from the less important details. This process often leads students to a deeper understanding of the author's intent.

Inferring Since students dramatize a text in their own words, they use inference as they create dialogue for their characters. When students enact scenes implied but not fully developed in a text, they use inference to make logical guesses about the characters' choices, motivations, dialogue, and actions.

Synthesis The process of story dramatization is synthesis. The students summarize the essential elements of a text in their own words. They transform the written word into a live drama. They make a personal connection with the text as they find their own words to convey their character's thoughts, feelings, motivations, and circumstances.

Drama and Theatre Connections

Story dramatization is a form of improvisation. Improvisation in its purest form is a spontaneous scene created by actors without a script. Story dramatization more closely resembles a planned improvisation—one in which there is a predetermined structure but no script. In story dramatization, a scene or story serves as the plot, but the characters' words are spoken extemporaneously. The dialogue, therefore, may be different each time the scene or story is dramatized.

Story dramatization may also include improvising scenes that are implied but not fully developed in a text. For these scenes, students must rely heavily on prior knowledge of the characters in order to achieve effective improvisations.

Directors use this process in rehearsing a play. Often, to get at the essence of a scene and to help actors make personal connections with their characters, a director will ask the actors to act out a scene in their own words. By temporarily leaving the words of the playwright behind and dramatizing the same sequence of action, actors often discover the deeper meaning of a scene. They make stronger personal connections with the feelings and circumstances of the characters. These discoveries often inform and affect the actors' performances when they return to speaking the words of the playwright. This technique is often used when the language of the play is not in modern vernacular.

Directors also often have actors improvise scenes that are implied in the play but not included in the script. Improvising these scenes deepens actors' understanding of their characters. They discover how their characters might behave outside the strict confines of the script. This breathes life into their characters and helps the actors understand their characters as fuller, richer human beings. This knowledge can profoundly enrich the actors' final performances.

Playwrights also find this process beneficial in the development of a new script. Improvisations conducted during rehearsals for a staged reading or production of a play can inform the playwright of necessary changes or scenes that need to be added to the script.

Figure 5–1 details the steps for conducting an effective story dramatization.

STEPS FOR EFFECTIVE STORY DRAMATIZATION

Preparing for Story Dramatization
Teacher Planning
    Step 1: Select an appropriate text.
- Identify the portion(s) of the text to dramatize.
  - Consider time.
  - Gauge skill levels.
  - Consider objectives.

    Step 2: Determine the key drama and reading comprehension objectives.
    Step 3: Choose a delivery approach for the text.
- Deliver the text aloud.
  - Determine listening tasks.
  - Deliver the text silently.

    Step 4: Determine a procedure for sequencing.
    Step 5: Organize the dramatization.
- Determine the structure of the dramatization.
  - narrative pantomime
  - simultaneous dramatization with dialogue
  - group dramatization
  - whole-class dramatization
- Identify a role for every student.
- Define the acting area.
- Create a plan for blocking the scene or story.
- Identify and plan how to dramatize challenging moments in the text.
- Plan the narration.

Student Preparation
    Step 6: Identify drama and reading comprehension objectives.
- Define the drama strategy.
- Conduct pertinent warm-ups.

    Step 7: Familiarize students with the text.
- Deliver the scene or story.
- Sequence the plot.

    Step 8: Describe the story dramatization guidelines.
- Define the acting area.
- Revisit the basics.
- Clarify roles.
- Rehearse challenging moments.
- Explain the blocking floor plan.

Conducting the Story Dramatization
    Step 9: Enact the scene or story.
- Transition from reality to fantasy.
- Narrate the action.
- Remain in the fiction.
- Transition from fantasy to reality.

Reflecting on the Story Dramatization
    Step 10: Assess the students.
- observational assessments
- reflective discussions
- written assessments
- assessment checklists

FIGURE 5–1   *Steps for Effective Story Dramatization*

Preparing for Effective Story Dramatization

Teacher Planning

Step 1: Select an Appropriate Text

Choosing an appropriate text is key for successful story dramatization. Because this strategy can be used for either a scene from a text or the entire story, you can use picture books as well as chapter books. The chart in Figure 5–2 may help you choose a text.

The story "The Monster Year: A Chinese New Year's Legend," retold by Lenore Blank Kelner, will be the text used as an example throughout this chapter. Please read the story so that all the references and examples are clear.

> **The Monster Year: A Chinese New Year's Legend,**
> **retold by Lenore Blank Kelner**
>
> Every year on New Year's Eve in a small fishing village in China, the great monster, Year, would rise up out of the sea. He would bring with him great huge waves of water that would wash up onto the shore and destroy all the homes in the village and take away all the villagers' possessions. Shoes, clothes, toys, candles, food—all would wash out to sea.
>
> After losing everything for many years, the villagers came up with a new plan. They agreed that on New Year's Eve day they would pack up all they could carry and move to higher ground—to the mountains—so they would be safe.
>
> One New Year's Eve day, the villagers were busy in their homes packing their most precious belongings. They moved swiftly, knowing they didn't have much time. Suddenly an old beggar appeared in the town and knocked on the door of one of the houses.
>
> "Excuse me," he called meekly. The door was ajar and so he gently pushed it open. "I am poor and hungry. Please can you give me some food?"
>
> But the family inside did not stop packing. They barely glanced at him. They just shouted out, "We can't help you now; Year is coming!"
>
> The exhausted beggar moved on to the next home and knocked on the door. This time no one answered even though he could hear people moving inside. "Please help me," he cried. "Can you spare just a few grains of rice?"
>
> But the family inside yelled back, "We can't help you now; Year is coming!"
>
> He went to a third door, asked the same question, and got the same answer.
>
> At last he saw an old woman feverishly packing a basket outside her home. He pleaded with her. "I beg of you, please give me something to eat or I will die from hunger."
>
> She quickly unwrapped some steamed rice cakes from her basket and handed them to the beggar and said, "You can't stay here! You must go with us to the mountains! Year is coming!"
>
> "Who is this Year?" asked the beggar as he devoured the first rice cake.
>
> "Year is a monster that comes out of the sea every New Year's Eve at midnight. He brings with him a terrible storm and huge waves. He takes with him our houses and all of our belongings! You must not stay!"
>
> The beggar wiped his mouth and looked into the eyes of the old woman. "I am not afraid, kind woman. I will face this monster, Year. Give me a lantern and a red cape. Give

GUIDELINES FOR SELECTING A SCENE OR STORY FOR DRAMATIZATION

The text should have *all* of these qualities:

- a scene or story that is developmentally appropriate for the students
- characters and objects that students have the drama skills to portray
- a text that connects in some way with classroom content objectives and has the potential for taking the content to a deeper level

The text should have some or all of the following qualities:

Setting
- an intriguing setting that has impact on the story
- a rich setting that students can dramatize (vocally and physically)
- a setting that opens new worlds to the students
- a setting that includes a maximum of four locations

Plot
- a plot that the students can clearly understand
- a plot with which students can identify
- a plot that intrigues the students
- a plot that includes a repetitive pattern in which several characters go through the same experience until there is a culminating event (especially for young children)
- a plot that revolves around a dramatic situation—an adventure or a quest
- a plot that has a clear conflict and/or tension
- a plot that has the potential to empower students through the dramatization
- a plot that engages students on a feeling and thinking level
- a plot that contains individual scenes for short dramatizations
- a plot that you can envision dramatizing successfully

Characters
- characters with whom the students can strongly identify so that they can easily and eagerly predict the characters' thoughts and feelings
- several minor characters (in addition to the protagonist and antagonist) that play significant roles in the story
- objects vital to the plot that can be played by students as speaking roles
- characters and objects that can be played by multiple students so that all have an opportunity to act
- enough characters so that all students have an opportunity to act, but not so many that the teacher or students will have trouble keeping track of the roles
- enough character dialogue clearly or implicitly stated that provides students with the necessary clues for creating their own dialogue

Theme
- a theme that students can understand
- a theme that's meaningful to the students
- a theme that is important for the students to consider

FIGURE 5–2 *Guidelines for Selecting a Scene or Story for Dramatization*

me two large knives and a chopping board. I will stay here and if my plan works, Year will never return."

The old woman hobbled inside her small house and brought out the beggar's requests. Then she and all the other villagers hurried to the mountains.

The beggar sat in front of the old woman's door. He put the red cape around his shoulders. Then he lit the lantern and waited. He watched the sea.

At midnight the monster lifted his head out of the sea. The ocean waves swelled. As soon as the beggar saw Year he began hitting the knives as hard as he could on the chopping block. This made a loud and frightening sound.

Year lifted his head out of the water and howled, "What is that noise?" Then he saw the red cape. He bellowed, "What is that red? It must be blood! Ahhhh!" Year screamed with fear and sunk back into the sea, never to be seen again.

When the villagers returned their village was safe. Their houses were not destroyed and all their possessions were in place. Both Year and the beggar were gone forever.

From that day on, every New Year's Eve the Chinese people dress in red and make loud noises with firecrackers that sound like big knives hitting a chopping board to remember the beggar and to keep the monster, Year, away.

IDENTIFY THE PORTION(S) OF THE TEXT TO DRAMATIZE

Once you have selected a text, decide if you are going to dramatize the entire story or chapter or just one or two scenes from the text. When you first conduct story dramatizations with your students, it is best to select one or two scenes to dramatize. Eventually you may choose to dramatize an entire story or a chapter from a book.

Dramatize Scenes Found Within the Text A scene is a moment of action in a story or play that has a beginning, middle, and end. Identify a scene(s) that includes enough action, characters, and/or objects so that all of the students can be involved. In story dramatization, several students can play one character. For some scenes or stories, the entire class can play one character or all the characters. Assigning roles for story dramatization is discussed in more detail in step 5. Use the chart in Figure 5–2 to inform your choice of scenes.

For the story "The Monster Year," a good scene that can involve all the students occurs at the end of the story when the monster rises from the sea. One or two students play the beggar and all the remaining students play the monster reacting to the noise and the fear of blood.

Another scene that can involve a large number of students is the one in which the villagers pack their belongings before the arrival of the monster. Groups of students play the villagers and one student plays the beggar coming to their homes, begging for food.

As you decide what scene or story to dramatize, you may want to do the following:

Consider Time

- What amount of time can you devote to the dramatization? Can you devote only one lesson or a series of lessons over several days?

- How long will each lesson be?

Gauge Skill Levels

- What is the drama skill level of the students? Are their acting tools and skills developed enough to effectively work with the text? How well can they cooperate? Concentrate?

- What is your skill level? What length of dramatization is comfortable at this level of development? What part(s) of the text can you envision dramatizing?

- How familiar are the students with the text?

Consider Objectives

- What reading comprehension objectives do you want the students to achieve through the story dramatization process?

- Based on those objectives, what scene(s) or story might best help meet them? If your reading comprehension objective is *determining importance*, you may want the students to distinguish between main events and details by asking them to dramatize key scenes. For example, in "The Monster Year," three of the key scenes are (1) the beggar arrives at the village and meets the old woman, (2) the monster appears and disappears, and (3) the villagers return to find their homes intact.

- If your objective is *synthesis* you may want the students to enact the entire story, as that will require students to summarize the text in their own words.

Step 2: Determine the Key Drama and Reading Comprehension Objectives

DRAMA OBJECTIVES

All drama strategies included in this text require students to use all the basic acting tools and skills. The following objectives, however, are the key drama objectives emphasized when planning, enacting, and reflecting on story dramatization.

Voice When they play roles, students will use aspects of voice to communicate information about their characters and the drama's circumstances. While acting, students will:

- vary vocal tone and pitch to create character voices and/or sound effects

- create and deliver dialogue that is in character—accurately communicates information about the character and the drama's circumstances

Body When they play roles, students will use aspects of body to communicate information about their characters and the drama's circumstances. While acting, students will:

- modify posture, poses, gestures, movements, and/or walk

Cooperation Because drama is a collaborative art form, students will work as members of an ensemble. When they plan, enact, observe, and reflect upon their work, students will:

- create a community of actors who work together and support each other as members of a team

READING COMPREHENSION OBJECTIVES

All of the reading comprehension objectives are a part of story dramatization; however, the following objectives are the key reading comprehension objectives for the planning, enacting, and reflecting upon story dramatization.

Determining Importance To find the essentials in a text, students will distinguish between the main ideas and the details of what they read. Students will:

- demonstrate comprehension of the important elements of the text
- list the sequence of key events
  - retell the plot (beginning, middle, and end)

Inferring To extend and enrich the meaning of a text, students will draw conclusions and make interpretations based on information provided, but not specifically stated, in the text. Students will:

- discover the implied information within the text—read between the lines
- combine clues found in the text with prior knowledge to make logical guesses

Synthesis To demonstrate their understanding of a text, students will take information from what they have read, combine it with prior knowledge, and create something new. Students will:

- respond personally to the text

The objectives listed above are the key drama and reading comprehension objectives for story dramatization as described in this chapter. Each time you use story dramatization you may wish to vary the objectives. In the teacher planning stage, it is important to determine which of the many drama objectives (see page 11) and reading comprehension objectives (see page 13) you wish to target.

Step 3: Choose a Delivery Approach for the Text

A delivery approach is the method by which you convey the text to the students. The appropriate approach is based on the age, grade, and ability level of the students. Since everyone loves to hear a good story, telling or reading all or part of it aloud is an option for all grade levels. Older students (intermediate and middle school) may read the text silently. For primary-grade students, you can tell or read the story aloud.

DELIVER THE TEXT ALOUD

It is beneficial when introducing a story to tell it rather than read it to the students. If that is not possible, it can be beneficial to read the story without showing the students the pictures. When students listen to a story without pictures, they are more apt to see the story in their minds. They create their own mental pictures of the characters and the circumstances the characters face. After the dramatization, you can read the text to the students and show the pictures and compare the two versions of the story.

As you tell or read the story aloud, create different voices for the characters so that the students are fully engaged, attentive, and focused. The vocal variety helps the students envision the characters and provides a model for students to consider when they take on the voice of their own characters in the drama.

However, not all stories can or should be told or read aloud without the visuals. The illustrations in some texts are essential for the students to comprehend the story. In other texts, the setting or action of the story may be so unfamiliar that students need the visual clues for understanding. For young students, students who are English Language Learners (ELL), or students with little real-world experiences, the pictures may be key for comprehension. For these students, it's best to show the pictures as you tell the story. This is often referred to as a "picture walk" of the text. You show the pictures and tell the story instead of reading it word for word.

As you tell or picture walk through the story, you will naturally abridge the text slightly. There will be details you will not include. There will be figurative language that you will leave out in the telling. When you read the text word for word after working with story dramatization, invite the students to compare and contrast the two versions of the story. Ask the students to raise their hands when they hear a detail you missed as you told the story. Stop during the reading to examine and relish the author's choice of words. Delivering a story in this manner makes the reading of the text the icing on the cake. The students yearn to hear the author's work. They make a deep personal connection to the text.

Several factors can influence your choice of a delivery approach to a text, including:

- your familiarity with the text

- the students' ability to comprehend the story without visuals

- the complexity of the story (How essential are the pictures to understanding the story?)

- the prior experience of the students

- the ability of the students to focus and attend

⌁ Teaching Tip

For young students, *Story Can Theatre* can be an effective method for telling a story. This storytelling technique involves using various objects and toys to represent the setting and characters in the story. For the story "The Monster Year," represent the ocean with a piece of blue felt, the beggar with a toy man, the old woman with a toy woman, and the monster with a monster finger puppet .

Place the items in an opaque container such as a can or a bucket. You can decorate the container to reflect the story's setting or country of origin.

Take the items out one by one as you tell the story. Lift each character as he or she talks in the story. Animate the items as you would a puppet by changing your voice for each character and moving the characters as they speak.

It is important to include items big enough for all students to see, but not so big that you lose the sense of them being toys. It is also important to be sure to set the toys on a surface so all the students can see.

This technique captures the attention of younger students, students who are English Language Learners, and students with little real-world experience. The toys engage them and help them envision the story. After dramatizing the story, students can read the actual text and compare the two versions in relation to the differences in the amount of detail.

Determine Listening Tasks

A listening task is a sound, word, or phrase and an accompanying gesture that the students respond to on cue as they listen to you tell or read a story aloud. One to three preplanned listening tasks per story are sufficient because if you include too many listening tasks, the students will be so busy listening for the cues that they will not be able to attend to the content of the story.

⌁ Teaching Tip—Benefits of Using Listening Tasks

A listening task:

- promotes focus and attention; students are engaged and have a purpose for listening

- promotes retention and comprehension since students are truly listening

- addresses various learning styles, especially the kinesthetic learner

- supports brain research on the importance of organized movement in stimulating brain connections

- supports brain research on the importance of including the mind, body, and emotions in the learning process

Teachers cue students by simply pointing to them when it is time for them to respond with the listening task or gesturing to them in some other consistent manner. If the story has a repetitive sentence or phrase, another effective cueing device is to simply stop telling or reading the story midsentence and wait for the students to provide the listening task that completes the sentence. Following are some sample listening tasks.

- *a repetitive word or phrase that is found in the text*
  Example: In "The Monster Year," students create gestures to correspond with the repetitive sentence "We can't help you now; Year is coming!" The teacher cues the students by starting the sentence: "The beggar asked for food and the villagers answered . . ."

- *a created repeating line that fits the story and maintains the integrity of the text*
  Example: The story "The Monster Year" does not include a repeating line that the beggar says when he knocks at each door, but the teacher and/or the students can create one as well as gestures to correspond with the line, such as "Please help me, help me! I am *so* hungry!"

- *repetitive sound effects that are integral to the text and/or the setting*
  Example: The students use their voices and arms to represent the waves and the sounds of the villagers packing in the story "The Monster Year." Point to the students each time the sound effect fits in the story. See the activity Environment Orchestra in Chapter 3 (page 30) for more information.

- *dialogue a character might say that is implied but not provided in the text*
  Example: The students can create dialogue and corresponding gestures that the monster might say as midnight draws near and the waves increase in size and strength, such as "Hmm, it is just about time for me to raise my ugly head and attack!"

DELIVER THE TEXT SILENTLY

When students read a text silently, it is beneficial to review the scene or story aloud before beginning the dramatization. The students need a basic knowledge of the plot in order to enact the scene or story. One simple way to gauge students' knowledge of the plot is through sequencing the main events.

Step 4: Determine a Procedure for Sequencing

Whether the text is delivered aloud or silently, students need to recall the main events in the proper sequence before they can dramatize the scene or story. If students demonstrate a basic knowledge of the plot and action of the scene or story, they can apply that knowledge in a deeper way during the dramatization.

There are a variety of ways teachers review the order of events in a story. Graphic organizers, sequence charts, and story maps are commonly used. Often, young students draw pictures of the sequence and write sentences to accompany each illustration. Any of these methods can be used in preparation for story dramatization. During the dramatization, leave the sequence of events visible to guide the dramatization.

Following are four methods for sequencing that help students get to the dramatization quickly.

A Preprinted List of the Sequence of Events

Prepare in advance a list of the sequence of events on a large piece of chart paper or a transparency. Cover the events so that students cannot see them. Ask questions that lead the students to identify each event correctly and then reveal that entry on the chart or transparency. The list should focus on key actions in the story and avoid detail. To streamline the process so that students' attention does not wane, make each entry brief and focused on an action. The class can review details orally.

Here is a sample of brief entries for the story "The Monster Year":

1. The hungry beggar arrives at the village.
2. No one feeds him.
3. Finally, an old woman gives him food and tells him to run away.
4. She explains about the monster.

A List of Characters

For some stories, a simple list of the characters in the order in which they appear in the story serves as a good sequencing tool.

- Beggar

- Family 1

- Family 2

- Family 3

- Old Woman

- Monster, Year

Pictures (Young Students)

Use illustrations or drawings of the text to sequence the events. Add a phrase or sentence to the bottom of each picture to reinforce the sequence. Write a number on each illustration to signify the order of the events in the story. Post the pictures as the students identify the events.

Toys (Young Students)

Use miniatures and toys to represent the sequence of the story (see the description of Story Can Theatre in the teaching tip on page 74). As students orally identify the event, take out a toy to represent the event. Line the toys up on a table from left to right (from the students' perspective). Lining the toys up in this way simulates the focus and direction students use when they read.

Step 5: Organize the Dramatization

The dramatization of a scene or story needs to be structured and carefully planned for students to reach their drama and reading comprehension objectives. Without planning, students can lose focus and behavioral issues may arise. If the dramatization is well organized, students understand expectations and remain on task. At the end of this chapter is a planning sheet (Figure 5–5) that reviews all the components in organizing a dramatization.

DETERMINE THE STRUCTURE OF THE DRAMATIZATION

Outlined in the following sections are various ways to structure a story dramatization. The list is organized from simple to complex, but it is by no means complete. As you become more proficient, you will find ways to combine several of these structures in one story dramatization, and ultimately you will develop your own structures. All of these structures share one basic principle—all students are involved. Every student has a meaningful role as a character or object in the dramatization.

Narrative Pantomime As you narrate the scene or story, students collectively mime the action. You provide all the language and the cues for the action. In silence, the students create the bodies for all the characters and enact the text sequentially while you speak.

This structure can be used as a warm-up activity for students who need extra exposure to the text before dramatizing it in their own words. As you narrate, increase volume or add emphasis to cue the students to become the next person or object. Adding descriptive words to the narration increases the effectiveness of the dramatization.

Sample Language: As I tell the story, act out all the characters in your personal space. This is a silent activity that focuses on your use of body. "Once upon a time a poor, hungry beggar went down a steep mountain and came to a village by the sea. . . ."

After students feel comfortable collectively miming all the parts of the story, the same process can be modified for small groups of three to five students, with each playing a separate role in a scene. Assign roles and have the students mime the scene as you narrate.

Simultaneous Dramatization with Dialogue All the students simultaneously play a character in the story. The teacher cues all the students to create the character's body and speak in the character's voice. Together, all the students spontaneously devise their own language and deliver a monologue of the character's thoughts and feelings. The teacher provides the cue to end the drama.

This is a good structure to use midstory before the students know the entire plot. It encourages students to predict what might happen in the story, to use inference to demonstrate their comprehension of the story up to this point, to explore the voice of a character, and to devise dialogue.

Sample Language: Actors, find your personal space. Everyone will now play the beggar. It is the moment the third family refuses to give you food. You are starving and do not understand why everyone has refused to help you. When I say, "Places," show me the body of the hungry beggar. Places. When I say, "Action," begin speaking as the beggar. What do you say to yourself? What are you thinking and feeling? Let me hear your inner thoughts. When I say, "Freeze," you will stop being the beggar. When I say, "Curtain," we will all be ourselves again. Action.

 Dramatic Detail—Objects as Characters

In story dramatization, students can also play objects that may or may not move or speak. Students can play the third family's house or the old woman's door. Students can infer what the door might say to the beggar—"You've come to the right house" or "Go away! Can't you see how busy she is?" or "What do you want?" and so on. In this chapter, any references to students playing characters also include students playing objects that move and speak.

Group Dramatization Divide the students into small groups of four to six. Provide each group with one scene of a text to dramatize. Assign roles or allow the students to decide which character each will play. Students create the bodies and voices of the characters, rehearse and revise the scene, and present it to the entire class or to another group.

Whole-Class Dramatization The remainder of this chapter discusses in depth the whole-class dramatization format. This structure can be a compilation of some or all of the other structures already described. In this format, an entire class works together to dramatize a scene or story. Individual student actors, pairs, and even small groups contribute to the sequential enactment of a scene or story. Students portray characters. The teacher narrates and cues the students to speak. The narration threads the story together, but the dialogue is spontaneously created by the students, revealing the students' ability to infer and synthesize the text.

IDENTIFY A ROLE FOR EVERY STUDENT

As defined in Chapter 2, drama is a process that focuses on the participants and is not meant for an audience. In story dramatization, it is therefore ideal if all students have a meaningful role in the drama. In drama, more than one person can play a role. People, animals, and even objects can talk. Boys can play girls and girls can play boys. This nontraditional form of casting helps you find substantial roles for everyone.

Determine how the scene or story will be cast to include all the students. Create a cast list that divides the roles and ensures that all students will participate. Assign the parts just prior to the enactment of the story. Students can volunteer for parts or you can assign them. Post the cast list so that the students see all the roles.

As you develop your cast list, examine your scene or story and list all the characters and objects that students could play. The list for "The Monster Year" could include:

The Beggar

Family 1

Door of the House of Family 1

Family 2

Door of the House of Family 2

Family 3

Door of the House of Family 3

Old Woman

Door of the House of Old Woman

Lantern

Cloak

The Monster, Year

"The Monster Year" has many characters, but even a story featuring as few as two characters can be dramatized by a large group. Here are some effective ways to involve every student in your classroom cast:

- Create a sound effects section—a group of students whose task is to create the sounds but not to overwhelm the action. They can include gestures or movements to accompany the sounds. (Note: The class might have already created some of the sounds in the warm-up activity Environment Orchestra; see Chapter 3, page 30).

- Have a small group of students play one character, such as the monster.

- Have students play objects that speak, for example, the lantern and the doors.

- Have pairs or small groups of students work together to play an object, such as the cloak or the door.

- Double-cast major roles. For example, have two students play the beggar or the old woman. (Pairing a verbal student with a less verbal student can work well for promoting language and full class participation.) You or the students can plan how they will share the role. They can speak simultaneously, divide the part, or alternate speaking lines.

- Vary the student playing a major role in each new scene of the story. For example, the role of the beggar can be played by five different students. The role switches each time the character interacts with a different character.

If possible, all characters and objects should speak.

See the following boxed sections for three possible cast lists for the story "The Monster Year" for a class of twenty-four students. The lists reflect the casting options just described. Experimenting with various methods for casting a story dramatization improves your skills as a facilitator and presents new challenges for students.

Cast List Option One: 1–24 Students

In this version, the students dramatize only the last scene of the story, when the beggar faces the monster. Groups of students plan how they will work together to create the voice, body, and dialogue for the beggar and Year before starting the dramatization. Cue the sound effects section during the dramatization so that they know when to make noise and when to be silent.

The Beggar (6 students)

The Monster, Year (6 students)

Lantern (2 students)

Cloak (1 student)

Sound Effects Section (9 students)

Cast List Option Two: 2–24 Students

In this version the students dramatize the entire story. One person plays the beggar throughout and students work in small groups to create the families and the monster. Provide students with a brief time to rehearse the dialogue, voice, and body of their characters.

The Beggar (1 student)

Family 1 (4 students)

Door of the House of Family 1 (1 student)

Family 2 (3 students)

Door of the House of Family 2 (1 student)

Family 3 (3 students)

Door of the House of Family 3 (1 student)

Old Woman (1 student)

Door of the House of the Old Woman (1 student)

The Monster, Year (5 students)

Lantern (2 students)

Cloak (1 student)

Cast List Option Three: 3–24 Students

In this version the students dramatize the entire story. The role of the beggar is played by five different students. The role switches each time the character interacts with a different character. This version allows more students to take on a main role.

The Beggar 1 (1 student)
Family 1 (2 students)
Door of the House of Family 1 (1 student)

The Beggar 2 (1 student)
Family 2 (2 students)
Door of the House of Family 2 (1 student)

The Beggar 3 (1 student)
Family 3 (2 students)
Door of the House of Family 3 (1 student)

The Beggar 4 (1 student)
Old Woman (1 student)
Door of the House of the Old Woman (1 student)

The Beggar 5 (1 student)
The Monster, Year (5 students)
Lantern (2 students)
Cloak (1 student)

 ## Dramatic Detail

There may be a few students who do not want to participate in the dramatization. These students may be willing to participate in the sound effects section or in a role played by a small group. It is best to encourage them but not force them to participate. The students will join in the drama when they feel safe and ready. This could take a few minutes or several days. It is best to focus on the students who are ready to work versus those who are not. Eventually all will join in.

DEFINE THE ACTING AREA

As discussed in more detail Chapter 3, adequate space is important in all drama work. For whole-class story dramatization, a large rectangle taped on the floor provides adequate space for all students to sit and stand. Students can sit or stand on or behind the tape line as they observe and/or wait for their turn to participate in the drama. The inside of the taped space serves as an informal stage.

The tape provides a home base for students. They know where to sit or stand before they play their parts and where to return when it is time for them to become good audience members. The tape is very effective for young students and for students who are extremely active. For very active students, it can also be helpful to assign seats on the tape.

Another space option is a drama circle. When it is time for students to enact a story, ask them to form a large circle. If you use the circle routinely and consistently and refer to it as the drama circle, students will understand the boundaries in the same way as those created by the tape.

Defining the acting area sets clear boundaries for the students. It helps them know when they are in and out of the drama; it provides them with entrance and exit locations and provides them with a clear place for transforming into attentive audience members. The acting area will also influence the blocking you plan for the scene.

CREATE A PLAN FOR BLOCKING THE SCENE OR STORY

Blocking is a theatre directing term that refers to the basic movements of the actors on the stage. Think as a director does and create a floor plan of how you want to block actors within the acting area so that all the student actors know when and where to go and all the audience members can see them. Generally, you do not want too many students on the stage at once, as they will have little room to move and the students observing will not be able to distinguish the characters and the action.

One simple blocking procedure is to ask all the students at the beginning of the drama to stand on or behind the acting tape (or drama circle). When it is their turn to act, they step into the middle of the acting area and perform their role. When their role is completed or if they are waiting to reenter the action, they return to standing on or behind the acting tape (or drama circle). This simplifies and streamlines the blocking. It also helps you maintain order during the dramatization.

It is helpful to sketch out a floor plan of the different settings of the scene or story within the acting area. One advantage to a rectangular-shaped acting area is that each corner of the rectangle can be a different location.

See Figure 5–3 for a sample floor plan of how the story "The Monster Year" could be blocked so that all can see.

There are many different ways to block a drama. The important thing is to make sure both you and the students know where the dramatic action occurs and where the audience can easily observe it.

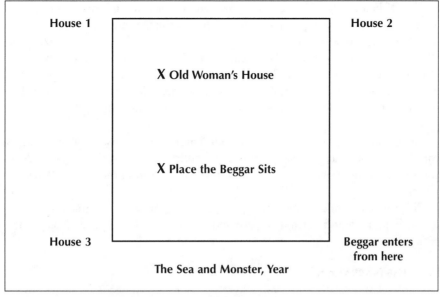

FIGURE 5–3 *Sample Floor Plan*

IDENTIFY AND PLAN HOW TO DRAMATIZE CHALLENGING MOMENTS IN THE TEXT

In many texts there is a scene or a moment that is highly physical or complicated to dramatize. It is helpful to plan a way to dramatize this moment before beginning the dramatization. Students are apt to get carried away if these scenes are not planned and rehearsed before the drama.

Challenging scenes often have:

- a physical struggle

- lots of characters in the acting area at one time

- many characters moving simultaneously

- an object or character that breaks, spills, is tossed, and so on

- high emotion of any kind; in particular, anger

- a moment where characters might touch

- a group of students playing one character

In the story "The Monster Year," the most physical moments are when the monster rises out of the sea and is then scared away. A group of students playing the monster could easily get carried away dramatizing these actions, thus disrupting the rest of the drama, breaking concentration, and possibly hurting one another. If before beginning the dramatization, you plan and rehearse a way for the monster to rise and disappear, you can usually eliminate these problems.

You might rehearse these monster actions by having the students playing the role stay seated on one side of the acting area until it is time for the monster to rise. On cue (a hand motion or head nod), the students begin to sway as if in the water; they move from a seated position to their knees, then they stand, and finally they rise up on their toes. When it is time for the monster to disappear, they reverse this process.

There are many ways to dramatize challenging moments. Let your students contribute their creative ideas for blocking a difficult moment. When the students contribute to the process, they are more invested in having the moment enacted successfully.

If groups of students are playing certain roles, consider how much time you will give the students to plan their parts and where in the room you will place each group of students.

PLAN THE NARRATION

In whole-class dramatizations, you also take on a role. You become the narrator—a key role in the dramatization. In a whole-class dramatization, the narrator:

- *Serves as the storyteller.* Change your voice so that it is different from your normal teacher's voice. Deliver the narration in vocal tones that reflect the action, mood, and dramatic circumstance of the text.

- *Supplies the thread that begins and ends the dramatization, introduces each character, and connects each event in the scene or story.* Familiarize yourself with the correct sequence of the scene or story so that you can retell (*not* read) it in your own words. The sequencing technique developed in step 4 and used in step 7 can serve as guide in helping you retell the story.

- *Cues the students to speak, but* does not *provide their dialogue.* The cue might be the beginning of a sentence. Your voice should indicate that dialogue is required by the student playing the character, who will finish your sentence with dialogue created spontaneously. The narrator promotes the language through descriptive cues and then waits while the students retrieve and create the language.

Descriptive Cues Cues need to be clear and highly descriptive. The more descriptive the cue, the more language it promotes. Often teachers rely on the cue "And then he *said* . . ." to prompt students to speak. This cue will work to some degree, but a more descriptive cue stimulates students to create dialogue that truly reflects the character and the drama's circumstance. This can lead to synthesis and a far deeper comprehension of the text.

Instead of relying on *said*, select a verb that promotes rich dialogue. Here is a list of verbs that stimulate strong character dialogue:

The character . . .

insisted . . .	argued . . .
begged . . .	praised . . .
pleaded . . .	consoled . . .
whispered . . .	chattered . . .
declared . . .	murmured . . .
announced . . .	growled . . .
explained . . .	cheered . . .
interrupted . . .	cried . . .
congratulated . . .	blurted out . . .
instructed . . .	yelled . . .
demanded . . .	

Use other rich, descriptive words to convey the feelings of the characters or the characters' reactions to their circumstances. These words will inform the students of how to portray their characters. They will provide clues as to how the character might say a line or react in the situation. Following are some suggested words that convey a feeling.

The character felt . . .

frustrated	terrified
angry	determined
hurt	surprised
scared	on top of the world
lonely	flattered
exhausted	elated
anxious	in charge
excited	thrilled
horrified	confident
on the verge of tears	

To prompt even greater language use, combine both types of descriptive words:

- The villagers were so *frustrated* with the beggar that they *shouted* . . .

- The *determined* beggar *declared* . . .

- The *anxious* old woman hurriedly *explained* . . .

- The *horrified* monster *cried out* . . .

- The *surprised* villagers *cheered* . . .

Sample Language: When the door of the first house opened, the beggar looked at the family and pleaded . . . [*student playing the beggar finishes the line*].

He moved on to the next house. When the door of the second house did not open, he got on his knees and begged . . . [*student playing the beggar finishes the line*].

When the beggar saw the old woman, he could barely speak. He was faint from hunger. Finally in a raspy voice, he blurted out . . . [*student playing the beggar finishes the line*].

Student Preparation

Step 6: Identify the Drama and Reading Comprehension Objectives

Post and review the lesson's key drama and reading comprehension objectives. Discuss their meanings and clarify any unclear terminology. Simplify the language to meet the grade and ability level of your students.

As students develop a level of proficiency with all of the basic acting tools and skills, you may want to introduce and review the Story Dramatization Assessment Checklist in Figure 5–4. The checklist includes a set of indicators of dramatic excellence in story dramatization. It identifies expectations and provides support for students as they strive to meet the key drama objectives and use additional acting tools and skills. Refer to the checklist when the students reflect and assess the effectiveness of their work at the conclusion of the lesson and set drama goals for the next story dramatization.

You may want to review the Reading Comprehension Strategies Assessment Checklist (see Figure 4–6) with the students so that they also can plan how they will meet the objectives in reading comprehension.

DEFINE THE DRAMA STRATEGY

Briefly describe story dramatization. Explain that the students will be using all of the acting tools and skills to act out a scene or story from a book. The students will envision and then play all the characters and the important objects, infer and deliver improvised dialogue, and enact all the events.

CONDUCT PERTINENT WARM-UPS

Post and review the basic acting tools and skills. Select acting tool- and skill-building activities from Chapter 3 that address the lesson's drama objectives. Acting tool- and skill-building activities that work well for whole-class story dramatization include Finding the Character's Voice (page 31), Bits 'n' Pieces: Bringing a Setting to Life (page 35), and Contrasts (page 34). In addition, the other structures for story dramatization discussed earlier in this chapter can be used as warm-ups.

Rehearsing the Body of the Character. Photo by Ali Oliver.

Step 7: Familiarize Students with the Text

Using the delivery approach you chose in step 3, familiarize students with the scene or story they will dramatize.

DELIVER THE SCENE OR STORY

Deliver the text as you planned it in step 3. If you are reading or telling the text aloud, include listening tasks to help students remain focused and to increase retention of the plot. If you choose to show the illustrations, be sure that all students can see them.

SEQUENCE THE PLOT

Sequence the scene or story as planned in step 4. A reliable gauge of students' fundamental knowledge of the plot is how well they recall the order of the story. Once you have reviewed the scene or story, identify for the students what part(s) of the text they will be dramatizing.

Step 8: Describe Story Dramatization Guidelines

DEFINE THE ACTING AREA

Clarify for the students the boundaries of the acting area that you planned in step 5. Identify the area in which students will act and the area(s) in which they will participate as attentive audience members.

REVISIT THE BASICS

During the delivery of the story, the students may have been seated for a long period of time. To prepare them to enact a scene or story, it is helpful to get students on their feet and refresh the basic acting tools and skills. Lead one or more warm-ups that connect specifically to the text and provide an opportunity for the students to devise language to use in the dramatization. The activity Finding the Character's Voice (Chapter 3, page 31) can easily be modified for this type of warm-up. All the students can become one or two characters as they revisit the basics in preparation for drama.

Sample Language: Sample Language: Actors, please find a place on the acting tape. Remember that your personal space is with you everywhere you go—even when you are right next to another person. Let's just warm up our acting tools and skills one more time before we dramatize the story. Remember that our two drama objectives for today are to change our movement to reflect our characters and to create dialogue that is in character. Our reading comprehension objective is to make inferences. So when I say, "Places," please take on the body of the monster, Year. When I say, "Action," please say what you infer the monster said as he approached the shore before he heard the noise or saw the red. Take a minute to think about what he would be saying to himself. Places. . . .

Students use their bodies and imaginations to play characters. Photo by Ali Oliver.

CLARIFY ROLES

Post the cast list you created in step 5. You may write a student's name next to his or her role or write the name on a sticky note and place the note next to the assigned role. If you use sticky notes you can reuse the cast list for another lesson. It is important that all students have a meaningful role.

Explain to students that you will be playing the role of the narrator. As student actors, they are to listen to your cues carefully. Your cues will alert them to begin acting and remind them of the sequence of the scene or story.

Remind students that after they play their parts, they should become attentive audience members. Their job is to observe without distracting the other student actors.

REHEARSE CHALLENGING MOMENTS

If in step 5 you identified any moments in the scene or story that are highly physical or potentially problematic, rehearse them now. Provide students with direction as to how to enact the scene safely and/or ask the students to help in this problem-solving process.

Sample Language: In the story, the monster screams in fear and races back into the sea, disappearing forever. How can we act out this part of the story safely? We do not want actors running in all directions. How can we show the monster's fear and his disappearance without anyone getting carried away or hurt?

You may want to experiment with several options before selecting one. Once you have selected and rehearsed the challenging moment, secure everyone's agreement to follow the plan during the dramatization.

Sample Language: Our plan for dramatizing that moment will work well. Those of you playing the monster need to agree to follow this plan. If anyone chooses to get carried away with this moment, I will say, "Freeze," and ask you to go back to your seat until you feel ready to make a more cooperative choice.

If you are having students work in groups to create a character or object, provide them time at this juncture to plan their roles.

EXPLAIN THE BLOCKING FLOOR PLAN

Review with the students your plan for the blocking that you created in step 5. Ask the students to take their places in the designated locations. You can post the floor plan you created or simply ask students who are playing the roles to take the positions you assign to them.

Middle school students enact the final scene of "The Monster Year."

Indicate clearly for the students where they are to be:

- before they enter the acting area as their characters

- when they are enacting their roles

- when they exit the acting area to wait to reenter as characters and/or become audience members

Sample Language: Students playing the monster please sit here until it is time for you to rise out of the ocean. Beggar, when it is time for you to beat the chopping block, please sit in the middle of the acting area, facing the monster. Let's put the old woman's house directly behind you.

Conducting the Story Dramatization

Step 9: Enact the Scene or Story

Once all the planning has been completed, students are ready to enact the story. The planning makes expectations clear so the students know what to do, when to do it, how to do it, and where they should be before, during, and after their role in the dramatization is complete.

TRANSITION FROM REALITY TO FANTASY

Distinguishing boundaries of the fictional world of the drama and the reality of the classroom is an important component in story dramatization. It mirrors the theatre convention of the curtains opening at the start of a play and closing at the end. Taking students clearly from the reality of the classroom to the fantasy of the drama is transformative. It elevates the experience and encourages students to suspend disbelief, to agree to pretend. It supports their transformation into another time, place, and character.

Language or sounds that help students transition from reality to fantasy and back to reality serve as a valuable control device. The students are clear when to begin and when to stop acting. For younger students who often prefer to remain in character, transitions help bring them back to the reality of the classroom and prepare them for the next step in the process.

Sample Language: We are ready to begin our dramatization. Close your eyes and listen to the sound of the wind chimes. When I count to three, the chimes will stop, you will open your eyes, and our dramatization of "The Monster Year" will begin. One . . . two . . .

🖉 Teaching Tip—Methods for Transitioning from Reality to Fantasy

Here are some suggested methods to help students enter and exit the fictional world of the drama:

- Ask students to close their eyes for a count of three upon beginning and ending the dramatization. The eyelids imitate the curtain rising and falling in the theatre. *This is a good and simple transition device to use alone or in combination with any of the other suggestions listed below.*

- Use a special sound or instrument—a whistle, a gong, a tambourine, a chime. The instrument you use can reflect the culture of the dramatized text.

- Use sounds students created for the Environment Orchestra (see Chapter 3, page 30). Have the sounds get louder as students enter the fictional world and quieter as they leave.

- Turn the lights on and off.

For young children:

- Sprinkle invisible magic dust on the students and gather it up when leaving the imaginary world.

- Wave a magic wand over the heads of the children.

NARRATE THE ACTION

Use the cues you planned in step 5 to narrate the scene or story. Try to accept the students' dialogue without criticism. Their dialogue will not be an exact replication of the language found in the text, but it should reflect the main ideas of the scene or story.

If the dialogue is not consistent with the main idea of the scene or story or if a student does not respond at all to a cue, simply say, "Freeze," to briefly stop the action. Quickly solicit the language from the other students. Once peers provide the dialogue, check to see if the student actor playing the character is now ready to say these words. Then reenter the world of the drama by saying, "Action."

Sample Language: Freeze! Class, what do you think the beggar said to the first villager? [*Class responds with "Please give me some food. I am starving!"*] OK, Vanessa, do you know what to say now? Great . . . and action!

If the student still does not deliver any dialogue, freeze the action again. Ask the student if she is still comfortable playing the role. If not, ask another student to take the part. If the student still wants to keep the role, but does not speak, invite another student to share the role. By double-casting the part, you allow a quiet student or ELL student to still fully participate.

REMAIN IN THE FICTION

Throughout the dramatization you and the students should maintain your roles as narrator and characters and objects consistently. After playing their roles, students should become attentive audience members. In your narrator role, referring to students as their characters, not by their real names, helps keep the illusion of the fictional world. For example, say, "And then the old woman appeared," instead of "Becky, it is time for you to be the old woman."

If at any point during the drama you feel you need to address an issue outside of the fictional world (behavioral concerns, interruptions, etc.), simply say, "Freeze!" Quickly resolve the problem and then say, "Action," to resume the dramatization.

TRANSITION FROM FANTASY TO REALITY

When the dramatization is complete, transition the students back to the reality of the classroom with the same device previously used for entering the drama. Once the students have returned to the classroom, have them show appreciation for their work. Applause often works well!

Sample Language: Close your eyes and listen to the sound of the wind chimes. When I count to three, the chimes will stop, you will open your eyes, and our dramatization will be over. We will be ourselves again and we will return to our classroom. One . . . two . . .

Story Dramatization—Whole-Group Format

Reflecting on the Story Dramatization

Step 10: Assess the Students

As discussed in Chapter 4, an arts-integrated lesson includes measurable objectives in both the arts and the nonarts curriculum areas. Assessment, therefore, is possible for both content areas. Included in the following sections are various ways to assess both the drama and reading comprehension objectives set for story dramatization in this chapter. As you experiment with story dramatization, you may choose to focus on different objectives.

OBSERVATIONAL ASSESSMENTS

Observing, listening, and taking notes as students plan, enact, observe, and reflect on their story dramatizations provide valuable information regarding the extent to which students have achieved the key drama and reading comprehension objectives for the lesson (see Chapter 4 for more information on observational assessments).

Use the procedure and note-taking form provided in Figure 4–2 to record your observations of three to five students over several story dramatization lessons. This information will be valuable in helping you understand the needs and progress of the students. Use the following points to guide your observations.

From a Drama Perspective

Voice

- Notice how well students playing characters vary their vocal tone.

- Notice who creates dialogue that is in character.

- Note how effective each group of students playing a character creates a collective voice.

Body

- Observe how the students modify their bodies to portray the characters.

- Note how the students adjust their walk, gestures, and movements.

- Consider how each group of students creates a collective body for their character or object.

- Notice whether students who are portraying objects pose their bodies to effectively resemble the objects.

Cooperation

- Consider how well the students listen to each other and to you.

- Observe how students work collaboratively to create group objects and characters.

- Note the manner in which students respect the opinions of their peers during the planning, enacting, and reflecting segments of the drama.

From a Reading Comprehension Perspective

Determining Importance

- Note how well students' dialogue conveys the main ideas of the scene or story.

- Consider which students know the sequence of the action and are prepared to enter and exit on cue.

Inferring

- Watch which students make logical predictions as you deliver the scene or story.

- Observe which students create actions that indicate they read between the lines of the text.

- Notice which students create dialogue that reflects effective logical guesses.

Synthesis

- During the drama, watch which students take on the personality of their character and speak and respond from that new perspective.

- Observe which students are able to devise dialogue for their character to convey the essence and meaning of the scene or story.

After several story dramatizations, review your observation notes. Use the trends you glean from the notes to guide adjustments for the next story dramatization.

REFLECTIVE DISCUSSIONS

Use the drama and reading comprehension objectives to guide discussions about the effectiveness of the story dramatization. These discussions allow students to examine their own work, become aware of how and when they met the lesson's objectives, consider the strengths and weakness of the experience, and set goals for future story dramatizations.

As outlined in Chapter 4, open-ended questions motivate the highest-quality reflective discussions. Pose questions that:

- recall elements of the drama experience

- encourage praise

- encourage change

Questions That Recall Elements of the Drama Experience Refer to the posted objectives and ask the students if, when, and how they saw each of the objectives met. Ask students to provide an example to support their statements. Here are some model questions you may want to use with your students. Select a question or two from each category that fit your students' age, abilities, and needs as well as your time constraints.

From a Drama Perspective

- Think about the group that played the sound effects section. What sounds did they make with their voices that were effective and helped us envision the setting?

- What dialogue did the students playing the doors create? Which lines seemed right for the situation?

- How would you describe the body movements of each student who played the beggar? What did you notice about their uses of body that were similar? What was different?

- During our dramatization, when did you feel that you belonged to a community of actors?

- How did you listen to one another in your groups and as audience members?

- Sound effects section, how did you use cooperation in deciding which sounds and gestures the group would use?

From a Reading Comprehension Perspective

- What words or phrases did we hear the characters repeat in this dramatization? Why were they repeated?

- How well did we remember all the events in the scene or story? Are there any main points we should have added?

- What important details did we remember? Which ones did we forget?

- When the monster yelled, "I'm getting out of here!" what reading comprehension strategy did that group use?

- One group playing a family did not say anything to the beggar when he knocked at the door. They just whispered to each other to "be quiet" so "the dirty beggar" would go away. Did the group's decision not to answer the beggar at all seem logical for this scene or story? Did it fit the drama's circumstance? Why or why not?

- What did you learn about legends through this dramatization?

- After you dramatized the scene or story, did you think about it in a new way? If so, how?

Questions That Encourage Praise As discussed in Chapter 4, it is beneficial for students to give positive feedback to their peers once they have a clear understanding of the acting tools and skills and the reading comprehension strategies. As students compliment each other, they build a sense of ensemble. Questions that encourage praise build a community that strives toward excellence.

When initially asking these questions, it is helpful if you give feedback first. Your praise of specific students or groups sets expectations that the students will strive to meet.

🖉 Teaching Tip

For young students, ELL, and low-ability students you may need to model the feedback for the first few discussions. These students can reflect on the drama, but you may need to simplify the questions or ask fewer questions. The students' answers may be only words or phrases. However, these students can still complete this task at their own level of language and thought. They can identify what went well and why in very simple, but clear, terms.

From a Drama Perspective

- Who surprised you with how much they sounded like the character or object? How did they accomplish this change?

- What group, other than your own, would you like to compliment for their use of body? Why?

- Which students participated in ways that helped us build our community of actors? What did they do?

From a Reading Comprehension Perspective

- Who surprised you with the details they remembered from the scene or story? What details added to our dramatization?

- Who picked up on a clue in this story you missed? What clue was it?

- Who added something new to the scene or story—an action, a phrase, a body position—that made the scene or story even better?

- What moment in the dramatization made you laugh or made you feel afraid? What did the actors do to make that happen?

Questions That Encourage Change

It is beneficial for students to self-assess and examine their own work. Questions encouraging praise focus outward to other classmates. Questions encouraging change focus on the self. Students examine their own roles in the drama and set goals for improvement.

From a Drama Perspective

- How would you like to improve on your use of voice for our next story dramatization?

- How do you wish you had used your body differently in this dramatization?

- How might you cooperate better with the other student actors in our next dramatization?

- What would you change about the way you behaved or treated another person during this dramatization?

From a Reading Comprehension Perspective

- What did you forget to say that you know was important in today's drama?

- How will knowing this help you in our next story dramatization?

- Did you use any dialogue that did not fit the character? If so, why didn't it seem right? How will this information help you in our next story dramatization?

- What clues did you miss in the scene or story that would have made your character stronger? What can you do to avoid missing clues for the next story dramatization?

- What would you like to change or revise if we dramatized this scene or story again?

In addition to the questions listed here, use the questions starters outlined in Chapter 4 to help you create questions that are appropriate for the lesson as well as the age and ability level of the students.

ⓘ Teaching Tip—Self-Evaluation

Since you have several roles in the drama—narrator, director, facilitator—it is helpful if you also consider what you did well and what you would want to change for the next story dramatization.

- Were you able to maintain your voice and role of the narrator throughout, or did you call students by their real names and use only your normal teacher voice?

- Did you provide descriptive cues for the students to speak, or did you tell the students what to say?

- Did you plan well?

- Did the students understand what to do and where they were to stand, move, and sit?

- Did you plan the blocking well? Could everyone see the action on stage?

Review the planning sheet in Figure 5–5 to consider what you did well and what you need to work on. You may want to share some of your self-assessment with students during the reflective discussions. This helps students know that you are part of the ensemble working to improve your acting tools and skills.

WRITTEN ASSESSMENTS

Story dramatization can be a strong writing motivator. Students are often eager to write after completing an effective dramatization. Written assessments provide another window into the students' comprehension of drama and the text.

From a Drama Perspective

Brief Responses

- Write one line you heard in today's dramatization that you feel was in character. Based on what we know about this character, give two reasons you feel this line was a good choice.

- List the sounds the sound effects section created. Star the ones that sounded the most realistic. Add two more you would have liked to have heard.

- List three words (adjectives) to describe the way you stand and move. List three words (adjectives) to describe the way the character you played stands and moves. Write and/or draw how you changed your body to become that character.

- In your journal, write and draw a description of the character you played in today's lesson.

- List two ways you think we worked well together in today's drama. List two ways you think we should improve for our next drama experience.

Extended Responses

- When Max played the monster, he started to wail and then cry as he disappeared. Do you think those sounds and actions fit the character? Why or why not? Include three reasons to support your answer. Include a prediction as to where the monster went after he disappeared.

- Imagine the monster is sharing his secret thoughts about what happened in this story with a friend. Write four secrets Year would say if no one else could hear the conversation. Be sure the dialogue is in character and reflects what we know about the character and his situation. (If you do not think Year would reveal his thoughts to anyone else, imagine he wrote in a journal.)

- Describe the way you envisioned the posture, movements, and walk of your character. Include the following:

  - Describe how you envisioned the character.

  - Compare the way you envisioned the character with how you portrayed the character.

  - What aspects of body did you do well?

  - What do you want to improve for the next dramatization?

- When did you feel you belonged to a community of actors during today's drama? Include in your response what that phrase means to you.

From a Reading Comprehension Perspective

Brief Responses

- Write and/or draw the three main events in this story. Include an event in the beginning, the middle, and the end of the story. Write one line of dialogue you remember from each of the three events.

- Summarize the entire scene or story we dramatized in five sentences.

- List two lines of dialogue from our story dramatization that did not seem to fit the character. Explain why they did not seem in character.

- Think about what could happen next if this story continued. Create a title for a sequel to this story. Draw a picture to go with it.

- Write one line of dialogue you wish you had said as your character.

- In your response journal, describe a moment a character in the drama made you smile, laugh, feel scared, or have some other reaction. What did the student actor do to make you feel this way?

- Write and/or draw a time you felt the same way a character was feeling in the story.

- List two of your favorite parts in the scene or story. Explain why they are your favorites.

Extended Responses

- Choose three details you heard in the dialogue of our dramatization and explain why they added to the effectiveness of the drama.

- Write a sequel to this scene or story that predicts what would happen next. Where does the monster go? Where did the beggar go? Include three inferences from what we know about the characters and the situation. Underline the inferences. Create a title for your story. We will dramatize several of the best stories.

- Sometimes characters say one thing but mean another. Think of two lines a character said in our dramatization that meant something else. Write the lines and explain what the characters really meant.

- The story is written from the perspective of the beggar. What if Year wrote the story? Rewrite the scene or story from Year's perspective.

- This story is a legend. A legend explains something. Write what you think this legend explains.

- Have you ever been afraid of something much bigger than you? Write in your journal about that time and what you did to face your fear.

ASSESSMENT CHECKLISTS

Figure 5–4 is an assessment checklist for the drama strategy story dramatization. Once the students are familiar with story dramatization and proficient with all the acting tools and skills, you may choose to present this checklist when you identify the key drama and reading comprehension objectives in step 6. Explain to the students that in addition to the key objectives, this checklist examines how well the students use all the acting tools and skills during the story dramatization. The checklist can be the basis of the reflective discussion after the lesson.

STORY DRAMATIZATION ASSESSMENT CHECKLIST

Student's Actor's Name _____

DURING THE STORY DRAMATIZATION, THE ACTOR . . .	CONSISTENTLY 3	USUALLY 2	RARELY 1	NEVER 0
Imagination/Mind				
. . . agrees to pretend.				
. . . interacts with real and/or imagined characters and objects.				
. . . reacts to imaginary sights, sounds, smells, tastes, and textures.				
Voice				
. . . varies vocal tone and pitch to create character voices and/or sound effects.				
. . . creates and delivers dialogue that is in character.				
. . . speaks with expression that reflects the personality, traits, thoughts, and feelings of the character.				
. . . projects—speaks loudly enough to be heard.				
Body				
. . . modifies posture, poses, gestures, movements, and/or walk.				
. . . uses facial expressions that communicate the thoughts and feelings of the character.				
Cooperation				
. . . works as a member of an ensemble/team.				
Concentration				
. . . focuses intently on the given drama task.				
. . . remains in character.				

Total _____

32–36 Standing Ovation
27–31 Round of Applause
22–26 Polite Clapping
0–21   Back to Rehearsal

Personal Goal: _____

_____

FIGURE 5–4   *Story Dramatization Assessment Checklist*

The checklist provides a tool for students to self-assess, for the teacher to assess the students, and for both the teacher and the students to collaboratively reflect on the drama work. Together students and teacher can set goals for future story dramatizations. See Chapter 4 for more details on the purpose and use of the assessment checklist.

This same process can be followed for the reading comprehension objectives. Refer to the Reading Comprehension Strategies Assessment Checklist in Figure 4–6. This checklist can be used with any of the drama strategies in this text.

TIME ALLOTMENTS

With practice, the teacher planning of a story dramatization lesson (steps 1–5) should only take 15–20 minutes. Once you and the students are familiar with the Steps for Effective Story Dramatization (see Figure 5–1 on page 67) and the students begin to use the basic acting tools and skills, the student preparation and conducting of the story dramatization (steps 6–9) can be completed in 20–45 minutes, depending on the length of the text. A scene may take only 20 minutes. A picture book or a chapter from a text may take 30–45 minutes.   The length of the assessment section (step 10) of lesson will vary based on the depth of the assessment.

Extending the Drama Strategy

Dramatizing Implied Scenes from the Text

Once students have experienced dramatizing scenes or stories within the text, they can dramatize scenes not explicitly presented in the text. Dramatizing a scene only implied in the story requires students to infer events not fully developed in the text. In "The Monster Year," for example, students might predict and enact a sequel to the story that includes where the monster goes after he disappears or how the villagers honor the beggar. Students can brainstorm what might occur in an implied scene as a whole class or in small groups. They can then dramatize the scene(s).

When developing an implied scene for dramatization, consider a scene that:

- Extends the story forward beyond the ending provided by the author. *What happens next?*

- Explores what might have happened before the story began. *What happened before?*

- Explores a moment(s) mentioned in the story, but not fully developed. *When did the monster first come to this village? What did that look like? How did the people react? What did he do?*

- Extends the story based on genre. *This story is a legend. It explains why firecrackers and loud noises are used to celebrate Chinese New Year. What legend could we create to explain why we have firecrackers on our Fourth of July?*

PLANNING SHEET FOR STORY DRAMATIZATION

Use this sheet to help you plan a whole-class story dramatization in which the teacher narrates and the students either in groups or with individual roles dramatize a scene or an entire story.

1. What are your drama objectives?

2. What are your reading comprehension objectives?

3. What skill-building/warm-up activities will you use to teach/reinforce your drama objective(s)?

4. How will you deliver the scene or story to the students? If aloud, what listening tasks will you use? How will you cue the students for the listening tasks?

5. How will you sequence the story/scene (transparency, chart, toys, pictures, etc.)?

6. After reading/telling and sequencing the scene or story, what other warm-ups will you use to refresh the students' acting tools and skills for the story dramatization?

7. How do your chosen warm-ups prompt students to create dialogue for the scene or story dramatization?

8. How will every student have a meaningful role in the story dramatization? (Groups play one character? Several students playing the same role? Students play inanimate objects?) Create a cast list that reflects your decisions.

9. What are the challenging moments in the story that need rehearsal before dramatizing the story? How will you decide how to stage these moments?

10. How will you define the acting area and plan the action so that all students know what to do and where to go and so that all the students can see? How will the students enter and exit the acting area?

Blocking Diagram (Acting Area Floor Plan)

11. How will you transition the students clearly from reality to fantasy and back to reality?

12. When you narrate, what descriptive language will you use to promote student dialogue? Write three cues using descriptive language that you would like to include in your narration:

    1.

    2.

    3.

13. How will you assess the story dramatization from both drama and reading comprehension perspectives?

14. How will you set goals for improvement for the next story dramatization?

FIGURE 5–5   *Planning Sheet for Story Dramatization*

6   *Character Interviews*

What Does an Effective Character Interview Look Like?

In character interviews, the teacher plays the role of the host of an imaginary television show, *Books Alive*. During each "show," the students play a book's characters, significant objects (such as the glass slipper from the classic story "Cinderella"), and/or author. They answer a series of interview questions posed by the host. These questions are carefully planned to promote inferential thinking and/or synthesis in relation to the text.

Drama Strategy: Character Interviews

Character interviews are a type of role drama. In role drama, the teachers and/or the students use their acting tools and skills to become someone or something else. Role drama is an improvisational strategy. This means it has no script. The dialogue and scenes are created extemporaneously. Role drama is not guided by a pre-described story or plot, as in story dramatization, but instead by an idea or objective. In the role-drama strategy character interviews, the text becomes the foundation or the springboard for the drama. The text serves as the guide, but the students make inferences beyond the text to play roles in which they answer questions about the story and the characters.

This chapter will focus on one format for using character interviews in which both teacher and students take on roles in the creation of a full-class role drama. The character interviews are conducted through a TV talk show format; the show is called *Books Alive*. The host of this show is Pat Pageworthy. The host interviews the students, who play important characters and objects from a text. After reading this chapter, you may want to create a name for your own television show and for your own host for the program. This will make the role drama more personal and, therefore, more meaningful.

Suggested Grade Levels

The recommended grade levels for this chapter's activities are grades 1 and above.

The Teacher's Role in the Drama

Here is an overview of the teacher's responsibilities in implementing this strategy. The teacher will:

- create an imaginary name for the host of the imaginary TV show

- create an imaginary name for the show itself

- select an appropriate text

- set drama and reading comprehension objectives

- generate questions (or facilitate the students in generating questions) for the various characters to be interviewed on the program

- take on the role of the host and lead the role drama

- lead the reflection and assessment of the drama experience from both drama and reading comprehension perspectives

The Students' Role in the Drama

The students' main responsibility is to portray the characters in a text and respond to questions as if they were those characters. To do this effectively, they must:

- recall the basic plot of the text

- understand the characters' thoughts, feelings, and motivations

- apply the basic acting tools and skills

- use inferential thinking to answer questions about the characters

- reflect on the experience in relation to the drama and reading comprehension objectives

The Rationale in Relation to Reading Comprehension

Character interviews integrate drama with all six reading comprehension strategies.

Developing Sensory Images For students to portray a character effectively, they must first use their imaginations to envision the character's appearance and hear the character's voice.

Building and Activating Schema Students make conscious and unconscious personal connections with a character's thoughts, feelings, and circumstances as they portray a character. They apply what they have learned about the character while reading the text. Their understanding is demonstrated in the dialogue they create, the manner in which it is expressed, and the actions they execute.

Questioning Character interviews require students to respond to and develop questions that probe the text. They wonder and speculate about a character's responses to interview questions and whether those responses are in character—whether they fit the character and the drama's circumstance.

Determining Importance Students' responses to the interview questions reflect their ability to recognize significant moments or facts from the text. When students portray the author of a text, they are better able to articulate the author's intent.

Inferring Character interviews involve students in answering a series of questions based on information not explicitly stated in the text. Students are required to make logical guesses and dig for the implicit meanings.

Synthesis Character interviews encourage students to synthesize the text. As they experience the world of the story from various viewpoints, their understandings of the text are enlarged and deepened. The students speak as the characters with new voices and new understandings (Mantione and Smead 2003).

Drama and Theatre Connections

> You never really understand a person until you consider things from his point of view . . . until you climb into his skin and walk around in it.
>
> *To Kill a Mockingbird*, by Harper Lee

Role drama, also known as *role play* or *process drama*, is an improvisational strategy. In role drama, actors take on roles to explore an event, issue, and/or relationship. Role dramas, like all improvisations, are unscripted and spontaneous. The strategy is often used in actor training to encourage actors to effectively utilize the basic acting tools and skills.

In the theatre, role drama is often used as a rehearsal technique. Actors take on the roles of the characters they will be portraying in a play. The director may put these characters in an improvisational situation that is in some way connected to the play but not fully described in it. As the actors improvise this situation, they may reach a deeper understanding about the characters they will portray and thus enhance their performance.

Character interviews are also used as a rehearsal technique. As actors become familiar with the roles they are playing, a director may use character interviews as a way to have the actors think more deeply about their characters. The director, cast, or the other actors in role may fire questions at one actor portraying a character.

The questions may or may not relate directly to the action of the play. The questions are designed to force actors to create full, well-rounded characters that have lives before, during, and after the confines of the play. This rehearsal technique is known as *hot seating*.

Before or after actors go through character interviews, a director may ask the actors to write an autobiography of their characters in another attempt to encourage actors to create more believable characters.

Role Drama in the Classroom

Teachers often use role drama when they ask students to speak from the first-person point of view as a character from a book or as a historic figure. Teachers also use role drama when they facilitate simulations such as reenacting the First Continental Congress or the American immigration experience.

Although teachers use role drama, they do not always take the time for the students to develop the skills needed to make it a rich dramatic experience. As a result, many of the role dramas are flat. Students do not have the true sense of becoming someone else or transporting to another time or place.

In some classroom role dramas, only the students take on roles (student-in-role). When students take on roles, they:

- examine others' perceptions and points of view

- integrate language, feelings, and thoughts

- develop skills in problem solving and decision making

- enlarge their experience

- research, read, and write about topics connected with the drama (Tarlington and Verriour 1991)

In other role dramas, the teacher takes on a role (teacher-in-role). In the character interviews discussed in this chapter, both teacher and students are in role. When teachers join role dramas, they keep the drama in motion by:

- questioning and challenging the students

- involving the students

- managing difficulties

- protecting a role drama from failure

- facilitating student responses

- summarizing ideas

- engaging the students in deeper dramatic action

There are many variations of character interviews, including the following.

Panel Discussions Students take on the roles of characters and, in a panel, respond to questions from other members of the class.

Group Role A group of students represents a single character who responds to questions from the teacher and/or other classmates. Anyone in the group who feels able to may answer as the character.

Mantle of the Expert This is a unique form of role drama defined by British drama specialist Dorothy Heathcote. In this type of interview, the teacher assumes a role of someone who seeks information or advice from a group of experts, played by the students. This is a reversal of the conventional teacher-student relationship. Here the teacher interviews the students, seeking their expertise.

Hot Seating A student or the teacher takes on a role (a literary character or historical figure, for example) and submits to questioning or interrogation by other members of the class. These class members may play detectives, news reporters, social workers, a court of inquiry, or any persons or characters with a need to question the hot-seated character(s).

The TV talk show format discussed in this chapter includes elements of each of these variations of character interviews. Figure 6–1 details the steps for conducting effective character interviews.

Preparing for Effective Character Interviews

Teacher Planning

Step 1: Select an Appropriate Text

A good text for character interviews is one that has intriguing characters, an engaging plot, and a conflict with which students can identify. The interviews are also enhanced if there are multiple perspectives presented in the text. Unresolved issues or questions can also enrich the character interviews. The drama strategy works well with many picture books and chapter books. See Figure 6–2 for a list of criteria for selecting an appropriate text for character interviews.

The criteria for text selection for character interviews are basically the same as outlined in Figure 5–2, page 69. A list of suggested books for story dramatization and character interviews can be found on page 218.

Step 2: Determine Key Drama and Reading Comprehension Objectives

Because an integrated arts lesson requires that objectives in both the art form and the nonarts curriculum be set and assessed, it maybe helpful to post one to four of the most important drama and reading objectives before starting the lesson. The students then understand that, as engaging and fun as drama may be, there is real work being accomplished. For young students, simplify the language for the objectives

STEPS FOR EFFECTIVE CHARACTER INTERVIEWS

Preparing for Character Interviews

Teacher Planning

    Step 1: Select an appropriate text.

    Step 2: Determine key drama and reading comprehension objectives.

    Step 3: Select the format.

- whole class
- small group

    Step 4: Identify the characters to be interviewed.

    Step 5: Develop questions for the character interviews.

- Clarify the purpose of the questions.
- Design questions to match the purpose.
- Limit the number of questions.

    Step 6: Prepare to take on the role of the TV host (teacher-in-role).

- Create names.
- Find a simple prop or costume.
- Create a voice and body.
- Create a sign.

Student Preparation

    Step 7: Identify the key drama and reading comprehension objectives.

- Define the drama strategy.
- Conduct pertinent warm-ups.

    Step 8: Acquire familiarity with the text.

- Use listening tasks.
- Sequence the text.

    Step 9: Prepare to take on the roles (students-in-role).

- Create the characters' bodies.
- Create the characters' voices.
- Create a gesture.
- Discuss questions (small group format)
- Define the acting area.
- Clarify the role of the audience.

Conducting the Character Interviews

    Step 10: Enter the fictional world of the drama.

- Transition from reality to fantasy.
- Introduce the show and the characters.

    Step 11: Interview the characters.

- Stay in character.
- Adjust the pace.

    Step 12: Respond to the characters' answers.

- Reinforce the fiction.
- Make a summary statement.

    Step 13: Close the drama.

- Sign off.
- Transition from fantasy to reality.

Reflecting on the Character Interviews

    Step 14: Assess the students.

- observational assessments
- reflective discussions
- written assessments
- assessment checklists

FIGURE 6–1   *Steps for Effective Character Interviews*

BOOKS FOR CHARACTER INTERVIEWS		
The books below work well for character interviews because they have . . .	a dramatic situation— a dynamic, intriguing plot	a clear conflict and/or tension
GRADES 1–2		
Caps for Sale, by Esphyr Slobodkina	x	
Gregory, the Terrible Eater, by Mitchell Sharmat		
The Mitten, by Alvin Tresselt or Jan Brett	x	x
The Day Jimmy's Boa Ate the Wash, by Trinka Hakes Noble	x	
Click, Clack, Moo: Cows That Type, by Doreen Cronin	x	
Nessa's Fish, by Nancy Luenn	x	x
GRADES 3–4		
Anansi and the Moss-Covered Rock, retold by Eric Kimmel	x	
The Great Kapok Tree, by Lynne Cherry	x	x
The Legend of the Bluebonnet, by Tomie dePaola	x	x
GRADES 5–6		
Katie's Trunk, by Ann Turner		x
Mufaro's Beautiful Daughters, by John Steptoe		x
Encounter, by Jane Yolen	x	x
GRADES 7–8		
A Wrinkle in Time, by Madeleine L'Engle	x	x
Scorpions, by Walter Dean Myers	x	x
Animal Farm, by George Orwell		x
Sundiata, Lion King of Mali, by David Wisniewski	x	x
Talking Eggs, by Robert D. San Souci	x	x
Nettie's Trip South, by Ann Turner	x	x

FIGURE 6–2   *Books for Character Interviews*

BOOKS FOR CHARACTER INTERVIEWS (continued)				
strong characters with whom students can identify	minor characters or objects to interview	a variety of perspectives	the ability to engage students on a thinking and/or feeling level	the ability to empower students
x			x	
	x			
	x			
		x	x	
x	x		x	x
x			x	
x	x		x	
x	x		x	x
		x	x	x
x	x	x	x	x
x	x	x	x	
x	x	x	x	x
x	x	x	x	x
x	x	x	x	x
x		x	x	x
x	x	x	x	x
x	x	x	x	

you post. You may even want to include a visual component with the written objectives.

KEY DRAMA OBJECTIVES

All drama strategies included in this text require students to use all of the basic acting tools and skills. The following objectives, however, are the key drama objectives for the planning, enacting, and reflecting on character interviews.

Voice When they play roles, students will use aspects of voice to communicate information about their characters and the drama's circumstances. While acting, students will:

- create and deliver dialogue that is in character—accurately communicates information about the character and the drama's circumstances

- speak with expression that reflects the personality, traits, thoughts, and feelings of characters

Body When they play roles, students will use aspects of body to communicate information about their characters and the drama's circumstances. While acting, students will:

- modify posture, poses, gestures, movements, and/or walk

Concentration When they play roles, students will use aspects of concentration to maintain the effectiveness of the drama experience. While acting, students will:

- focus intently on the given drama task
- remain in character

KEY READING COMPREHENSION OBJECTIVES

Most of the reading comprehension objectives are a part of the character interview process; however, these are the key reading comprehension objectives in the planning, enacting, and reflecting on character interviews.

Questioning To explore unresolved issues, concerns, and ideas raised during and after reading a text, students will engage in questioning. Students will ask or develop questions that:

- clarify evidence in the text
- probe for deeper meaning
- seek to discover new information
- promote wondering

- speculate on possibilities
- search for answers to problems

Inferring To extend and enrich the meaning of a text, students will draw conclusions and make interpretations based on information provided, but not specifically stated, in the text. Students will:

- combine clues found in the text with prior knowledge to make logical guesses

Synthesis To demonstrate their understanding of a text, students will take information from what they have read, combine it with prior knowledge, and create something new. Students will:

- extend and apply the information in the text to different contexts
- respond personally to the text
  - gain new perspectives

The objectives listed above are the key drama and reading comprehension objectives for the example of character interviews described in this chapter. Each time you use character interviews, however, you may wish to vary the targeted objectives. (See pages 11–16).

Step 3: Select the Format

Character interviews may be conducted with students playing roles in two different ways. Consider your students, their previous drama experience, and their ability to work in groups, and select either a whole-class format or a small-group format, described in the following sections.

WHOLE-CLASS FORMAT

When first using the character interviews TV talk show format, it is helpful if the entire class plays every character. This is a safe, low-risk way for all students to be included, to understand the process of character interviews, and to clarify expectations. For young children who do not read well and have difficulty waiting for turns, it is the best way to conduct character interviews.

When you conduct the show in this way, everyone plays every role. The entire class is Cinderella, or the entire class is the prince, and so forth. Everyone takes on the physical and vocal characteristics of that one character. As you pose questions, you will select individual students to answer. Not everyone will get to answer a question, but all students will have an opportunity to physicalize the character and feel like part of the drama.

One advantage to this format is that it can be done in a short amount of time. You can choose to interview only one character or several, but because the interviews are occurring without much time for student preparation, the interviews can be done quite quickly.

SMALL-GROUP FORMAT

Once students can read independently, the small-group format is preferable as it is much more challenging for the students. In this format the students are divided into groups. Each group is assigned one character or group of characters; for example, one entire group could be the prince (one character) and another group could all be the mice (a group of characters) in the story "Cinderella," by Charles Perrault (1965). Choose a maximum of five characters (five groups) for the show.

It may only be possible to interview one character in a day or to interview the five characters over the course of several days. You may also choose to interview all five characters as one lesson. There is no rule as to how to do this. Base the length of time you spend on the interviews on your time constraints and the students' ability to focus and concentrate. However, if you do an entire program in one lesson, more than five character interviews generally causes students to become restless.

> ## 🖉 Teaching Tip
>
> Once the students are familiar with the strategy of character interviews, conducting one interview in the whole-class format can serve as a warm-up before sending students into groups to discuss questions for the small-group format.

Step 4: Identify the Characters to Be Interviewed

Once you have selected the text and you are clear about your objectives for the students, select the characters and/or objects to be interviewed. Select a maximum of five characters and/or objects to be interviewed at one time. Here is a list of characters you may want to consider for the interviews:

- the protagonist

- the antagonist

- a major character who supports or contributes to the actions of the protagonist or the antagonist (for example, Cinderella's fairy godmother)

- a significant object in a story (for example, the glass slipper or magic wand in "Cinderella")

- a minor character who contributes to the action or may have an interesting perspective on the events of the story (for example, if the mice knew of Cinderella's plight)

- any character or object that might have a unique perspective on the events of the story or the thoughts and feelings of the characters

- the author

If the text has many intriguing supporting characters, and/or if the book is written from the protagonist's point of view, you may want to eliminate the protagonist and interview the other characters. If you are working with a chapter book, you can interview the same character(s) over time so that the students can see how the character(s) grows and changes, or you can interview different characters each time you conduct the interviews.

You can also interview the author. You can design questions to determine the author's intent. For older students, you can also include questions about language, foreshadowing, and style.

The following characters from "Cinderella" are used as examples in this chapter: the prince, the stepmother, the fairy godmother, the glass slipper, and the mice.

🔟 Teaching Tip—Cultural Sensitivity

For many cultures, myths and legends are sacred; therefore, anthropomorphizing gods can be offensive. This is definitely true in the Native American tradition. Therefore, it is best to not interview a deity on the *Books Alive* show. Greek and Roman gods are probably safe, but it is best to do research before including any deity in character interviews.

In drama, objects can also talk. Here, a fourth grader playing a tree answers interview questions. Photo by Barbara S. Holden.

Step 5: Develop Questions for the Character Interviews

Before conducting the interviews, devise the questions that the students will respond to in character. For the first few interview shows, you will develop the questions, but as you continue using this drama strategy, the students can contribute to or take over this preparatory step.

CLARIFY THE PURPOSE OF THE QUESTIONS

Think through your purpose as you develop your questions. Consider carefully what you want your questions to accomplish. Do you want your questions to:

- promote sequential knowledge of the text?

- differentiate main ideas from details?

- recall facts from the text?

- develop inferential thinking?

- promote synthesis of the text?

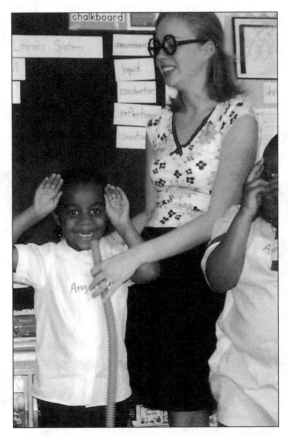

A teacher interviews a happy little mouse from "Cinderella." Photo by Ali Oliver.

The type of questions you create will affect the type of responses you get from the students. The most effective questions for character interviews are those that promote prediction, inference, and synthesis. These types of questions require the students to use higher-level thinking skills. They stimulate a deeper understanding of the text and help students to synthesize the text. This allows them to meet all the reading comprehension objectives stated previously.

Keep in mind that predicting is closely related to inferring, but when students predict an outcome or ending to a story, the events of the text either confirm or contradict the prediction. Inference is more open-ended. Students can infer things that will remain unresolved at the end of the story (Harvey and Goudvis 2000).

You may, however, decide that your purpose is to simply review or recall factual information from the story. If you have young children, English Language Learners (ELL), low-ability students, or students with low-language skills you may want to include a variety of questions—factual as well as inferential—so that every student is successful in the role drama. However, do not underestimate the skills of any student. Most students, in their own way, can answer deep and penetrating questions. Their responses may be only one word or a simple phrase, but they can still reveal higher-level thinking.

The inferential questions you create should prompt students to draw upon information supplied in the story and use this information to develop a creative response based on the text, but not specifically found in the text. The best questions are open-ended, allowing for many possible answers. Try to avoid those that can be answered with *yes* or *no*. When students answer open-ended questions appropriately, they are making steps toward synthesizing a text.

DESIGN QUESTIONS TO MATCH THE PURPOSE

Once you have clarified for yourself the purpose(s) for your questions, begin to develop questions that address that purpose(s). Since the objectives for the questions in this chapter are to promote inference and synthesis, following are some types of questions that would lead students to use these higher-level thinking skills. The well-known story "Cinderella," by Charles Perrault, is used as a model text throughout this chapter.

As you develop your questions, keep in mind that you will be delivering them as the TV host, not as the teacher. To intensify the fictional world of the drama, increase the quality of the students' responses, motivate them to include details, and encourage them to remain in character, create questions that are:

- *conversational*—phrased in a chatty, informal manner

- *immediate*—phrased as if the events referred to in the question are happening in the moment (present tense) or the recent past and responses to them are urgent

- *specific*—phrased realistically with added details from the text and from prior knowledge

For example, consider this question: *"Cinderella, what did you think about when you had to do all that work for your sisters?"* You could improve this question by making it more conversational, immediate, and specific: *"Cinderella, I am going to ask you something right now that I know you have never told anyone before: What were your secret thoughts as you cooked your stepsisters' food and washed their dirty stockings?"*

Questions That Promote Inference

1. Ask a character what he or she would like to say to another character: *"Now that you know the true owner of the glass slipper, Prince, what would you like to say to Cinderella's stepfamily?"*

2. Ask characters about their feelings and thoughts at the climactic moment in the story. (Be sure to include the words *think* and *feel*, not just *feel*, or the students will just answer in one word, such as "fine or "good."): *"Prince, when you picked up the empty glass slipper, what were your first thoughts and feelings?"*

3. Ask the characters to explain something hinted at in the text, but not fully explained: *"Stepmother, why were you so mean to Cinderella?"*

4. Ask the characters to describe a key event in the story: *"Cinderella, describe your transformation from a maid to a beautiful young woman in a gorgeous gown. Describe everything you remember that happened at that moment in time."*

5. Ask the characters to explain what happened before the story began: *"Stepmother, how did you react when Cinderella's father first told you he had a daughter from a previous marriage?"*

6. Ask the characters their plans for the future: *"Stepmother, now that Cinderella is the princess, what are your plans for yourself and your daughters in the future? What do you hope will happen to all of you?"*

7. Ask the characters to explain why they did something that may be questionable or unclear: *"Cinderella, you suffered for a long time. Why didn't you tell your father about the way your stepmother and stepsisters treated you?"*

Questions That Promote Synthesis

1. Ask the characters what they learned from their experiences: *"Stepmother, what did you learn from what happened to you and your daughters in this story?"* **Please note:** The student portraying this character might say, "I should have tossed Cinderella out of the house years ago!" or "I was terribly mean, so I got punished." If the stepmother remains cruel when she responds, the student is indicating comprehension of the character and the character's motivation. This is consistent with the story and is a valuable response for the class to reflect upon at the conclusion of the drama experience. If the student indicates the stepmother is remorseful for her hateful behavior, she is also indicating that she comprehended the nature of the character. By acknowledging that the stepmother has been cruel and blind to the truth, the student has drawn from details in the text to support the

character's change during the character interviews. Therefore either answer could be valid.

2. Ask the characters to express an opinion about something that happened in the story and explain their feelings: *"Stepmother, what are your secret thoughts about the prince marrying Cinderella and rejecting your other daughters?"*

3. Ask the characters if and how they would change things if they could do things over again: *"Stepmother, if you had a chance, what would you do differently in this story?"* **Please note:** The student could reply that he would not change anything, or that he would do something extremely cruel, or that he would have treated Cinderella differently and state why. Any of these responses could work, depending on the details of the answer. See note in question 1.

4. Ask the characters what has changed because of the events of the story: *"Cinderella, now that you are the princess, how does your stepmother treat you?"*

5. Ask the character(s) to explain how they are similar to or different from the character(s) in another version of the story: *"Cinderella, we recently had on the show the characters from the book* Mufaro's Beautiful Daughters, *by John Steptoe (1987). Tell us how you are like Nyasha in that story. How are you different?"*

6. Ask the author of the book the purpose for writing the story and why it is important for readers to consider: *"Charles Perrault, you are often the author given credit for the Cinderella story. However, a similar story can be found in many cultures around the world. Why do you think this story is so popular? What is it that you and so many other authors hope people will learn by reading this story?"*

After using character interviews several times, the students can share in the process of creating questions for the characters. Students will reveal through their questions the internal probing and wondering they often experience while they read. Writing their own questions helps students develop a key reading comprehension strategy (questioning). You can then screen their questions and select ones that are appropriate.

LIMIT THE NUMBER OF QUESTIONS

Limit the number of questions you create for each character. If you are doing multiple characters using the whole-class format, try to ask only two to three questions per character. In the small-group format, try to include enough questions so that each student in the group has an opportunity to answer one question. Try to keep the group size to four to five students.

At the end of the chapter are two sets of sample questions that may provide further clarification. One set of questions, for the book *Anansi and the Moss-Covered Rock*, by Eric A. Kimmel (1988) (an elementary-level text), is for the whole-class format. The other set of questions, for the book *A Wrinkle in Time*, by Madeleine L'Engle (1962) (a middle school text), is for the small-group format. Figure 6–3 may also help you develop questions for a text of your choice.

PLANNING SHEET: DEVELOPING EFFECTIVE QUESTIONS

Review the book you selected. Choose two characters you would like to interview on your TV show. Develop three inferential questions for each character. Use pages 117–19 as resources to help you develop good inferential questions.

Try to make the questions:

- *Conversational*—phrased in a chatty informal manner
- *Immediate*—phrased as if the events referred to in the question are happening in the moment (present tense) or the recent past and responses to the questions are urgent
- *Specific*—phrased realistically with added details from the text and from prior knowledge

Book Title _____

Character #1 _____

Questions: 1.

2.

3.

Character #2 _____

Questions: 1.

2.

3.

FIGURE 6–3 *Developing Effective Questions*

Step 6: Prepare to Take on the Role of the TV Host (Teacher-in-Role)

CREATE NAMES

Come up with an original imaginary name for the show and for the television host you will portray. In this chapter, the show is called *Books Alive* and the host of the show is Pat Pageworthy. Other names teachers have created are *Take a Look at Books* with host Bud Bookworm; *Stories Alive!* with host Lettie Literature; *Talking Books* with host Nancy News; and *Cook with Books!* with host the Magic Chef.

FIND A SIMPLE PROP OR COSTUME

Using a simple prop or costume for your host character helps to establish the character for the students. An unusual hat, a scarf, a beard, or a pair of funny-looking glasses can serve as an effective costume piece. If you play several different talk show hosts, use a different prop or costume piece for each.

If you choose glasses as your costume, you can buy inexpensive glasses at a dollar store. If they are sunglasses, decorate the frame and punch out the lenses. It is important for the students to see your eyes. This helps them focus and connect with the character. These glasses must be used solely for the portrayal of a single and specific character. Otherwise, the students will get confused as to what character you are portraying.

You will also need to find an object that can be used as an imaginary microphone. A thick marker, an eraser, or a bottle of water can work well as an imaginary microphone. You do not need to use a toy microphone. An imaginary microphone helps the students create and envision a fictional world.

CREATE A VOICE AND BODY

Establish a voice and body for your character. It may be helpful to watch some TV game shows and talk shows as you plan your character. Notice the high energy of many of these hosts. The energy and pace of the host drive the show forward. This is an important consideration for the character you create, as the students need the show to move forward at a pretty fast rate in order for them to maintain focus.

Whatever character you create, the energy, voice, and body of the character must be different from your normal teaching style. It is helpful if the TV host is intense and creates a sense of urgency when posing each question to the characters. This adds to the magic of the show and helps the students stay invested in the action.

Before the character interview show, rehearse your character so that you are comfortable in your role and can maintain the voice and body you have created throughout the role drama. See Figure 6–4 to help develop your TV host character.

CREATE A SIGN

Post a sign that states in large and bold letters the name of the TV show. In this chapter the sign will say Books Alive. Your sign will reflect the title of your program. This sign could even be as simple as the show's name written boldly on the blackboard. The host should refer to the sign at the opening and closing of the show.

Student Preparation

Step 7: Identify the Key Drama and Reading Comprehension Objectives

Post the key drama and reading comprehension objectives for the students. Prepare students to meet the objectives by reviewing the meaning of each objective. The remainder of the preparation to meet the reading comprehension objectives occurs throughout the step-by-step process leading up to the character interviews. During this process, the students are developing familiarity with the text. They are reading

PLANNING SHEET: CREATING A TV SHOW HOST

In preparation for creating your own TV host character, you may want to watch a few television quiz shows to see what types of TV hosts are effective. This may help you in planning your own show.

List the name of your TV show:

List the name of your TV host character:

Describe the character traits/personality of the host you wish to portray (jot down words and phrases that have meaning for you).

Envision your TV host character:

- See the character you wish to create.

- Note the character's physical features.

- Observe how the character stands and moves.

- Hear the voice of your host introduce the show.

- Observe the energy and pace of the character.

Describe in words and brief phrases how this character:

- Looks (face and body)

- Sounds (voice tone, tempo, and pitch)

- Moves (posture, gestures, walk, movements)

- Describe the energy and pace of this character.

With another person or in front of a mirror, rehearse your introduction to the show.

Go back and look at the name of your TV host and the name of your TV show. Does it reflect the character you created? If not, modify the name to fit the character you created.

May be copied for classroom use. © 2006 by Lenore Blank Kelner and Rosalind M. Flynn, from *A Dramatic Approach to Reading Comprehension* (Heinemann: Portsmouth, NH).

FIGURE 6–4   *Creating a TV Show Host*

or hearing the story. They are sequencing the plot. They are discussing, developing, and/or answering questions about the characters. They are predicting and making inferences. The entire preparation for the character interviews TV show sets the groundwork for the students to meet all the reading comprehension objectives.

Once students develop a level of proficiency with the acting tools and skills, you may want to use the Character Interview Assessment Checklist in Figure 6–9.

This checklist provides a set of indicators of dramatic excellence in character interviews. It identifies the key drama objectives as well as additional acting tools and skills. You may photocopy and distribute or enlarge and post the checklist.

Explain to students that the left-hand column of the checklist identifies the all the acting tools and skills (indicators) used in a high-quality character interview. (Each indicator is thoroughly explained in Chapter 4.) Take time to review and possibly demonstrate each element with the students so that expectations are clear. Students may also refer to the checklist later during reflective discussions and written assessments. The checklist ends with space for students to set personal goals for their participation in the next set of character interviews.

DEFINE THE DRAMA STRATEGY

Briefly describe for students the drama strategy. Explain that they will portray characters from a book on an imaginary TV show. Refer to the sign you created to familiarize them with the name of the show. You will portray the host of the show and interview these characters by asking them questions about the book. Share with the students the host's name you created and show them the costume piece you will don when you begin the program.

Clarify for the students that the answers to the questions they will be asked are not found in the book. The questions will be inferential, requiring students to know the characters and plot well so that they can use their imaginations and their minds to make logical guesses about the answers. Ask the students a model question and have them support their answers with details from the text.

Sample Language: Today we are all going on to be on a TV show called *Books Alive.* Are we really going on TV? No, we are going to use our imaginations and agree to pretend. I will be the imaginary TV host, Pat Pageworthy, and you will all be various characters from "Cinderella."

I will ask you questions and you will answer them as if you were the character in the book. But these are a very special kind of question. Their answers are not found in the book. These kinds of questions are called *inferential questions.* They require us to make logical guesses based on what we already know about the characters and the story.

 Dramatic Detail

It will help the students maintain concentration if you put on the glasses or costume piece you will be using for the host before starting the character interviews. This allows students to see you look a bit silly and get their giggles out before they enter the fictional world. Then, take the glasses or costume off until you begin the show.

Conduct Pertinent Warm-Ups

In order for students to meet the drama objectives, it is essential that they review and warm up the basic acting tools and skills. Acting tool- and skill-building activities that work well for character interviews include Finding the Character's Voice (page 31), Imaginary Mask (page 27), and Contrasts (page 34).

Step 8: Acquire Familiarity with the Text

The students need to know the story or chapter well if they are going to draw inferences from the text. If your text is a chapter book, it is not essential that students finish the book before they participate in character interviews. In fact, a series of interviews based on the same book with the same characters can be extremely beneficial for the students. Throughout the course of the book, the students gain understanding of how characters change and evolve.

Use Listening Tasks

A listening task is a sound and gesture that the students create and respond with on cue as they listen to a story being read aloud. It helps students stay focused and increases their recall of the story because they are kinesthetically involved. (Please refer to Chapter 5, page 74, for a deeper discussion on the definition and importance of a listening task.)

When the stepsisters say, "Cinderwench, sweep the floor," for example, the students might mime sweeping with a broom and create sweeping noises. Each time the fairy godmother uses her wand, students' listening task might be to wave an imaginary wand and say, "Zip, zip, zoop!"

Using two or three listening tasks when reading a story aloud will increase students' focus, engagement, and recall of the plot.

Sequence the Text

After the students hear or read the story, choose a way to review the sequence of key events. As recommended in Chapter 5, you may:

- prewrite the order of events on a transparency and review it with students
- ask students to recall the key events and record them in sequence on a chart
- duplicate pictures of key events from the text and have students arrange them in the correct order
- arrange toys or miniatures in the proper order to represent the key events—a small doll to symbolize Cinderella, a miniature broom or rag to represent her work, a miniature scroll (rolled-up piece of paper) to represent the messenger's announcement, and so on

Whatever your sequencing method, work to focus on key events and avoid detail.

Once the students recall the events of the story, they are ready to explore the text through *Books Alive*. During the character interviews, it is helpful to keep the sequence of events posted for the class to use as a reference.

Step 9: Prepare to Take on the Roles (Students-in-Role)

Just as the teacher has to prepare for taking on the role of the TV host, the students need to prepare for their roles.

CREATE THE CHARACTERS' BODIES

Whole-Class Format As you prepare students to enter the fictional world of the TV talk show, rehearsal helps students discover and create an appropriate body stance for their character(s). Ask the students to envision the character they will play. Have them close their eyes while you orally review the character's features and traits. This will allow them to envision in greater detail.

Sample Language: Actors, please stand and find your personal space. Now close your eyes and see the stepmother in the story "Cinderella." Envision how she stands, what her face looks like. See her giving an order to Cinderella. See her call Cinderella "Cinderwench."

Ask the students to show you silently how they would stand, pose, or gesture as the character.

Sample Language: When I say, "Places," would you please open your eyes, focus on a point of concentration, and take on the body of the stepmother in "Cinderella"? I do not want to hear her voice. I just would like to see her body. Places.

Look at the students' poses and comment on effective stances and facial expressions.

Sample Language: Good. Hold those poses for a minute. I like how some of your faces are all twisted. You look very mean. I see a lot of fingers out, pointing and giving orders. Think about what you like about your pose and how you would like to revise it to make it better. When I say, "Curtain," you may relax and be yourselves again. Curtain.

Have the students revise and improve their choices to capture in more detail their vision of the character. Suggest that they put more energy into the pose or encourage them to include more facial expression. Repeat this process for all the characters that will be interviewed.

Small-Group Format The same process described in the previous section could be used with the small-group format. However, after the students have participated in several lessons using character interviews, they can be responsible for creating the bodies of their characters on their own in their groups.

CREATE THE CHARACTERS' VOICES

Whole-Class Format Once the students have rehearsed the body of the character, repeat the process, adding the character's voice. It is helpful if the students rehearse one line that they will all say as the character when the interview begins, such as "It is great to be here," or "I am happy to be on the show," or "Thank you for inviting me here today." Saying one line in unison helps the students establish the vocal characteristics of the character and reinforces the format of the show. Repeat this process for all the characters you plan to interview (four to five maximum).

Sample Language: This time when I say, "Places," try to see the body of the stepmother and when I say, "Action," hear her voice say, "I am happy to be on the show." Places. Good, I see the stepmother very clearly now. Let me hear her—action. Let's revise it to make her sound a bit older and tougher. Let's try it again—action. Much better. And curtain. Nice work. Let's do the same thing for the next character you will play on the show, the fairy godmother.

Small-Group Format The same process described in the previous section can be used for this format. However, after the students have participated in several lessons using character interviews, they can be responsible for creating the voices of their characters on their own in their groups. Before starting the interviews, have each group present their character's body and voice, saying the one rehearsed line.

Sample Language: Would the group playing the prince please stand. When I say, "Places," let me see the body you have created for the prince. When I say, "Action," can I hear his voice say, "I'm happy to be on the show"?

 Dramatic Detail

If an animal or object is being interviewed, the students will need to experiment with the same process described in step 9 to discover the vocal and physical characteristics of this animal or object. Encourage the students to create their animals in a standing position rather than on all fours. They can do much more interesting and creative work with their bodies and voices in upright positions.

CREATE A GESTURE

A fun and effective way to deepen the fiction and increase students' concentration is to create a gesture that the characters will use to indicate they are ready to answer an interview question. Rather than just raising their hands, the students and/or the teacher can use a gesture that is in keeping with the character. If the character is an animal, the gesture should reflect some characteristic of that animal. For example, if the students are playing mice, they might wiggle their noses to indicate that they have an answer for a question posed by the host. For a human character, the action should reflect a quality about that character. A stepsister might flip her imaginary long hair off her shoulders or fan herself to signify she has a response. Asking the students to respond in this specific manner encourages them to maintain concentration throughout the drama and increases the sense of fantasy. The gesture can be used in both the whole-class and small-group formats.

DISCUSS THE QUESTIONS IN GROUPS—SMALL-GROUP FORMAT

Break the students into groups and provide each group with a set of interview questions to discuss. As mentioned earlier, the teacher and/or the students may generate these questions.

On the top of the page of questions, summarize all that you want the students to do in their groups and during the character interviews. This again will remind students of your expectations and can be done very simply for younger students or in detail for older students. See the examples in Figures 6–5, 6–6, and 6–7. Along with the page of questions, if possible, pass out a copy of the text for the students to use as a reference for their answers.

Discussing the Questions for Character Interviews—Small-Group Format. Photo by Barbara S. Holden.

FIGURE 6–5   *Small-Group Character Interview Instructions, Grades 1–2*

Each group should be given approximately ten minutes to brainstorm possible answers to the questions. Alert students that on *Books Alive* they could be asked any or all of the questions. They cannot know what question they will be asked; therefore, every group member needs to be prepared to answer all the questions. Include enough questions so that each student has the opportunity to answer one. The group may or may not come to consensus on their answers, but it is always nice if they do.

Give younger children only one or two questions and let them brainstorm multiple answers to the same questions. Depending on the complexity of the book, the difficulty of the questions, and the age of the students, you may need to vary the time you give the students to brainstorm responses.

🔊 Teaching Tip

For English Language Learners (ELL) or low-ability students, you may want to divide the class into pairs rather than groups. These students may need more structure. Give each pair of students one or two interview questions to discuss. It may help them to know exactly what questions they are responsible for answering. For some students, giving the questions beforehand may help them feel comfortable taking risks during the drama experience. Some students may even need to write their answers in order to feel comfortable speaking on the show. However, they should not refer to their papers or read their answers while on the show. These simplifications may increase participation, oral language, and comprehension.

FIGURE 6–6   *Small-Group Character Interview Instructions, Grades 3–5*

DEFINE THE ACTING AREA

Whole-Class Format As discussed in Chapter 3, set up a defined area of the classroom to designate as the acting area or stage. Tape a large rectangle with painter's tape on the classroom floor. For the whole-class format, the students can stand in their personal space or sit on three sides of the rectangle. If your class is large, use all four sides. Since all the students will be playing the same character simultaneously, you will be moving around the acting area, interviewing various student actors as they indicate they have an answer to the question (see "Create a Gesture" on page 127).

Small-Group Format The same taped rectangle described in the previous section can be used for this format; however, the fourth side of the rectangle should serve as the TV studio's stage. On actual television programs, there is often a tape line or mark that designates where to stand in relation to the camera. Therefore, this fourth tape line is in keeping with the fiction of being on a television program.

Once the groups have discussed the answers to the questions and created a body and voice for the character, the students should sit with their character groups

Small-Group Character Interview Instructions, Grades 6–8

Title of Book: _____ by _____

Name of Character: _____

Everyone in your group plays the character of _____

Each of you will answer as if you are this character.

Discuss these questions and be ready to answer any of them. You do not know what question you will be asked. Try, if possible, to agree as a group on the answers you plan to share.

As you discuss the questions, keep in mind what you have learned about this character so far. What is the character's personality? What are the character's successes? Failures? Concerns? Desires? Frustrations? Fears? What are the character's attitudes toward self and others?

Create a voice and body for your character. Be sure you use concentration to stay in character throughout your presentation. You are to be your character from the minute you are called up to the TV studio stage to the minute you return to your seats. Once you are seated, you become part of the audience.

Questions for the Character Interviews

1. _____
   _____ ?

2. _____
   _____ ?

3. _____
   _____ ?

4. _____
   _____ ?

FIGURE 6–7   *Small-Group Character Interview Instructions, Grades 6–8*

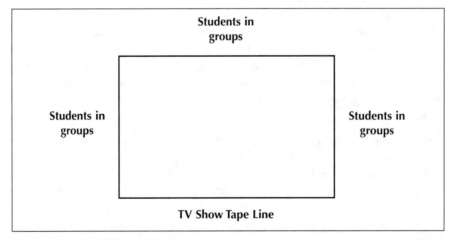

FIGURE 6-8 *Sample Floor Plan*

on the three sides of the taped rectangle on the floor. The host calls each character (group of student actors) up to the fourth tape line. Encourage the student actors to walk as their characters to the tape line. It is best if the characters remain standing throughout the interview, as this requires them to use their bodies throughout the presentation. They respond to the questions in character and return as their characters from the stage back to sit on the one of the other sides of the rectangle to become audience members. (See Figure 6–8.)

🎭 Dramatic Detail

For both the whole-class and small-group formats, it is best if you set up the tape line in such a way that allows you, as host, to interview the characters from the side or from behind instead of standing in front of the students. As you interview the character, place the imaginary microphone in front of the responding student actor's mouth. Standing in front of the characters with your back to the the majority of the class, makes it hard for the students playing the audience members to see and hear and, therefore, may cause them to get restless.

Another option is to have your back to the students being interviewed but face the remainder of the students. Just keep in mind that whenever possible, try not to have your back to the majority of the class.

If the class is very well behaved, you may not need to tape a rectangle on the floor at all for this drama lesson. The students can sit with their groups randomly on the floor, facing the single strip of tape that designates the TV stage.

For older students who may not want to sit on the floor and for a class that is somewhat difficult to manage, the students can remain at their desks until called up to the tape line on the floor, which designates the TV studio stage.

Don't be surprised if a student gets so involved in the fiction of the show that he grabs the microphone out of your hand when it is his turn to respond to a question. If this happens, let the student answer and then gently take the microphone away and move on to the next student actor.

CLARIFY ROLE OF THE AUDIENCE

Explain to the students that whenever they are not playing a character, they are part of the audience. As audience members, they are to listen attentively to whoever is speaking. This is part of working as an acting ensemble. Students should "demonstrate respect for the work of the actors" (see page 13). Actors always share the stage space and give respect and attention to whoever is on stage.

In the small-group format, before the student actors are called up to the tape designating the TV stage and once they return to their seats, they are the *Books Alive* audience members. Therefore, the students need to know that they play two roles: the TV audience and a character from the book.

To reinforce this idea when first conducting character interviews, have each group rehearse walking onto the stage, saying their character's opening line ("I'm happy to be on the show"), and returning in character to their seats. Once they sit down, they should become attentive audience members.

The host stands behind the characters so all the students can see and hear the action. Photo by Ali Oliver.

Dramatic Detail

One way to extend the role of the audience is have the students, as audience members, call out the name of the show at the beginning and end of the program. The host points to the sign indicating the title of the show and the students call out the name.

Sample Language: At the beginning of the show:
Host: Welcome everyone to [*points to the sign*].
Audience: *Books Alive!*

At the end of the show:
Host: This is Pat Pageworthy signing off for this week on [*points to sign*].
Audience: *Books Alive!*

Teaching Tip

As students become proficient with character interviews, they can also take on an additional role during the show. While they are audience members they can also be students who listen carefully for a good example of inference made by another student actor. They can then share this example during the reflective discussion and/or describe it in a written assessment. The students should be able to support their inferences with one or two details from the text.

Conducting the Character Interviews

Step 10: Enter the Fictional World of the Drama

TRANSITION FROM REALITY TO FANTASY

As discussed in Chapter 5, transitioning the students from reality to fantasy is an important part of any drama experience. Once everyone is ready to begin, ask the students to close their eyes. Then turn around so your back is facing the students and don your host costume piece (glasses, hat, funny nose, etc.). This can serve as the way in which you transition the class from reality to fantasy, or you may add an additional sound effect (noisemaker, musical instrument, etc.) or lighting effect (classroom lights off during the transition and on when the show begins).

All of these devices help the students enter and envision a fictional world. It is important that the students know when they are in the fictional world and when they are not—when the drama experience begins and when it ends. Not only is this a drama objective (see Chapter 2), but it also aids in class control. The students need to know when to start and stop acting.

Sample Language: Close your eyes, close your eyes. [*put on your host's costume piece*] At the count of three, if we use our imaginations, I will be Pat Pageworthy, you will be the studio audience, and we will all be on the television program *Books Alive*. One, two, three.

There are many other conventions that you can employ to make this reality-to-fantasy transition smoothly. Please consult Chapter 5, page 91, for more information on this process.

Once the transition from reality to fantasy occurs, the entire class enters the fictional world of the drama. Ideally, the students remain in character as either the studio audience or a character from the text for the entire show, until you transition them back to reality.

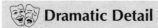 **Dramatic Detail**

During the transitions from reality to fantasy, there will be some students who do not close their eyes. Do not focus on them or single them out. You might reinforce the importance of closed eyes by saying, "I hope you all will close your eyes. It helps us feel the magic as we enter the imaginary world."

? Dealing With Difficulties

Often there are interruptions that interfere with the flow of the interviews. Sometimes the students break the fantasy by calling you by your real name instead of your character's name to ask if they can go to the bathroom or the nurse. Outside forces can break into the fictional world—a knock on the door or an announcement over the school PA system, for example. If this happens, simply call, "Freeze!" take off your costume piece, and deal with the interruption as quickly as possible so as not to lose the momentum of the drama. When the issue has been resolved, resume the drama by putting the costume piece back on and calling, "Action."

You can use this same procedure if a student chooses not to participate in a cooperative manner. If a student begins to show off or disturb the class while another person or group is presenting, you can call, "Freeze!" remove the host's costume piece, and deal with the problem.

Sample Language: I am sorry you made the choice not to use your cooperation. You will need to sit outside the acting space and watch for a while until you are ready to work as an ensemble (work together) with your fellow actors. Please go and take your seat.

You may request that the student sit out for a few minutes or for the entire role play. If an entire group of students who are playing one character is disruptive, that group may not get to act at all on that day. It helps if you set up behavioral expectations and consequences for poor behavior at the beginning.

If *Books Alive* features a character that might get out of control, for example, a wolf or a monster, it is best to place that character in imaginary constraints, such as in a cage or behind an invisible wall, to avoid any potential behavior problems during the drama.

INTRODUCE THE SHOW AND THE CHARACTERS

It is important for you as the host to have a strong introduction to the show. Introduce each character using rich descriptive language. This language will serve as a reminder for the students to use their acting tools and skills. Deliver this reminder in character as the host so as to not break the fiction of the drama.

Sample Language: Welcome to *Books Alive*. I am Pat Pageworthy, and we have a fabulous show for you today. We are going inside the amazing story "Cinderella," by Charles Perrault, and talk to the characters. So let's get started. Our first character today is the fairy godmother. Will you please stand and take your place on the *Books Alive* stage? Just *float* your *sweet chubby* self on over and find a place on the tape. Thank you so much for being here. Could I hear you say in your *syrupy, soft* voice, "I am happy to be on the show!" Let me hear you now. Thank you and welcome to the program.

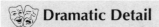 **Dramatic Detail**

As you plan the order of characters to be interviewed on the show, try to alternate the serious and funny characters. There usually is a progression that makes sense for the show. Often it is best to save the main character for last and to have the antagonist go before the protagonist. This order allows you to end the show on a positive note.

Step 11: Interview the Characters

STAY IN CHARACTER

As the host of the program, it is important that you stay in character throughout the show. Your commitment to your character sets the tone for everyone. One challenge to your concentration is keeping in mind that if the entire class or a group of students is portraying one character, it is important to respond to each student actor as one character. As you move from student actor to student actor, simply refer to each of them as the same character.

For example, as you approach one student actor, you might ask: "Prince, what would you like to say to the stepsisters for trying to keep Cinderella away from you?" As you move to the second student actor playing the prince, you could say, "Prince, what else would you like to say to those stepsisters?"

Interviewing One of Cinderella's Stepsisters. Photo by Barbara S. Holden.

Try to avoid saying something like "And what does the next prince think?" or "Justin, what do you think the prince is thinking?" These statements jar the student actors out of the fictional world of the drama. By calling the students by their real names, you also have stepped out of character and are once again the teacher. If everyone, including the teacher, stays in character, the students take the experience more seriously. Their answers reflect deeper thought and they make more connections with the text. All of this leads to more inferential thinking and sets the stage for synthesis.

 Dramatic Detail

If you should mistakenly refer to the students by their real names or make any other incorrect reference, do not call attention to it. Continue on and reenter the drama. You can discuss this lapse with the class later during the reflection section of the lesson.

ADJUST THE PACE

Keep in mind that *Books Alive* must move along rather quickly. In the small-group format, it is best not to ask the same question to each student playing the same character. This will work only when you are interviewing younger students who are answering only one or two questions on the show. In the whole-class format, if you ask every student the same question, the show will go on endlessly. You do not want the students to get restless. In general, ask one question of each student. However, there are usually one or two questions that are so rich that having two or more students respond is appropriate.

There may also be students who are so creative that they are able to quickly improvise answers to almost any question. Therefore, once the students are comfortable with the format, you can introduce off-the-cuff questions that have not been previously screened by the students. This can elevate the excitement and immediacy of the drama and force the students to do some fast and furious inferential thinking.

As you select student actors to answer questions in the small-group format, there is no need to go in any particular order. This random questioning will also pick up the pace of the drama and infuse it with an air of excitement and unpredictability. Randomly choosing students to respond helps keep the show fresh and focuses the students' attention. However, it is important to also be sure that all students, including English Language Learners, have an opportunity to respond. Try to sense when the pace is dragging, and when you feel this, decide how to pick up the pace. Consider asking a new question, interviewing a different character, or ending the show.

Step 12: Respond to the Characters' Answers

REINFORCE THE FICTION

After the characters answer the questions, it is important for the TV host to respond to the questions in a way that reinforces the fiction of the show. Again, watching talk shows and game shows on television may provide some good examples of responses. Here are some possible responses:

- "Thank you so much for that thoughtful answer."

- "You heard it here first, ladies and gentlemen, on *Books Alive!*"

- "I never knew that was going through your mind at that moment. I am amazed!"

- "I can tell you are feeling very bad about what happened. Thank you for sharing that with us today."

- "Amazing! Absolutely Amazing!"

- "Who would have ever dreamed you felt that way?"

- If a student is silent or having trouble getting out the words, you might say: "I can tell you are really thinking. Thank you for taking our show so seriously," or "I can tell you are so upset you are speechless!"

- If a student playing an antagonist in the story does not change and continues to answer the questions in a hostile manner (which in this context can be good, as it reflects comprehension of that character and his or her motivation), you might want to respond with: "Well, I can see nothing has changed. You did not learn a thing from this experience. I certainly hope you will think about what happened."

- If a character does something heroic in the story, you might respond with: "You are incredible! What a brave character you are! Let's give this wonderful character a round of applause [or possibly a standing ovation]."

- If you get many different answers from the students and some of them conflict, or the answers reflect many varying but valid points, your response can be a summary of the points the students made: "I understand you have a lot of conflicting [mixed, opposite] feelings about the situation. That is totally understandable. On one hand you feel _____, and you also know that _____ is true. At times you want _____ but also you know that _____ could happen. You have given us a lot to think about."

- If the book is a chapter book and the same characters are being interviewed several times during the course of studying the book, the responses should reflect the changes the character has experienced: "We know that you finally understand why you had to go through so many tests in this book. We are all so proud of your newfound maturity."

MAKE A SUMMARY STATEMENT

After each group finishes the interview, the host needs to make a summary statement. This response should include a cue to remind students to continue to use their bodies as they return to their seats, such as "As you heard, the mice have seen so much that Cinderella has gone through over the years. We are so glad they got this chance to really support Cinderella. Let's give the mice a round of applause and thank them for being on *Books Alive*! Please *scurry* back to your seats in the audience."

 Dramatic Detail

There will be books that are so exciting and characters that are so intriguing that the students will not let go of their characters when they are supposed to be audience members. They will maintain their roles throughout the character interviews TV show. They may frown or talk back to characters that are on camera. They may heckle or even boo hostile antagonists. As the teacher, you should decide how you want to handle this situation. Some teachers are thrilled to find their students so involved. They find this an extremely exciting and engaging experience. Other teachers become fearful of losing control.

If at any time you are not comfortable with the reactions of your students when they are portraying audience members, just say, "Freeze!" Take off your host costume piece and quickly remind the students that they are audience members when they are no longer on the stage. Once you are ready to go back to the show, put your costume piece back on and say, "Action!"

If your students' enthusiasm excites and delights you, you can respond to the behavior as the television host. For example, when the stepsisters answer questions, the students portraying the fairy godmother may hiss or call them liars. As the host you could say, "Oh my goodness, ladies and gentlemen, the stepsisters are getting quite a reaction here today on *Books Alive*. Many people seem upset with how they treated Cinderella. I understand everyone's feelings, but please quiet your responses so that all our viewers way out there in TV land can hear what every character has to say. You know the rule on *Books Alive*: every character gets equal time on the show."

Step 13: Close the Drama

SIGN OFF

When it is time to close the role drama, develop a creative ending to the show, also referred to as the sign-off. This ending should be in keeping with the host's character and the general tone of the program. A brief summary of key points could also be included.

Sample Language: We have had a wonderful show today and learned so much about these characters. We are amazed that Cinderella is such a forgiving soul that she has built a new house for her stepfamily, and we certainly hope the apologies we heard from the stepfamily today were sincere. This is Pat Pageworthy saying good-bye until next week. Who knows what book we will enter next week on [*point to the sign so the audience responds in unison*] *Books Alive?*

TRANSITION FROM FANTASY TO REALITY

As soon as the TV show is over, instruct the students to close their eyes and use the same convention that you previously used for the transition from reality to fantasy to return them back to the reality of the classroom.

Sample Language: Close your eyes, close your eyes [*turn your back and take off the host's costume piece*]. At the count of three, we will be done being actors for today. We will be students again, back in our classroom, and we will give ourselves a nice round of applause for a job well done.

After they have transitioned back to the reality of the classroom, the students should show appreciation for their hard work. Applause often serves as a great validation.

Reflecting on the Character Interviews

Step 14: Assess the Students

Use the following assessment models as you reflect upon and assess students' work in character interviews.

OBSERVATIONAL ASSESSMENTS

Observing, listening, and taking notes as students plan, enact, observe and reflect on character interviews provide important information regarding the extent to which students have achieved the key drama and reading comprehension objectives.

Use the procedure and note-taking form provided in Figure 4–2 to record your observations of three to five students over several lessons using character interviews. This information will be valuable in helping you understand the needs and progress of the students. Following are some questions you may want to consider as you observe your students.

From a Drama Perspective

Voice

- Listen for instances of students who create dialogue that is in character—accurately reflects the character and the drama's circumstance.

- Note which students speak with expression that reflects their character's personality.

Body

- Look for examples of students modifying their bodies.

- Notice whether students adjust their walks, gestures, and movements.

Concentration

- Notice which students stay focused during the drama experience.

- Notice students who remain in character throughout the interview process.

From a Reading Comprehension Perspective

Questioning

- As students discuss the interview questions, note the type of questions students ask each other during their group work.

- Note students who revisit the text to search for facts to support their answers to the questions.

- Note the types of interview questions students develop on their own.

Inferring

- Listen for responses to interview questions that reflect logical guesses.

Synthesizing

- Listen for responses that indicate that students extended information from the text to different contexts.

- Note evidence of students responding personally to the text.

- Note responses that reflect that the students explored or gained new insights, opinions, or perspectives.

REFLECTIVE DISCUSSIONS

Discussing with students the effectiveness of the drama experience can serve as an initial form of informal assessment. Using the drama and reading comprehension objectives to guide the discussion allows students the opportunity to self-assess.

As recommended in Chapter 4, facilitate effective reflective discussions by posing open-ended questions that

- recall elements of the drama experience

- encourage praise

- encourage change

Questions That Recall Elements of the Drama Experience

From a Drama Perspective

- What answers to interview questions contained information that was not found in the story, but seemed right for the character?

- Consider the group that played the glass slipper. How did each person use his or her body in a different way?

- How did concentration improve the drama?

- Were there any distractions that interfered with concentration?

- What other acting tools and skills did you use during the drama?

From a Reading Comprehension Perspective

- What interview questions encouraged you to speculate upon what might happen next in the text?

- What interview questions did your group find challenging and why?

- What were some good inferences about Cinderella's feelings toward her stepfamily?

- When Eve said as Cinderella that she "understood how the slaves must have felt" and that she sometimes dreamed she had "an underground railroad," what reading comprehension strategy was she using?

- Describe how it felt to take on the perspective of your character and think differently. How is your character like you? How is your character different?

- What other reading comprehension strategies did you use to prepare for or act in our character interviews?

Questions That Encourage Praise These reflective questions ask students to give positive feedback to their peers. This type of assessment builds a sense of community. As the students compliment each other, they set a standard for themselves for quality drama work. As discussed in Chapter 4, it is helpful to model the praising of others. This clarifies expectations for students.

From a Drama Perspective

- What were some of the most imaginative answers you heard today? Think about answers that that fit the character but were not found in our book.

- Let's think about the use of voice. What person or group, other than you or your group, used voice in an effective way today? Tell me what you heard and why it was so effective for the character.

- What person or group, other than you or your group, used the body in effective ways today? Tell me what you saw and why it was so effective.

- Who, other than you or your group, used good concentration and stayed in character from the minute their character was introduced to the minute their character was asked to sit down?

From a Reading Comprehension Perspective

- Who in your group asked good questions that helped shape the answers your character presented on the show?

- Who other than you demonstrated the use of inference in the way they created the body and voice of their character?

- What clue from the story did someone include in his or her answer that surprised you?

- Who made a comparison between their character and a historical figure? What reading comprehension strategy did they use?

Questions That Encourage Change The questions that ask for change are self-directed. These questions ask students to look inward at what they can do better in the next drama experience. Structuring the reflection in this way avoids student criticism that could undermine the sense of community (ensemble) that is vital to drama.

From a Drama Perspective

- Think about the answers you gave as your character today. Which answers do you wish you could revise? How would you revise them?

- Did you like the voice you created for your character? What changes would you like to make if you play that character again?

- Think about how you changed your body for your character. Were you able to maintain your character's body throughout the interview, just in the beginning, or off and on during the drama? How would you like to improve on your use of body for our next character interviews?

- When was it most difficult for you to maintain your concentration? When did you lose concentration?

- What do you think will help you maintain your concentration for the next drama we do?

- How might we improve our audience behavior to help the student actors?

From a Reading Comprehension Perspective

- What questions do you wish you had asked your group to clarify information about your character?

- Which of the questions that you created for a character needs revision? Why?

- What inferences did you make that did not fit the character? What can you do for the next character interviews that will help you improve upon the inferences you make?

- What clues do you wish you had included in your answers?

- What new information did you learn about your character from listening to other people in your group?

- How well did you take on the perspective of your character and think in a new way? How could you improve upon this for the next character interviews?

WRITTEN ASSESSMENTS

Character interviews can be strong motivators for writing, which provides additional opportunities for assessing students' understanding of drama and a text.

From a Drama Perspective

Brief Responses

As described in Chapter 4, a brief response is when students write a few lines or paragraph in reply to a writing prompt.

- Think about one question your character was asked today. Write a different answer that would be in character for this question.

- Identify a student actor who you think spoke with expression and captured the personality of the character you envisioned in this story. Name the student actor and the character he or she portrayed, and write three sentences describing how this person captured the character.

- In your response log, make a list of three things you liked about your use of body for the character you played today and three things you would change.

- List three moments in today's character interviews where it was hard for you to keep concentration. Describe why it was hard.

- Write three sentences that explain why concentration is important when doing drama.

Extended Responses

An extended response requires more detail.

- Choose one character in the story, and in your journal, write a secret letter to Cinderella from that character. What would the letter say? Be sure to include at least three secrets not heard on today's show.

- Imagine your character is interviewed again on *Books Alive*. The host asks: "Describe yourself. What are you like? Tell us about your personality, the kind of person/object you are, the friends you have, and what you do for fun. Include your thoughts and feelings about Cinderella and everything that happened to her." Write your answer to the host of the show and be prepared to read it aloud to the class in the voice of the character.

- Create a Venn diagram that compares the body (voice) of the stepmother with the body (voice) of Cinderella. Find at least five similarities and five differences.

- Write about a moment in the drama when you broke concentration. Describe what happened and how, if ever, you got your concentration back.

- Write three personal goals you have for using concentration in our next character interviews. Explain why these are your goals.

From a Reading Comprehension Perspective

Brief Responses

- Based on what you heard today, write a question about something you still wonder about the character of the fairy godmother.

- Write two questions your character hopes no one will ever ask.

- Dennis, as the prince, said about the stepfamily, "They are not coming to live in my palace!" Do you think that was an accurate inference for him to make as his character? Why or why not? Write a paragraph stating two reasons for your opinion.

- List two things you learned about the story by participating in the character interviews.

- Create a Venn diagram comparing Cinderella with Nyasha in *Mufaro's Beautiful Daughters*, by John Steptoe. Draw and/or write at least four ways these characters were alike and four ways they were different.

Extended Responses

- Imagine that you interview the stepsisters twenty years after Cinderella marries the prince. What five questions would you ask them?

- Identify one character from the story that did not appear on *Books Alive*. Write a set of five interview questions for that character.

- Based on what you heard on today's show, do you think Cinderella invited her stepfamily to the wedding? Why or why not? Write your opinion and support your answer with facts from the story. Draw a picture of the wedding that shows your answer and the feelings of the characters.

- There is a similar story to "Cinderella" in many cultures around the world. Why? What does this story teach us? Why is it an important lesson for people around the world to consider? Write a three-paragraph response in your journal.

ASSESSMENT CHECKLISTS

As mentioned earlier in the chapter, if the Character Interview Assessment Checklist in Figure 6–9 is introduced in the beginning of the lesson when you identify the key drama objectives (see step 7), the students can refer to this checklist as they assess the drama experience and set personal goals for the next character interviews. The students can also use this checklist to guide their reflective discussions or to self-assess. You can use the entire checklist or just parts of the list. Time and experience will dictate the length of the checklist.

This same process can be followed for the reading comprehension objectives. Refer to the Reading Comprehension Strategies Assessment Checklist in Figure 4–6. You can use that checklist with any of the drama strategies in this text.

TEACHER SELF-ASSESSMENT

As the host of the show, you may also have some reflections about your own character portrayal. Perhaps you laughed and broke concentration or perhaps you did not stay in character throughout the show. If so, it is important for you to indicate to the students what improvements you want to make the next time you take on a role. By sharing the changes you want to make in this process, you are setting a positive example for the students. You are making it safe for them to act and reflect upon their work. You are creating an atmosphere of continually raising the bar for improvement as actors.

At the end of the reflective discussions, the class can set goals for the next drama experience. These goals can be posted and referred to as part of step 2 for the next set of character interviews.

Sample Goals for the Next Character Interviews

Students

- use our voices more consistently

- stay in the fictional world of the drama—use concentration

- use cooperation so that we don't talk to our friends when other students are acting

Teacher

- keep concentration and do not laugh when the students answer in imaginative ways

CHARACTER INTERVIEW ASSESSMENT CHECKLIST

Student Actor's Name _____

DURING THE CHARACTER INTERVIEW, THE ACTOR . . .	CONSISTENTLY 3	USUALLY 2	RARELY 1	NEVER 0
Imagination/Mind				
. . . agrees to pretend.				
. . . interacts with real and/or imagined characters and objects.				
. . . reacts to imaginary sights, sounds, smells, tastes, and textures.				
Voice				
. . . varies vocal tone and pitch to create character voices and/or sound effects.				
. . . creates and delivers dialogue that is in character.				
. . . speaks with expression that reflects the personality, traits, thoughts, and feelings of the character.				
. . . projects—speaks loudly enough to be heard.				
Body				
. . . modifies posture, poses, gestures, movements, and/or walk.				
. . . uses facial expressions that communicate the thoughts and feelings of the character.				
Cooperation				
. . . works as a member of an ensemble/team.				
Concentration				
. . . focuses intently on the given drama task.				
. . . remains in character.				

Total _____

32–36   Standing Ovation
27–31   Round of Applause
22–26   Polite Clapping
0–21   Back to Rehearsal

Personal Goal: _____
_____

FIGURE 6–9   *Character Interview Assessment Checklist*

After your first attempt at character interviews, however, you need to consider how well the students remained focused during the lesson. If concentration and attention began to wane, shorten the length of the next drama experience. It is important not to get angry with the students if they become restless or disruptive. The behavior is simply a sign of what the students are capable of doing at that moment in time.

TIME ALLOTMENTS

When you conduct the first whole-class format character interviews for one or two characters each answering three questions, the Teacher Planning section (steps 1–6) will take approximately 20 minutes. The Student Preparation and Conducting of the character interviews should take 20–30 minutes. The length of the assessment section (step 14) of lesson will vary based on the depth of the assessment. After you and the students are familiar with this process, the time will significantly decrease.

The first time you conduct the small-group format for four characters each group answering 4–5 questions as part of one lesson on the same day, the Teacher Planning section (steps 1–6) will take approximately 30–40 minutes. The Student Preparation and Conducting of the character interviews will take approximately 30–50 minutes. The length of the assessment section (step 14) of lesson will vary based on the depth of the assessment.

Once you and your students are comfortable with the process the length of time to prepare and conduct the small-group format character interviews will significantly decrease. You will discover many ways to divide the process over several days, shorten the steps, and increase the students' involvement by having them devise the questions.

Sample Questions

Following are two sets of sample character interview questions. The questions for the elementary-level book *Anansi and the Moss-Covered Rock*, by Eric A. Kimmel, are designed for the whole-class format. There are questions for two characters.

The sample questions for the middle school–level text *A Wrinkle in Time*, by Madeleine L'Engle, are designed for the small-group format. Included is a set of questions for a group of students to portray the author. These questions may be helpful models for questions you create for other texts.

Whole-Class Format

Title of Book: *Anansi and the Moss-Covered Rock*, by Eric A. Kimmel (1988)

Character: Anansi
1. Anansi, in almost all of your stories, you try to trick someone. Why do you do it? Why do you enjoy tricking everyone?
2. You stole the food belonging to many of your animal friends. What would you like to say to them now?

3. Anansi, after all you went through in this story, you ended up with nothing. What did you learn from this experience?
4. Can you give us a big news tip—what is your next trick?

Character: Little Bush Deer

1. Why did you feel it was your job to teach Anansi a lesson?
2. When you delivered the food back to the animals, what did they say and do for you?
3. What would you like to say to Anansi now that you never had the courage to say before?

Small-Group Format

Title of Book: *A Wrinkle in Time* (Chapter 1), by Madeleine L'Engle (1962)

Character: Meg Murray

1. Why did you beat up those boys who said something about your "dumb baby brother"?
2. You are having a very hard time sleeping in this chapter. Could you share with us some of the things you are worried about right now?
3. Deep in your heart, where do you think your father has gone?
4. When you hear the postal lady and the other gossips in town whisper about you and your family, what do you wish you could say to them?
5. If you had three wishes, what would you wish for tonight?

Characters: Town Gossips (The Postmistress, Mrs. Buncombe, and Others)

1. You always whisper to each other when you see Meg walking down the street. What are you saying?
2. What nicknames do you and your friends have for Meg and Charles Wallace?
3. What do you imagine happened to Mr. Murray? Why do you speculate he has disappeared?

Character: Author, Madeleine L'Engle

1. Why do you start off your book with Meg alone in her attic with a terrible hurricane going on outside? What are you trying to foreshadow for the reader?
2. What important facts do you want the reader to know about Meg, Charles Wallace, and the Murray family by the end of Chapter 1?
3. What do you want the reader to predict as the main conflict of the book, based on these first pages?
4. Are there any hints or secrets in this first chapter that you want us to notice and wonder about?

Extending the Drama Strategy

Once the students have done character interviews in the formats described here several times, you may want to add a few variations to the drama experience.

Hot Seat

Divide the students into groups. Assign one group a character to play; have a different group secretly develop inferential questions to pose to that character. The students in the group playing the character take their places on the TV stage tape. They are in the hot seat. The group that developed the inferential questions then interviews this character. The student actors must extemporaneously respond to questions that are posed to their character. They do not have time to prepare or consider their answers. Repeat with new characters and groups.

News Reporters

Instead of playing audience members when they are not being interviewed on the show, students can portray news reporters. As news reporters, they:

- ask additional impromptu questions of the characters being interviewed

- take notes on one character's answers and write a newspaper article about what news-breaking information the interviews revealed

- write an article that summarizes in more general terms the information revealed during the interviews

Compare and Contrast

Two groups of students can play the same character, who appears on two different episodes of *Books Alive*. In each episode, the host can ask the character the same questions. After the two shows, the students can discuss or write about which answers seemed to fit the character best and why, supporting their answers with facts from the text.

7

Tableau

What Does an Effective Tableau Look Like?

The students, assuming the roles of characters in a text, freeze in poses that represent a significant moment in the text. Their expressive faces, body poses, and arm and hand positions, as well as how they pose in relationship to one another, all contribute to the creation of a living photograph, sculpture, or painting. It is a carefully planned live visual image of characters in a circumstance found in a text. The final product results from choices students have made about poses and facial expressions. This tableau is a synthesis of their decisions about (1) how actors use their faces and bodies to communicate actions, circumstances, and emotions, (2) how characters in this dramatic circumstance would likely think and feel, and (3) how incorporating actions or expressions not explicitly stated in the text may enhance the frozen picture. The student actors remain silent, still, expressive, and focused.

Drama Strategy: Tableau

In the classroom, a tableau involves groups of students who play roles and position themselves to create a silent frozen picture that represents a significant moment in a story.

Suggested Grade Levels

While students in grades 3 and younger can participate in tableau drama activities, the recommended grade levels for this chapter's activities are grades 4 and above.

The Teacher's Role in the Drama

In this drama strategy, the teacher functions as facilitator, director, and coach. The teacher will:

- lead students through the process of creating and improving a tableau

- encourage students to use and return to the text for information that will accurately shape their tableau

- view the frozen picture with the eye of a stage director and suggest adjustments to enhance the tableau dramatically

- coach student actors to infuse the roles they play with expression, energy, and the discipline to focus and concentrate

- lead reflections and assessment of tableau experiences

The Students' Role in the Drama

To create tableaux, students experience the kind of thinking that actors, directors, and playwrights practice when they consider how to bring a text to life on the stage. The students will:

- examine the text, discussing and planning how the characters in the frozen picture will pose

- rehearse their tableaux

- play characters by freezing in expressive positions to create a living photograph of a moment described in a text

- participate as audience members who view and critique tableaux

- reflect on and revise their tableaux

The Rationale in Relation to Reading Comprehension

As they read, good readers envision the action and events described in a text. They create a mental movie. A tableau is one frame of that movie. Students first read and imagine what the text describes and then they work together to create a live visual image of the words. Through the planning and presenting of a tableau, students strengthen their ability to visualize the written words, develop and present sensory images, and thus gain a deeper understanding of the text's meaning.

The process of creating and staging tableaux involves students in all of the reading comprehension strategies.

Developing Sensory Images Before beginning work on a tableau, students create mental pictures of what the overall scene and individual characters might look like. While presenting a tableau, student actors respond to sights, sounds, smells, textures, and tastes that are not physically present.

Building and Activating Schema Students call upon their background knowledge about people and circumstances when choosing tableau poses and expressions.

Questioning Because they must solve the problem of how to create a tableau, students question themselves and others about the text and answer those questions.

Determining Importance Because a tableau is a distillation of one particular moment described in words, students must sort out the significant information in the text and use it to create a meaningful frozen picture.

Inferring In the process of planning the frozen picture, students make inferences about characters, emotions, and circumstances that inform their choices about individual poses and the overall look of the tableau.

Synthesis A tableau is a dramatic visual representation. It organizes and summarizes the reading and thinking processes necessary for meaningful comprehension of text. A well-executed tableau, therefore, is a synthesis of a piece of text because it encapsulates the meaning of the written words.

Drama and Theatre Connections

NTC's Dictionary of Theatre and Drama Terms defines tableau as "a grouping of silent, motionless actors representing an incident . . . and presenting an artistic spectacle. The tableau may conclude an act—as when actors freeze at the curtain line—or may be one in a series of tableaux that make up a pageant" (Mobley 1995, 149).

Tableau as a theatre convention is frequently used by directors to create striking visual images. The battle pose struck by actors at the conclusion of Act I of the musical *Les Miserables* is a tableau. In *Mamma Mia*, when the music stops and disco dancers freeze in dancing positions, they create a tableau.

The tableau drama strategy and theatrical convention also have their roots in nineteenth-century theatrical entertainments and parlor games. Called *tableaux vivants*, meaning "living pictures," these presentations featured performers or models or just groups of friends who struck and held poses for extended periods of time. Paintings were often the source of their poses. Spectators were welcome to view the live frozen pictures, but the participants, like statues, could not respond to them. Far earlier instances of tableaux were the costumed sacred, historical, or cultural scenes pulled on wagons through the streets of medieval Europe.

Tableau as a classroom drama strategy is well known and used by drama educators worldwide (Heinig 1992; Morgan and Saxton 1987; O'Neill and Lambert

1987; Tarlington and Verriour 1991; Wilhelm 2002; Wilson 2003, for example). Other names for the tableau drama strategy include *depiction*, *human sculpture*, *group sculpture*, *living statue*, *living portrait* or *picture*, *still image*, *freeze-frame image*, and *frozen picture*.

The word *tableau* comes from the Old French word *tablel*, diminutive of *table*, a surface prepared for painting. Its plural form is *tableaux*. This chapter is devoted to providing in-depth explanations of how to introduce and lead students in creating dramatically effective and meaningful tableaux. Figure 7–1 details the steps for conducting an effective tableau.

STEPS FOR AN EFFECTIVE TABLEAU

Preparing for the Tableau

Teacher Planning

Step 1: Choose the tableau scene(s).
- Determine cast size.

Step 2: Determine the key drama and reading comprehension objectives.

Student Preparation

Step 3: Identify the key drama and reading comprehension objectives.
- Define the drama strategy.
- Share assessment checklist.
- Conduct pertinent warm-ups.

Step 4: Describe the tableau scene(s) and characters.
- Reread, review, and discuss pertinent sections of the text.
- Invite students to visualize character poses.

Step 5: Describe the tableau guidelines.
- Define the acting area.
- Explain the tableau cues.
- Provide time for planning and rehearsal.
- Emphasize concentration, stillness, and silence.

Conducting the Tableau Presentation

Step 6: Present the tableau.
- Cue the student actors to begin the tableau.
- View the tableau.
- Cue the student actors to end the tableau.

Reflecting on the Tableau

Step 7: Revise the tableau.

Step 8: Re-create the tableau.

Step 9: Repeat tableau revisions and re-creations.
- Re-create the tableau again.

Step 10: Assess the students.
- observational assessments
- reflective discussions
- written assessments
- assessment checklists

FIGURE 7–1 *Steps for an Effective Tableau*

Preparing for the Tableau

Teacher Planning

Step 1: Choose the Tableau Scene(s)

Examine your text for moments to dramatize as tableau scenes. The most effective moments involve a group of characters engaged in an activity or observing something of interest. When using a piece of literature as the source of your tableau scene, look for:

- action—scenes in which characters do something, interact with one another, move, react

- scenes or sequences in which characters react emotionally to an event

- incidents that are mentioned only briefly in the text, but when dramatized may increase understanding of the text and characters

- scenes that would make good book illustrations

- scenes that would make interesting photographs

- dream or nightmare scenes

- scenes that occur in a character's imagination

- moments that are unusual, funny, or require exaggerated expressions or interesting body positions

Here are some text elements to avoid:

- descriptive text with little or no action

- scenes in which there is much dialogue but little action

- love scenes

- scenes that involve magic or special effects too difficult to depict

DETERMINE CAST SIZE

In theatre, a cast is the group of actors who perform in a play. In a classroom, your cast size will vary according to the scenes you choose to dramatize. The number of students involved in a tableau scene is determined by the number of characters in the chosen scene. Consider the scene or scenes from your text that you would like to dramatize, and decide whether to use the small-group format or the whole-class format.

Small-Group Format When scenes from the text involve small numbers of characters, small groups of students create the tableaux. Each group can work on depicting a different scene in the text, or several groups can work on presenting tableaux based on the same text passage. The number of characters in a scene drives the number of students required for the cast in each small group. The small-group format for tableaux is more completely discussed in the second part of this chapter.

Whole-Class Format A scene from a text that involves a large number of characters provides an opportunity for a greater number of students to be involved in the acting. When you introduce the tableau drama strategy, it's best to find a scene in the text that allows every student in your classroom to be involved as an actor. Whole-class involvement increases student interest and learning. See Figure 7–2, Tableau Examples—Whole-Class Format, for ideas from various pieces of literature.

A whole-class tableau is used as the model in this portion of the chapter. The source for the whole-class tableau is the funeral scene in *The Adventures of Tom Sawyer*, by Mark Twain (1994). The town presumes that Tom Sawyer, Huck Finn, and Joe Harper are dead. The citizens are gathered in the church, listening to the

TABLEAU EXAMPLES—WHOLE-CLASS FORMAT		
CHARACTERS	**SETTING**	**CIRCUMSTANCE**
Citizens of Hannibal, Missouri	In church for the funeral of Tom Sawyer and two other boys—all presumed dead	Reacting to the three boys who appear at their own funeral (*The Adventures of Tom Sawyer*, by Mark Twain)
Harry Potter and classmates	Hogwarts school grounds	Watching a game of quidditch (*Harry Potter and the Sorcerer's Stone*, by J. K. Rowling)
Guests at the palace	The prince's ball	Noticing the arrival of Cinderella ("Cinderella," by Charles Perreault)
Fans	A high school basketball game	Reacting as one of your cheerleaders cheers for the other team (*Stargirl*, by Jerry Spinelli)
Students	A classroom	Reacting to the doll made by Molly (*Molly's Pilgrim*, by Barbara Cohen)
Students	A classroom	Reacting to Andrew's blue "freckles" (*Freckle Juice*, by Judy Blume)
Members of the community	An auditorium during the Ceremony of Twelve	Reacting to the selection of Jonas as the next Receiver of Memory (*The Giver*, by Lois Lowry)
Citizens of Chicago in 1919	A beach	Watching or participating in a race riot (*Color Me Dark*, by Patricia C. McKissack)
A crowd in Paris, a hundred years ago	A street over which a high wire (tightrope) has been erected	Watching as Mirette stretches her hands out to Bellini (*Mirette on the High Wire*, by Emily Arnold McCully)

FIGURE 7–2   *Tableau Examples—Whole-Class Format*

minister's funeral sermon, when the three "dead" boys appear in the church. The text from Chapter 17 reads:

> The congregation became more and more moved, as the pathetic tale went on, till at last the whole company broke down and joined the weeping mourners in a chorus of anguished sobs, the preacher himself giving way to his feelings, and crying in the pulpit.
>
> There was a rustle in the gallery, which nobody noticed; a moment later the church door creaked; the minister raised his streaming eyes above his handkerchief, and stood transfixed! First one and then another pair of eyes followed the minister's, and then almost with one impulse the congregation rose and stared while the three dead boys came marching up the aisle, Tom in the lead, Joe next, and Huck, a ruin of drooping rags, sneaking sheepishly in the rear! They had been hid in the unused gallery listening to their own funeral sermon! (146–47)

Step 2: Determine the Key Drama and Reading Comprehension Objectives

DRAMA OBJECTIVES

Every drama strategy included in this book requires students to use most or all of the basic acting tools and skills. The following objectives, however, are the key drama objectives emphasized when planning, enacting, and reflecting on tableaux.

Body When they play roles, students will use aspects of body to communicate information about their characters and the drama's circumstances. While acting, students will:

- modify posture, poses, gestures, movements, and/or walk
- use facial expressions that communicate the thoughts and feelings of characters

Cooperation Because drama is a collaborative art form, students will work as members of an ensemble. When they plan, enact, observe, and reflect upon their work, students will:

- create a community of actors who work together and support each other as members of a team

Concentration When they play roles, students will use aspects of concentration to maintain the effectiveness of the drama experience. While acting, students will:

- focus intently on the given drama task

READING COMPREHENSION OBJECTIVES

When planning, enacting, and reflecting upon their work, the students will work toward these key reading comprehension objectives.

Developing Sensory Images To enhance their understanding of a text, students will use multiple senses to create mental images when they read. Students will:

- visualize the setting, characters, and action of the text (create a mental movie)

Inferring To extend and enrich the meaning of a text, students will draw conclusions and make interpretations based on information provided, but not specifically stated, in the text. Students will:

- discover the implied information within the text—read between the lines

Synthesis To demonstrate their understanding of a text, students will take information from what they have read, combine it with prior knowledge, and create something new. Students will:

- extend and apply the information in the text to different contexts

The objectives listed above are the key drama and reading comprehension objectives for the sample tableaux described in this chapter. Each time you use tableaux, however, you may wish to vary the targeted objectives. In the teacher planning stage, it is important to determine which of the many drama objectives (see pages 11–13) and reading comprehension objectives (see pages 14–16) you wish to target.

Student Preparation

Step 3: Identify the Key Drama and Reading Comprehension Objectives

Share the targeted drama and reading comprehension objectives with students. For easy reference, you may wish to post them in the classroom. Ensure that students comprehend each objective by reviewing, clarifying, or simplifying the language and offering examples as necessary for your students.

DEFINE THE DRAMA STRATEGY

Be sure that students understand that a tableau is a silent frozen picture made with people who pose as characters. Posting this definition of a tableau in the classroom is a helpful reinforcement for students. Make your tableau explanation more vivid by asking students to envision these still images: a newspaper photo of a crowd, a painting of human figures, a frame of a comic strip, a video or DVD on pause, and a frame of a movie. When live actors assume and hold the poses and facial expressions of the characters in these still images, they create tableaux.

SHARE ASSESSMENT CHECKLIST

Once students develop a level of proficiency with the acting tools and skills, you may want to provide a checklist of indicators of dramatic excellence in tableaux. This checklist identifies the key drama objectives as well as additional acting tools and skills. Figures 7–6 and 7–7 contain sample assessment checklists that you may photocopy and distribute or enlarge and post.

Explain to students that the left-hand column of the checklist identifies the all the acting tools and skills (indicators) used in a high-quality tableau. (Each indicator is thoroughly explained in Chapter 4.) Take time to review and possibly demonstrate each element with the students so that they understand the criteria. Students may also refer to the checklist later during reflective discussions and written assessments. Each checklist ends with space for students to set personal goals for their participation in the next tableau experience.

CONDUCT PERTINENT WARM-UPS

Discuss the acting tools and skills with students. If you created a chart of these tools and skills, as suggested in Chapter 3, use that as a guide.

Lead the class in acting tool- and skill-building activities that correlate with the drama objectives. For example, to reinforce the acting skill of concentration, lead the students in Group Mirror (page 25). To give students practice in modifying their posture and body positions, creating strong facial expressions, and freezing in silence, conduct a few Shake and Freeze exercises (page 41) and Show-Me Facial Expressions activities (page 38).

Step 4: Describe the Tableau Scene(s) and Characters

Describe to students the moment, characters, and setting chosen for the tableau.

Sample Language: You will create a tableau from Chapter 17 of *The Adventures of Tom Sawyer*. The characters you will play are the citizens of Hannibal at the funeral service for Tom, Huck, and Joe. The tableau will be the moment in which you, the mourning citizens, spot the three "dead" boys marching up the aisle of the church.

REREAD, REVIEW, AND DISCUSS PERTINENT SECTIONS OF THE TEXT

Even if the students have previously read the pertinent section of the text, they need to reread and examine it. Students must read to find and infer information that will inform the tableau. In a text, this information may be explicit, or students may have to call upon their prior knowledge (from the text or their own experiences) and make inferences that they can use in creating their characters.

Review any unfamiliar vocabulary in the text (*congregation, mourners, anguished, pulpit,* and *transfixed,* for example). Then help students examine the text and consider their prior knowledge to determine the following information for their tableau:

- *Setting*—Where and when does the event occur?

- *Characters*—Who is involved?

- *Circumstance*—What is happening?

- *Feelings*—How might the characters be feeling?

- *Thoughts*—What might the characters be thinking?

- *Actions*—What are the characters doing?

Sample Language: Let's take another look at the part of the chapter that describes this incident. Look for important information for our tableau. What is the setting? [a church in Hannibal, Missouri, in the 1800s] Who are the characters? [the townspeople, family, and friends of the three boys] Why are the characters in a church? [They are listening to a preacher give a funeral sermon.] At first, what are the characters doing? [They are listening, weeping, and sobbing.] Think about whether you have ever experienced anything like what is happening in these paragraphs. How might these characters be feeling? [mournful, anguished, sad, sorrowful, miserable, gloomy] Then, when the characters spot the three boys they thought were dead, what do they do? [They stand up and stare at the boys.] What can you infer about how the characters are feeling? [shocked, amazed, disbelieving, frightened, angry, relieved, joyful] What might the characters be thinking? [They might figure out that they have been tricked; they might be relieved that the boys are alive.]

INVITE STUDENTS TO VISUALIZE CHARACTER POSES

Encourage students to think in silence like actors who must use their bodies and faces to communicate information about the characters they play within the drama's circumstances. Before actually doing the tableau, ask students to visualize how they could show what their characters are doing, thinking, and feeling.

Sample Language: You will need to freeze in a pose that communicates what your character is doing, thinking, and feeling. Close your eyes and picture those three boys—the boys you thought were dead—marching up the church aisle. Before you strike your pose, imagine the expression on your face. Visualize how you might stand. What will you do with your arms and hands to show the emotions of your character? Close your eyes and envision the scene and yourself as a character in it.

These instructions and questions are not meant to be discussed. Their intent is to stimulate students' thinking. Keeping their eyes closed will help some students visualize; others may prefer to keep their eyes open. Give the students a few moments to silently envision their dramatic choices, but avoid discussing their ideas.

Step 5: Describe the Tableau Guidelines

DEFINE THE ACTING AREA

When you introduce the tableau drama strategy by using the whole-class format, identify the acting area as being in or around the students' seats. You may indicate to the students that their imaginary audience is in the front of the classroom where you are standing.

In *The Adventures of Tom Sawyer* tableau, as in many other dramatizations, you will need to establish a focal point—a spot in the room where student actors should focus their dramatic attention. In this case, the student actors need to know where the imaginary characters Tom, Huck, and Joe are as they march up the church aisle, so that they may focus on this point when they create their frozen picture.

Sample Language: You will create your tableau in the area around your seats. Let's imagine that your theatre audience is up in the front of the classroom, here where the blackboard is. This aisle between our classroom desks will be the aisle of the church. You should imagine that Tom, Joe, and Huck are just about to this spot between these two desks—the front of the church—when you strike your frozen poses.

 Dramatic Detail

Tell student actors to pick a point of focus in the room (a numeral on a clock, a sign, a floor tile, for example) and direct their vision to it during the tableau presentation. Keeping their eyes on this point, called a *point of concentration*, will help them maintain stillness and concentration.

EXPLAIN THE TABLEAU CUES

For actors, a cue is their signal to perform an action or begin a line. Describe tableau cues to students so that they will know when to strike their frozen poses ("freeze") and when they may move again ("relax"). Clear cues help student actors distinguish between the time for dramatizing and the time for discussing.

Sample Language: When it's time to present your tableau, I will cue you by saying, "Action . . . two . . . three . . . freeze!" You may begin to get into your pose as soon as you hear me say the word action. When I say, "Freeze," remain perfectly still and hold your pose until I say, "Relax."

PROVIDE TIME FOR PLANNING AND REHEARSAL

Give the students a small amount of time to discuss their characters, consider one another's ideas, ask questions, and practice their poses. The time allotted for this step may be as short as thirty seconds or as long as fifteen minutes. Time allotments vary according to the difficulty of the text passage, the number of tableaux being planned, the number of characters per tableau, and the class' previous experience with the drama strategy tableau.

EMPHASIZE CONCENTRATION, STILLNESS, AND SILENCE

When it is time to begin, give students quick reminders about how the quality of a tableau is increased when actors use concentration and remain still and silent.

Sample Language: An excellent tableau requires actors who use the skill of concentration and pose perfectly still in silence. Your tableau may show characters who are crying or gasping, but as actors, your job is to strike and hold your pose without laughing or making a sound.

Conducting the Tableau Presentation

Step 6: Present the Tableau

CUE THE STUDENT ACTORS TO BEGIN THE TABLEAU

Slowly call, "Action . . . two . . . three . . . freeze!" Silently observe the student actors create and hold their tableau poses.

VIEW THE TABLEAU

Take a look at each student actor and at the overall frozen picture. Note whether students have chosen poses that accurately communicate information about the characters and the circumstance in the text. Observe which students maintain concentration and stillness. Initially, about ten seconds is long enough for student actors

Student actors create a tableau.

to remain frozen in their tableau poses and experience the drama strategy. You may choose to lengthen this amount of time for presentations of subsequent tableaux.

CUE THE STUDENT ACTORS TO END THE TABLEAU

Call, "Relax," and express your appreciation for the students' work. Compliment students who remained still and silent. Praise interesting and accurate poses and facial expressions.

Reflecting on the Tableau

Step 7: Revise the Tableau

Occasionally, the student actors' first version of a tableau is superb. More often than not, however, the students benefit from some dramatic coaching. In an excellent tableau, actors choose character poses that accurately reflect the meaning and mood of the dramatized situation. After students have created their first tableau, it's time for revision. The following are some dramatic coaching points to share with students when considering how to revise a tableau.

Energy and Expression In a high-quality tableau, actors pose with energy and expression, maintain their concentration, and stay still and silent. Hold a discussion with students about what makes a photograph of people, and therefore a tableau, visually compelling—energy in their bodies, expression in their faces.

Demonstrate (or choose a student to demonstrate) the difference between a low-energy pose and facial expression and a high-energy version of the same reaction (for example, shock at having a bunch of people unexpectedly jump out and yell "Surprise!" on your birthday). See Figure 4–5 on page 60 for further clarification of dramatic energy and expression.

A Variety of Levels A visually compelling tableau, like an interesting photograph or painting, has a variety of levels—some figures are at a high level (standing, reaching, stretching), some are at a medium level (bending, leaning, sitting), and some are low to the ground (stooping, crawling, lying).

Theatre directors who help actors create stage pictures are concerned with levels. Varying levels strengthens the visual impact of a scene or tableau and highlights characters' relationships to one another. Explain to students that they can create more dynamic stage pictures or tableaux by incorporating levels—posing close to the floor, crouching or sitting midlevel, or standing and reaching high.

The Audience's Perspective Directors also continually consider the audience's perspective: Is this character's face visible? Can this action be seen? Are the important actions staged conspicuously? Ask students to think about whether they need to adjust their frozen poses so that, if they had an audience, all of the characters and actions in the tableau would be more visible.

Upstaging Upstaging is a theatre term that refers to anything that inappropriately takes the audience's attention away from the intended focus of the dramatic

A Low-Energy Pose   A High-Energy Pose

moment. Upstaging in a tableau could be an inappropriate pose, gesture, or facial expression, deliberate movements, a pose by one student actor that blocks the audience's view of another student actor, or anything that diminishes the intended mood or meaning. Discuss the concept of upstaging with students. Ask them to consider whether they need to revise a frozen pose because it might be considered upstaging.

After discussing these coaching points, have students revise the tableau by repeating it.

Step 8: Re-create the Tableau

Rehearsal is an indispensable element of theatre. Especially for students' first exposure to this drama strategy, repeated practice in presenting the same tableau strengthens their acting tools and skills. Continue this drama groundwork by asking students to consider their first tableau a rehearsal. Encourage them to think about how to revise their first tableau by improving their energy, expression, positions, and variety of levels in a second tableau of the exact same situation. Then, have students re-create the tableau so that, by incorporating those elements, it is dramatically more powerful.

Step 9: Repeat Tableau Revisions and Re-creations

After their second tableau presentation, discuss with students the revisions they incorporated. Overwhelmingly, the dramatic coaching inspires an improved second tableau. Invite students to consider the increased energy and expression in their individual poses, the quality of their concentration, any variations in the levels of their poses, and how well they were able to remain still and silent.

RE-CREATE THE TABLEAU AGAIN

Because the entire group was part of the first two presentations of the tableau, you are the only person who got to view the frozen picture. It's time now for some of the students to view others in tableau and experience the presentation as an audience and also as stage directors. Invite about half of the students to re-create the same tableau while the other half observes.

Since the first two tableaux were created in the area where the students sit, you may want to shift the acting area to the front of the room or to any classroom area that permits easy viewing. Defining the acting area helps focus both the student actors and the audience.

While the first half of the class re-creates the tableau, invite the remaining half—the student audience—to view the frozen picture and think like stage directors who help actors improve a tableau. As they view the tableau, ask the observing students:

- Which student actors remain still and maintain concentration?

- Which student actors use their bodies to communicate exactly what their characters are thinking and feeling?

- What variations in body positions might improve the tableau for the audience? Variations in body may include adjusting the following:

  - *stance*—sitting, standing, kneeling, stooping, leaning

  - *gestures*—pointing fingers, shielding eyes, covering mouths

- What variations in facial expressions might improve the tableau for the audience? Variations in face may include showing expressions of fear, awe, skepticism, or relief.

If this discussion gets lengthy, allow the student actors to relax their tableau poses, but have them remain in the acting area to continue discussing and responding to suggestions from the observing students. During the exchange of these suggestions, remind the student actors to listen and think about whether they will incorporate the suggestions. In the end, the student actors will make their own choices. Time spent defending, arguing, and rationalizing is time taken away from dramatizing.

After an appropriate amount of time spent discussing the previous questions, have the same student actors re-create the tableau. Many will incorporate the suggested changes; some will not. After this and each tableau presentation, encourage the student audience to show their appreciation for the student actors. Typically, a simple round of applause will do.

Following the same procedure, invite the students who were the audience to change places with the first group of student actors and present their version of the same tableau. Have the students observe, suggest revisions, and re-create the tableau as previously described. During this introduction to the drama strategy, therefore, your students will present six separate versions of the same tableau.

Step 10: Assess the Students

The assessment process is the same for effective tableaux (just described) and for an extension of this drama strategy detailed in the next section of this chapter—effective tableaux with dialogue. Therefore, please consult the section titled "Step 10: Assess the Students" that begins on page 178.

Extending the Drama Strategy

Creating a silent frozen picture is an effective drama and reading comprehension strategy. That may be as far as you wish to work with tableau. If, however, you would like to deepen the connection between drama and reading comprehension, the next step involves incorporating dialogue—lines or words spoken by actors playing characters—into the tableau. Used within a tableau, a strategy called *shoulder touch*, (also referred to as *tapping in*, *thought tracking*, and *voice in the head*) is commonly known among educational drama practitioners and writers (Macy 2004; Wilhelm 2002; Tarlington and Verriour 1991; O'Neill and Lambert 1987; Tarlington 1985, for example).

Shoulder touch used in conjunction with tableau is a strategy for stimulating dialogue appropriate to the still image and providing opportunities for students to verbalize in role as their characters. While student actors hold their frozen positions, the teacher circulates among them and touches the shoulder of each individual in turn. This is a cue for the individual to speak as his or her character. Adding language to a tableau deepens students' understandings of the tableau and the text. Students infer, create, speak, and hear a character's thoughts (called *subtext* by actors) or words that could be lines of dialogue (such as a playwright might write) as if this tableau were a scene from a play.

The next section of this chapter details a process for creating tableaux with dialogue. (See Figure 7–3 for an outline of the steps for effective tableaux with dialogue.)

STEPS FOR EFFECTIVE TABLEAUX WITH DIALOGUE

Preparing for Tableaux with dialogue

Teacher Planning

   Step 1: Choose the tableau scene(s).
   - Determine the cast size(s).

   Step 2: Determine the key drama and reading comprehension objectives.

Student Preparation

   Step 3: Identify the key drama and reading comprehension objectives.
   - Define the extension of the drama strategy.
   - Explain the use of shoulder touch.
   - Conduct pertinent warm-ups.

   Step 4: Describe the tableau scene(s) and characters.
   - Reread, review, and discuss pertinent sections of the text.
   - Choose tableau participants.
   - Invite students to visualize character poses.
   - Invite students to create lines of dialogue.

   Step 5: Describe the tableau guidelines.
   - Define the acting area.
   - Explain the tableau cues.
   - Provide time for planning and rehearsal.
   - Emphasize concentration, stillness, and silence.

Conducting the Tableau Presentation

   Step 6: Present the tableau.
   - Cue the student actors to begin the tableau.
   - View the tableau.
   - Touch each student actor's shoulder to prompt dialogue.
   - Cue the student actors to end the tableau.

Reflecting on the Tableau

   Step 7: Revise the tableau.
   Step 8: Re-create the tableau.
   Step 9: Repeat tableau revisions and re-creations.
   Step 10: Assess the students.
   - observational assessments
   - reflective discussions
   - written assessments
   - assessment checklists

FIGURE 7–3   *Steps for Effective Tableaux with Dialogue*

Preparing for Tableaux with Dialogue

Teacher Planning

Step 1: Choose the Tableau Scene(s)

From a text, choose one or several moments for students to present in tableaux. As previously recommended, look for moments within a text that feature characters engaged in an activity or observing something of interest. See the recommendations in Figure 7–4 for examples.

TABLEAU EXAMPLES—SMALL-GROUP FORMAT		
TEXT	**CHARACTERS**	**CIRCUMSTANCE**
Liang and the Magic Paintbrush, by Demi	Liang Emperor Emperor's family members	After the emperor orders Liang to paint a sea full of fish and a boat, the emperor's family joins him on the boat. Then he tells Liang to paint wind. Liang does, and soon wind is blowing and waves are crashing.
Marianthe's Story: Spoken Memories, by Aliki	Marianthe Her brothers Her mother	Marianthe, her twin brothers, and her mother leave their beloved village to travel to America, where her papa waits for them.
Sarah, Plain and Tall, by Patricia MacLachlan	Papa Sarah Anna Caleb	Papa yells to Sarah, Anna, and Caleb, "A squall!" They see a huge, horribly black cloud moving across the fields toward them.
Morning Girl, by Michael Dorris	Morning Girl Father	So that Morning Girl can see what she looks like, Father instructs her to look deeply into his eyes.
Little House on the Prairie, by Laura Ingalls Wilder	Laura Mary Ma Two Indians	Laura and Mary enter their log cabin and find two Indians with fierce expressions waiting while Ma cooks them cornbread.
Wringer, by Jerry Spinelli	Palmer Beans Mutto Henry	Fighting back tears of joy and relief, Palmer greets his three birthday-party guests as they shove gifts at him and storm into his house.
Daniel's Story, by Carol Matas	Storm Trooper Mrs. Werner	A storm trooper with a gun stands outside the door of Daniel's father's store. Mrs. Werner, a brassy ninety-year-old, taps the storm trooper's boot with her cane and informs him that she has no intention of observing the boycott of Jewish shops.
The Sign of the Beaver, by Elizabeth Speare	Matt Two Indians	After Matt almost drowns, he awakes on dry ground to find two Indians bending over him.
Ella Enchanted, by Gail Carson Levine	Ella Olive Hattie	As Ella obeys the sisters' demands for the necklace, Hattie begins to figure out that she can always make Ella follow her orders.
A Wrinkle in Time, by Madeleine L'Engle	Meg Calvin Charles Wallace Mrs. Who Mrs. Which Mrs. Whatsit	Meg, Calvin, Charles Wallace, Mrs. Who, Mrs. Which, and Mrs. Whatsit travel in the fifth dimension, called a tesseract. After a violent gust of wind, there is complete darkness and silence. Meg screams, but no sound comes out. She and the others experience the sensation of existing without a body. They seem to "evaporate."

FIGURE 7–4 *Tableau Examples—Small-Group Format*

Determine the Cast Size(s)

Identify the number of characters needed in each of your chosen scenes. Scenes with large numbers of characters—crowds, citizens, spectators, for example—lend themselves to the previously described whole-class format.

Most pieces of literature offer tableau opportunities for small groups of students to play the roles of characters and work together to create a tableau. A small group might be as few as two student actors or as many as seven. See the chart in Figure 7–5 for a variety of tableau ideas from *The Adventures of Tom Sawyer*.

Remember that you do not have to have a different scene for each small group. Several small groups of students can work on creating tableaux of the same scene. This practice can lead to interesting discussions of each group's decisions about essential information, visual and sensory images, and inferences that led them to the artistic choices they made in their journey from the page to the stage.

The tableau detailed in this section of the chapter models the process of working with a small group of students and adding dialogue to a tableau. You will work with one group of student actors while the rest of the students observe and learn the process.

Small-Group Format When they work independently in small-group format, students will:

- examine and discuss the section of the text that they are to depict in tableau

- identify the characters and determine which student will play each character

- identify the circumstance and rehearse possible character poses

- create a line of dialogue that each will speak when prompted with shoulder touch during the enactment of the tableau

- help one another with ideas for lines of dialogue and character poses

- work together to create their tableau

The source for the small-group tableau in this model is a schoolroom scene in *The Adventures of Tom Sawyer*, by Mark Twain. Tom protects Becky, the girl he loves, by taking responsibility for the page of the teacher's book that she tore. The text from Chapter 20 reads:

> The next moment the master faced the school. Every eye sank under his gaze. There was that in it which smote even the innocent with fear. There was silence while one might count ten—the master was gathering his wrath. Then he spoke: "Who tore this book?"
>
> There was not a sound. One could have heard a pin drop. The stillness continued; the master searched face after face for signs of guilt.
>
> "Benjamin Rogers, did you tear this book?"
>
> A denial. Another pause.

"Joseph Harper, did you?"

Another denial. Tom's uneasiness grew more and more intense under the slow torture of these proceedings. The master scanned the ranks of boys—considered a while, then turned to the girls:

"Amy Lawrence?"

A shake of the head.

"Gracie Miller?"

The same sign.

"Susan Harper, did you do this?"

Another negative. The next girl was Becky Thatcher. Tom was trembling from head to foot with excitement and a sense of the hopelessness of the situation.

"Rebecca Thatcher" [Tom glanced at her face—it was white with terror.]—"did you tear—no, look me in the face" [her hands rose in appeal]—"did you tear this book?" A thought shot like lightning through Tom's brain. He sprang to his feet and shouted—"I done it!"

The school stared in perplexity at this incredible folly! (1994, 168–69)

Step 2: Determine the Key Drama and Reading Comprehension Objectives

To the previously established objectives for tableaux (see page 156–57), add the following drama objective:

Voice When they play roles, students will use aspects of voice to communicate information about their characters and the drama's circumstances. While acting, students will:

- create and deliver dialogue that is in character—accurately communicates information about the character and the drama's circumstances

Student Preparation

Step 3: Identify the Key Drama and Reading Comprehension Objectives

Share the targeted drama and reading comprehension objectives with students, emphasizing the addition of the voice drama objective. You may wish to post the objectives in the classroom.

DEFINE THE EXTENSION OF THE DRAMA STRATEGY

Review the characteristics of a tableau with students. Explain to them that the drama strategy remains the same, and oral language is added. The students will learn the process of adding dialogue to a tableau by observing a small group model a tableau. When they work in small groups, they will use the same process to add dialogue to their tableaux.

TABLEAU EXAMPLES FROM *THE ADVENTURES OF TOM SAWYER*, BY MARK TWAIN (SMALL-GROUP FORMAT)

CHARACTERS	SETTING	CIRCUMSTANCE
Tom Sawyer Ben Rogers	The fence outside of Tom Sawyer's house.	Tom whitewashes the fence. Ben ridicules him for having to work instead of going swimming. Tom pretends to prefer painting.
Tom Sawyer Sid Sawyer	Tom and Sid's bedroom	Sid is alarmed by Tom's painful groans as Tom pretends he's dying.
Tom Sawyer Sid Sawyer Mary Sawyer Aunt Polly	Tom and Sid's bedroom	Tom wails in pain over his sore toe. Aunt Polly, Sid, and Mary run to Tom's room.
Tom Sawyer Huck Finn	The cemetery	Late at night, Tom and Huck are so frightened by noises that they scarcely breathe.
Muff Potter Injun Joe	The cemetery	Potter wakes up and questions Injun Joe about the knife he holds.
Tom Sawyer Huck Finn Joe Harper	An island on the river	Hearing a deep boom, the three boys hurry to the shore, part the bushes, and peer out over the water.
Tom Sawyer Becky Thatcher	A dark cave	Becky fears that they are lost. Tom tries to remain confident.

FIGURE 7–5   Tom Sawyer *Tableau Examples—Small-Group Format*

EXPLAIN THE USE OF SHOULDER TOUCH

Tell the student actors that, while they are holding their frozen tableau positions, you will circulate among them and touch the shoulder of each individual. That is the cue for each to speak in character. Share the following information about dialogue and subtext.

Dialogue Explain to students that dialogue is the words or lines spoken by actors playing characters in a play. The main way playwrights communicate a story to an audience is through character dialogue—what characters say about themselves, others, or situations. Invite students to think like playwrights who write lines of dialogue for actors to speak.

Sample Language: If a playwright were writing a line for your character to speak at this moment in the tableau, what might that line be? When I touch your shoulder, that's your cue to speak a line that could be said by your character in this circumstance.

Subtext Explain to students that when actors are not speaking on stage, they must still remain in character. Good actors work to think and feel as their characters do even if they have no dialogue to express those emotions. *NTC's Dictionary of Theatre and Drama Terms* defines *subtext* as "the thoughts, feelings, and reactions implied but never stated in the dialogue of a play" (Mobley 1995, 145).

Sample Language: Even when they are not speaking lines, actors must think and feel as their characters do. These thoughts in their heads are what actors call subtext. When I touch your shoulder, the line you choose to speak could be your character's unspoken thoughts—subtext.

CONDUCT PERTINENT WARM-UPS

Remind students of the acting tools and skills. If you posted a chart of these tools and skills, draw students' attention to it.

Lead the class in acting tool- and skill-building activities that correlate with the drama objectives. For example, to reinforce the acting skill of concentration, lead the

Use the shoulder touch to promote dialogue. Photo by Dennis M. Kelner.

students in Shake and Freeze/Point of Concentration , described on page 41. To practice modifying posture, body positions, facial expressions, and freezing in silence, conduct a few Show-Me Characters and Show-Me Facial Expressions (see pages 36 and 39). To experiment with ways of speaking lines in character, use Finding the Character's Voice (see page 31).

Step 4: Describe Tableau Scene(s) and Characters

Describe to students the tableau moment or moments from the text. To introduce the use of shoulder touch to motivate dialogue, demonstrate with one group of students.

Sample Language: To demonstrate the use of shoulder touch, a small group of students will create a tableau from Chapter 20 of *The Adventures of Tom Sawyer.* The characters are the schoolmaster and students in the Hannibal schoolroom. The tableau will be the frozen moment in which the schoolmaster confronts Becky about the torn page in his book. Tom protects Becky by taking the blame, and the students stare at him in disbelief.

REREAD, REVIEW, AND DISCUSS PERTINENT SECTIONS OF THE TEXT

Students must read or reread the pertinent portion of the text for elements that will inform the tableau. Discuss any unfamiliar vocabulary. As in the whole-class format, determine the characters, setting, circumstance, and characters' thoughts, feelings, and actions.

Sample Language: Let's look at the part of the chapter that describes this incident and find information for our tableau. What is the setting? [a schoolroom in Hannibal, Missouri, in the 1800s] Who are the characters? [the schoolmaster and the students—Tom, Becky, Benjamin, Joseph, Amy, Gracie, and Susan] What is happening? [The schoolmaster is questioning each student to discover who ripped his book.] At first, what are the characters doing? [The students are watching, listening, and answering the teacher.] Think about whether you have ever experienced anything like what is happening in these paragraphs. How might these characters be feeling? [the teacher—mad, angry, furious; the students—scared, frightened, petrified, speechless, terrified, worried] Then, when Tom Sawyer stands up and takes the blame, what do the other characters do? [The students stare at him because they cannot believe how crazy he is to tell on himself.] What can you infer about how the characters are feeling? [The students might feel relieved, incredulous, confused, shocked, or amazed. The teacher may be annoyed, satisfied, enraged, or furious.] Take a moment to think about what the characters might be thinking.

CHOOSE TABLEAU PARTICIPANTS

Once students are familiar with the tableau material from the text, decide (or allow the students in the small group to decide) which students will play each role in the designated tableau scene. (During the modeling of the small-group tableau, the rest of the students will observe as audience members.)

INVITE STUDENTS TO VISUALIZE CHARACTER POSES

Encourage student actors to envision how they can use their bodies and faces to communicate information about what their characters are doing, thinking, and feeling. Before striking tableau poses, ask them to visualize (in silence) their characters in the drama's circumstance.

Sample Language: Your frozen poses must communicate to the audience what your character is doing, thinking, and feeling. Before you participate in the tableau, envision your character's facial expression and body position. Picture in your mind how you will use the acting tools to play this character in this circumstance. It may help you to close your eyes.

The intent of these instructions and questions is to stimulate students' thinking. Allow a few moments for students to silently envision their dramatic choices, but avoid discussing their ideas.

Middle school students strike tableau poses. Photo by Barbara S. Holden.

INVITE STUDENTS TO CREATE LINES OF DIALOGUE

Allow the student actors an appropriate amount of time to think of what they will say in role when you touch each one's shoulder. Some students will need only a few moments to create the lines that they will speak. Others may require some time to compose their lines in writing. Others may need additional help from you or a classmate.

If desired or necessary, remind the student actors to choose appropriate dialogue—no profanity or anachronisms, for example. The words should enhance the intended mood of the tableau and be consistent with the characters who will speak them in this time and place.

Sample Language: When you create the tableau, I will enter into your frozen picture and touch each student actor's shoulder. That's your cue to speak a line of dialogue that your character would say at this moment in time. Think of the line you will say. Don't share it now. Wait until you present the tableau so that the audience and I will hear all the lines for the first time while we view the tableau.

 Dramatic Detail

To the extent that it is appropriate for your students and the tableau scene, it may be helpful to establish guidelines like the following, especially before incorporating dialogue:

When you choose your frozen poses and create your line of dialogue, your character may not use:

- violence
- weapons
- profanity
- references to drugs or alcohol
- gang symbols
- words that intentionally hurt or humiliate another person

Step 5: Describe the Tableau Guidelines

DEFINE THE ACTING AREA

Because a small group of student actors will present for an audience, you will need to define where the tableau will be staged. Choose any clear area of the classroom that can be easily seen by the students watching as audience members. Having the audience view tableaux head-on (rather than having an audience on three sides or completely surrounding the student actors) increases visibility of student actors' poses and facial expressions. A space that is about three to six feet deep and at least eight feet wide can accommodate a small group of student actors.

Sample Language: You will create your tableau in the space in the front of the classroom. When you strike your poses, keep your audience in mind. Pose so that the audience can see your face and body. Try not to block the audience's view of another character.

EXPLAIN THE TABLEAU CUES

Establish how you will signal student actors to strike their frozen poses ("freeze") and to end ("relax") the tableau.

Sample Language: When it's time to present your tableau, I will cue you by saying, "Action . . . two . . . three . . . freeze!" While you are frozen, I will circulate among you and touch each person's shoulder. After each character has spoken, I will say, "Relax," and you may stop posing.

PROVIDE TIME FOR PLANNING AND REHEARSAL

Give the student actors some time to collaborate on how they will pose and what words they will speak. Encourage them to do more than discuss what they will do; they must actively rehearse their tableau scene. A rehearsal period of five to ten minutes is generally adequate. During the modeling of the small-group tableau, lead this rehearsal by encouraging the observing students to offer ideas to the student actors.

EMPHASIZE CONCENTRATION, STILLNESS, AND SILENCE

Although dialogue will eventually be a part of this tableau, concentration, stillness, and silence are still important elements. Just prior to beginning, remind student actors that unless it is their turn to speak, they should remain silent, still, and concentrated.

Sample Language: Remember that in this tableau, one of your drama objectives is to use the acting skill of concentration. Another objective is to use your body to communicate information about your character and the drama's circumstance. Your body must remain perfectly still even when you receive your shoulder-touch cue. Of course, your mouth will need to move when you deliver your dialogue, but otherwise, remain in your silent frozen pose until you hear the cue to end the tableau.

 Dramatic Detail

One drama objective requires that students, as audience members, willingly accept the fictional world of the drama they observe. To aid student actors with concentration and to model good audience behavior, it may be helpful to tell the student audience that they are welcome to laugh appropriately if they enjoy what they see and hear in a tableau, but they are not to make comments. Comments, even positive ones, can make it difficult for student actors to maintain focus and keep from reacting and laughing.

Conducting the Tableau Presentation

Step 6: Present the Tableau

CUE THE STUDENT ACTORS TO BEGIN THE TABLEAU

Slowly call, "Action . . . two . . . three . . . freeze!" and observe the student actors create the tableau.

VIEW THE TABLEAU

Observe each student actor and the overall frozen picture.

TOUCH EACH STUDENT ACTOR'S SHOULDER TO PROMPT DIALOGUE

Circulate among the frozen student actors and touch each shoulder to motivate dialogue. The remaining students, as audience members, should observe and listen. If necessary, request that the student actors speak loudly, clearly, and with expression.

Sample Lines of Dialogue from *The Adventures of Tom Sawyer* **created by student actors:**

Tom: I tore your book, Sir!

Becky is sure going to like me now!

I done it! [*The student actor playing Tom Sawyer may choose to deliver his line exactly as written in the text.*]

Becky: He's the nicest boy in the world!

My savior!

Students: The schoolmaster is going to whip him!

Tom Sawyer must really have a crush on Becky Thatcher!

Tom must be nuts to tell on himself!

He's crazy!

Schoolmaster: Tom Sawyer—as usual!

I should have known!

CUE THE STUDENT ACTORS TO END THE TABLEAU

About ten seconds after you have touched the last student actor's shoulder and he has spoken his dialogue, call, "Relax." Encourage the student audience members to show their appreciation for the tableau presentation. Applause is the typical way for audiences to honor actors' work.

Reflecting on the Tableau

Step 7: Revise the Tableau

After the small group of student actors has presented the tableau, invite the observing students to reflect on the frozen picture and think like stage directors who help actors improve their work. Begin with the dramatic coaching points explained under "Revise the Tableau" on pages 162–63:

- energy and expression

- a variety of levels

- the audience's perspective

- upstaging

In addition, focus on the voice drama objective by asking for responses to these questions:

- What examples of dialogue created by the student actors were in character and appropriate to this setting and circumstance?

- What suggestions do you have for making the lines of dialogue reflect more information about this scene and its characters?

Guide student actors to revise and improve dialogue by including some of the following elements in their lines:

- use of character names

- use of dialect or slang

- references to setting

- references to prior plot elements

- longer lines that elaborate on feelings, thoughts, and actions

- inclusion of information about characters, action, plot, and so on

Step 8: Re-create the Tableau

After discussing the coaching points and questions in the previous step, revise the tableau by inviting the same small group of student actors to re-create it. Encourage them to incorporate elements that will strengthen their tableau both dramatically and vocally.

Step 9: Repeat Tableau Revisions and Re-creations

Most groups of students are eager to repeat a tableau with a new set of student actors. If desired or necessary, you may continue modeling the small-group tableau by selecting another set of students to play the same characters and create a tableau of the same situation. Emphasize to the new student actors that while their tableau depicts the same situation, they may make different choices about their poses and lines of dialogue. Just as different actors will deliver different interpretations of the same role, different student actors may vary the ways that they portray the same characters in a tableau.

Independent Small-Group Work After students have experienced and observed the small-group format for tableaux with dialogue, you may have them work in independent small groups to create and present tableaux. Follow the same established steps for effective tableaux with dialogue, abbreviating information and instructions where necessary.

Allow a brief but reasonable amount of time for the small groups to plan and rehearse their tableaux and lines of dialogue. (As stated previously, five to ten minutes is usually sufficient.) After the planning and rehearsal time, bring the entire class back together for the conducting, reflecting, revising, and re-creating of each small group's tableau.

Step 10: Assess the Students

OBSERVATIONAL ASSESSMENTS

Observing and listening to the students as they plan, enact, observe, and reflect on the tableaux provide ongoing information about the extent to which they achieved the key drama and reading comprehension objectives. See Chapter 4 for additional information on observational assessment. Use the following categories to provide focus for your observations.

From a Drama Perspective

Body

- While the students play roles, note how they use their bodies to communicate information about their characters and the drama's circumstances.

- Note whether they modify and maintain their posture and body positions.

Cooperation

- When the students plan, enact, observe, and reflect upon their work, observe whether they help one another explore options and make choices.

- Look for instances of students working together and supporting one another as members of a team.

Concentration

- While the students are acting, watch for instances in which their deliberate attention helps maintain the effectiveness of the drama experience.

- Observe instances of students focusing intently on any aspect of the given drama task.

For tableaux with dialogue, also consider the following.

Voice

- When the students play roles, note whether their vocal expression communicates information about their characters and the drama's circumstances.

- Listen for the creation and delivery of dialogue that is in character.

From a Reading Comprehension Perspective

Developing Sensory Images

- When students dramatize a tableau scene, observe whether their frozen picture accurately reflects the setting, characters, and action described in the text.

Inferring

- As students discuss and rehearse their tableaux, note whether they read between the lines to extend and enrich the text's meaning.

- Listen for examples of the student actors' dialogue that include elements implied in the text. Note whether students are drawing conclusions and making interpretations based on information provided but not specifically stated in the text.

Synthesis

- Consider the extent to which the students' tableaux are effective examples of extending and applying information in the text to different contexts.

REFLECTIVE DISCUSSIONS

Classroom conversations can serve as initial informal assessments. Student responses to reflective discussion questions that focus on key drama and reading comprehension objectives will give you insight into the depth of their understanding. The goals of such questions are to (1) encourage students to recall the drama experience more deeply and learn from their participation in it, (2) let students commend and support one another, and (3) have students reflect on their own work to acknowledge strengths and areas in need of improvement.

Incorporate drama and reading comprehension vocabulary (strategy names) into your questions. If you used one of the assessment checklists (Figures 7–6 and 7–7), you and your students may refer to it during reflective discussions. The checklist can help you focus your conversations on students' use of all the acting tools and skills that contribute to high-quality tableaux. Following are some reflective discussion questions to pose after tableaux experiences.

Questions That Recall Elements of the Drama Experience

From a Drama Perspective

- What did you learn about the characters and the drama's circumstances by observing students in poses as characters in tableaux?

- How did expressive faces contribute to the quality of the tableaux?

- How did the lines of dialogue increase your understanding of this moment in the story?

- What other acting tools and skills did you use to create your tableaux?

From a Reading Comprehension Perspective

- What sensory images were evident in the tableaux?

- What were the differences between the mental movie you made while you read the text and the tableaux that you and/or others created?

- How did you use the reading comprehension skill inferring when posing or speaking in a tableau?

- How did observing or participating in a tableau make you think differently about the text?

- What other reading comprehension strategies did you use in creating your tableaux?

Questions That Encourage Praise

From a Drama Perspective

- Which student actors used their bodies effectively to communicate information about their characters and the drama's circumstances? How did they pose? Why were those poses effective?

- What facial expressions were particularly effective in communicating the characters' thoughts and feelings?

- What are some examples of dialogue that were especially in character?

- Who do you think worked particularly well as a member of our ensemble? What are some examples of teamwork that occurred as we worked on tableaux?

- Which student actors maintained their concentration during a tableau presentation? Who would you ask to share some strategies for keeping focus?

- Who, as an audience member, was especially good at demonstrating respect for the work of the student actors? Why is respectful audience behavior important? How does an audience's behavior positively or negatively affect the actors?

From a Reading Comprehension Perspective

- Which student actors' poses and/or facial expressions helped you visualize the scene particularly well?

- What inferences did you see in other student actors' poses and facial expressions?

- What inferences did you hear in their lines of dialogue?

- What new information about the characters or circumstances did you learn by viewing the tableaux of others?

- How did a tableau created by other student actors increase your understanding of the text?

Questions That Encourage Change

From a Drama Perspective

- The next time you participate in a tableau, how might you improve your use of the acting tool body?

- How might you use the acting tool voice more effectively the next time you participate in a tableau with dialogue?

- How can you improve as a member of our ensemble?

- What concentration goals might you set for the next time we do tableaux?

From a Reading Comprehension Perspective

- In the next tableau you work on, how might you communicate sensory images more effectively?

- When preparing your next tableau, how might you work to make and include deeper inferences? Consider the preparation involved in reading, posing, and creating lines of dialogue.

- If a tableau can serve as a synthesis of a text we read, how can we work together to create the highest-quality tableaux possible?

WRITTEN ASSESSMENTS

Observing and participating in the tableau drama strategy provide many ways for students to respond in writing about their drama and reading comprehension. Design writing prompts to elicit students' thinking based on their use of the acting tools and skills and the reading comprehension strategies. Journal entries, reading response logs, tableau captions, newspaper-style reports, and other written responses can all be fashioned to address the stated objectives. Student responses to writing prompts like the following can confirm their understandings of the text via tableaux.

From a Drama Perspective

Brief Responses

- Describe three ways that your character's body is different from your own body.

- Write down a line you spoke in a tableau with dialogue. Add new words or an additional sentence to your line so that your words communicate more information about your character and the drama's circumstances.

- State three reasons why it is important for actors to work together as members of an ensemble.

- Describe two examples of how the use of concentration by actors improves the drama experience for the audience.

Extended Responses

- Provide a detailed description of how and why your pose in the tableau communicated information about your character and the drama's circumstances. Include specifics about your posture, arm and leg positions, and facial expression. You may also want to sketch your pose.

- Meet with the other student actors in your tableau. Recall and record the lines of dialogue each of you spoke in the tableau. Create a short script (ten to twenty lines of dialogue) based on your tableau scene, using and adding to your original lines of dialogue.

- Recall how one student actor worked well as a member of your team of actors. Describe how that person's words and actions improved your tableau. Give at least three examples.

- In a five- to six-sentence paragraph, describe how you maintained your concentration while you were acting. If you lost concentration during a tableau, write an additional three- to four-sentence paragraph explaining how you will work to improve your concentration in future acting tasks.

From a Reading Comprehension Perspective

Brief Responses

- Write a compelling one-sentence caption that fully describes what is happening in the Tom Sawyer funeral tableau.

- Recall this line spoken by the schoolmaster: "I should have known!" State two things you might infer about this character based on this line and the way it was spoken.

- Choose one tableau you observed today. Draw a cartoon of the characters in the drama's circumstance. Include speech bubbles with the lines of dialogue you recall.

Extended Responses

- The characters Tom, Joe, and Huck were not actually in the first tableau you created. They were characters you needed to imagine. When you acted in the tableau, you were asked to picture these imaginary characters walking into their own funeral. Write a paragraph that describes these characters. What do you think they looked like? Use a variety of adjectives to describe each character's body, clothing, face, and attitude.

- Pretend you are playing one of the students in that Hannibal schoolroom. What sensory images—sights, sounds, smells, touch, or taste—might you include in your line of dialogue for this tableau? Write three new lines your character could speak that would communicate sensory images to an audience. For example: "Someone better admit to ripping that book!" or "I don't want to have to stay after school on this beautiful day!"

- Recall the body pose and facial expression of one student actor in the *Tom Sawyer* funeral tableau. Based on that student's use of the acting tool body, what might you infer about that character's thoughts and feelings?

- Pretend you are either Tom or Becky. In your secret diary, fill up a whole page (at least one hundred words) with your thoughts and feelings about the schoolroom event depicted in the model tableau with dialogue.

ASSESSMENT CHECKLISTS

The tableau assessment checklists in Figures 7–6 and 7–7 provide additional ways to assess students in a written format. You may determine the extent to which each student has achieved the described indicator and place a check mark in the appropriate column. Students may use the checklists to assess themselves and create a written record of their achievement of the dramatic criteria.

Please note that Figure 7–6 ends with space for students to set personal goals for their participation in the next tableau experience. This is an opportunity for the students to consider all the aspects of a high-quality tableau and record in writing how they plan to improve in one or more drama objectives.

For a reading comprehension strategy assessment checklist that can be used with any of the drama strategies in this text, refer to Figure 4–6.

ADDITIONAL ASSESSMENT IDEAS: TECHNOLOGY

Technology can be valuable in providing a record of student progress and evidence of achievement. Photos and recordings allow both teachers and students to review and monitor the uses of the acting tools and skills.

Photographic Records Photos of tableaux, especially digital photos that can be taken and viewed immediately, provide evidence of students' tableau skills. Photos allow students to view the tableau in which they participated and assess themselves individually and the tableau as a whole. Tableau photos may be reviewed and critiqued as ongoing assessment tools.

TABLEAU ASSESSMENT CHECKLIST

Student Actor's Name _____

DURING THE TABLEAU PRESENTATION, THE ACTOR . . .	CONSISTENTLY 3	USUALLY 2	RARELY 1	NEVER 0
Imagination/Mind				
. . . agrees to pretend.				
. . . reacts to imaginary sights, sounds, smells, tastes, and textures.				
Body				
. . . modifies posture, poses, gestures, movements, and/or walk, including: ■ varies levels. ■ poses with an audience's perspective in mind.				
. . . uses energy when modifying or adjusting body.				
. . . uses a facial expression that communicates the thoughts and feelings of the character.				
Cooperation				
. . . works as a member of an ensemble/team.				
. . . remains silent when cued.				
. . . remains frozen when cued.				
Concentration				
. . . focuses intently on the given drama task.				
. . . remains in character.				

Total _____

26–30   Standing Ovation
21–25   Round of Applause
18–22   Polite Clapping
0–17   Back to Rehearsal

Personal Goal: _____
_____

FIGURE 7–6   *Tableau Assessment Checklist*

TABLEAU WITH DIALOGUE ASSESSMENT CHECKLIST

Student Actor's Name _____

DURING THE TABLEAU PRESENTATION, THE ACTOR . . .	CONSISTENTLY 3	USUALLY 2	RARELY 1	NEVER 0
Imagination/Mind				
. . . agrees to pretend.				
. . . reacts to imaginary sights, sounds, smells, tastes, and textures.				
Voice				
. . . creates and delivers dialogue that is in character.				
. . . speaks with expression that reflects the personality, traits, thoughts, and feelings of the character.				
. . . projects—speaks loudly enough to be heard.				
. . . articulates—speaks clearly enough to be understood.				
. . . modifies word tempo—speaks slowly enough to be understood.				
Body				
. . . modifies posture, poses, gestures, movements, and/or walk, including: ■ varies levels. ■ poses with an audience's perspective in mind.				
. . . uses energy when modifying or adjusting body.				
. . . uses a facial expression that communicates the thoughts and feelings of the character.				
Cooperation				
. . . works as a member of an ensemble/team.				
. . . remains silent when cued.				
. . . remains frozen when cued.				
Concentration				
. . . focuses intently on the given drama task.				
. . . remains in character.				

Total _____

40–45 Standing Ovation
34–39 Round of Applause
28–33 Polite Clapping
0–27   Back to Rehearsal

FIGURE 7–7   *Tableau with Dialogue Assessment Checklist*

Recordings (Video or Audio) Recording the final presentation of a tableau also provides a useful reference for assessment. Video recordings permit students to observe and assess themselves in terms of body and concentration. Both audio and video recordings preserve a record of the actual lines of dialogue. Hearing the actual words spoken can help confirm student achievement of the voice drama objective.

TIME ALLOTMENTS

The introduction to the tableau drama strategy, including the identification of objectives and text section, the conducting of a whole-class format tableau, and the reflection, revisions, and re-creations of the tableau should take about an hour. You will need another hour to conduct the same tableau with both halves of the group, and reflect upon, revise, and re-create the tableaux. The amount of time required for assessment will vary according to the types of assessment you use.

Introducing the tableau with dialogue drama strategy and conducting a model tableau with dialogue takes about 30 minutes. To reflect on, revise, and re-create the model tableau with dialogue takes another 15–20 minutes.

The time needed for planning, rehearsing, conducting, revising, and re-creating of each small group's tableau with dialogue varies according to the number of tableaux. Allowing about 15 minutes per tableau should result in enough class time to complete the steps involved.

8

Human Slide Shows

What Does an Effective Human Slide Show Look Like?

A group of students playing characters create several tableaux or slides. When these slides are presented in sequence, they show the progression of events in a scene from a text. Although the student actors remain frozen in each individual slide, the tableaux viewed as a slide show depict a sequence of action. The student actors vary their poses and facial expressions from one slide to the next. This human slide show is a synthesis of students' decisions about (1) which events or moments within the scene are the most important to represent as slides, (2) the order of events—what happened first, second, third, and so on, (3) how characters in this dramatic circumstance would likely think, feel, and move, and (4) how actors use their faces and bodies to communicate actions, circumstances, and emotions. In each slide, the student actors remain silent, still, expressive, and focused as they strike the rehearsed sequence of poses.

Observers participate in the human slide show presentation by closing their eyes when cued with the word *blackout* to simulate a lighting blackout used in the theatre while actors change positions. When they hear the cue "Lights up," observers open their eyes to view each slide.

Drama Strategy: Human Slide Show

In the classroom, a human slide show involves groups of students who play characters in several silent frozen pictures that depict a sequence of events in a scene from a text.

Suggested Grade Levels

This drama strategy is most successful when the participants are in grades 4 and above.

The Teacher's Role in the Drama

As in the tableau drama strategy, when conducting human slide shows, the teacher functions as facilitator, director, and coach. The teacher will:

- determine the scenes from a text to dramatize with human slide shows

- lead students through the process of creating, conducting, improving, and reflecting on a human slide show

- instruct students to examine the scene from the text and determine the most important events or moments to include in their human slide show

- view each individual slide with the eye of a stage director and suggest adjustments to enhance the human slide show dramatically

- coach student actors to infuse the roles they play with expression, energy, and the discipline to focus and concentrate

- lead reflections and assessment of the human slide show experience

The Students' Role in the Drama

When students participate in human slide shows, they plan by thinking like theatre directors who consider how to create effective stage pictures to tell a story. They also participate as actors who execute the determined poses in the stage pictures and as observers who collaborate in the process of viewing a human slide show. The students will:

- examine the portion of text—the scene—that they will dramatize in a human slide show and determine the characters and important events or moments of action to represent

- discuss, plan, and experiment with character poses in each slide

- rehearse the human slide show

- play characters by freezing in a series of expressive poses to create a human slide show of a scene described in a text

- participate as observers of a slide show who follow cues to open and close their eyes

- reflect on and revise their human slide shows

The Rationale in Relation to Reading Comprehension

As they read, good readers call upon sensory images to create a mental movie of the text's action and events. Human slide shows provide a way for students to dramatize the most significant frames of that mental movie. To do so, students read and visualize what the text describes and collaborate to produce several live still images that represent their interpretations of the words. Human slide shows motivate students to (1) create mental images evoked by written words, (2) make choices about which moments described in a scene are the most compelling ones to depict as still images, and (3) experiment with and select character poses that best communicate the action and events, thus strengthening their understanding of the text.

Creating and staging human slide shows involves students in all of the reading comprehension strategies.

Developing Sensory Images To produce a human slide show, students must imagine the sights, sounds, smells, tastes, and textures described in the text. Those sensory images supply the information they need to transform their ideas into live still images that use human beings to portray the characters experiencing the events described in the text.

Building and Activating Schema To portray characters involved in a scene, students draw upon their previous life and learning experiences. They consider how events they have lived through, witnessed, or read about inform the acting choices they make as they rehearse and present a human slide show.

Questioning The planning and revising of human slide shows prompt students to ask themselves and others a variety of questions. These questions help them clarify information in the text, discover new information, and search for solutions to the challenges of staging a human slide show.

Determining Importance A human slide show is a distillation of a limited number of the significant moments in a scene from a text. Students must discriminate between key events and those less vital to represent dramatically.

Inferring The text serves as a road map for human slide shows. The students' task is to read and follow the text, and also to enrich their dramatic interpretation of the text by making decisions about the implied information it contains. The conclusions they draw by combining their prior knowledge with clues found in the text inform their dramatic choices.

Synthesis The human slide show that the students create and present is the synthesis—the extension and application of information from the text to create something completely new.

Drama and Theatre Connections

The staging of a human slide show allows students to experience a small taste of what actors and directors do when they rehearse and present a scene from a play. Instead of using a script as the structure for the dramatic work, students use a small portion—a scene—of the text. *Blocking*, for example, is a theatre term for the movements, grouping, or arrangement of actors during a play. When students make decisions about when and where characters stand, sit, lie, turn, climb, or flee, they experience the theatrical problem solving involved in blocking.

When they consider why characters behave in certain ways, students are thinking like actors who continually explore character motivation. They look within the text for clues to character behavior and relate the character's choices to their own life experiences and feelings. Actors also rely on emotional recall to play their roles convincingly. Similar to the reading comprehension strategy building and activating schema, emotional recall is the identification of specific emotional responses from past experiences used to understand and portray character behavior. Participation in human slide shows requires students to consider emotional recall.

As stated in the previous chapter on tableaux, *NTC's Dictionary of Theatre and Drama Terms* defines *subtext* as "the thoughts, feelings, and reactions implied but never stated in the dialogue of a play" (Mobley 1995, 145). When students discuss a character's possible inner thoughts, feelings, and reactions, and experiment with ways to show them in silence, they are exploring subtext.

"Lights up" is the cue for brightening the stage lights. "Blackout" is a lighting cue that signals the immediate darkening of the entire stage. In a recent production of the musical *Crowns* at Arena Stage in Washington, D.C., the actors created a human slide show when, during blackouts, they struck and held different poses that were visible to the audience each time the lights came up. Their sequence of poses represented photos taken at a wedding celebration. These two cues from the theatre—"blackout" and "lights up"—are the same ones used to cue actors and observers of human slide shows.

Human slide shows as a classroom drama strategy are also known as *freeze frames*, *slide shows*, and *linked still images*. Figure 8–1 details the steps for conducting effective human slide shows.

Preparing for Human Slide Shows

Teacher Planning

Step 1: Choose the Human Slide Show Scenes

A scene is a segment of a story or play that has a beginning, middle, and end. In a text that is part of your curriculum, search for scenes that describe a sequence of events. To determine whether your text contains scenes that are appropriate for human slide shows, look for:

- action—scenes in which characters do something, interact with one another, move, react

- a sequence of events that is mentioned only briefly in the text, but when dramatized may increase students' understanding of the text and characters

- scenes that, if filmed, would have interesting action and movement

STEPS FOR EFFECTIVE HUMAN SLIDE SHOWS

Preparing for Human Slide Shows

Teacher Planning

Step 1: Choose the human slide show scenes.
- Determine cast sizes.

Step 2: Determine the key drama and reading comprehension objectives.

Student Preparation

Step 3: Identify the key drama and reading comprehension objectives.
- Define the drama strategy.
- Conduct pertinent warm-ups.

Step 4: Describe the human slide show scenes and characters.
- Reread, examine, and discuss pertinent sections of the text.
- Brainstorm possible events or moments to depict as slides.
- Determine the four or five most important moments to depict as slides.
- Create a sequence-of-events chart listing each slide in the slide show.
- Invite students to visualize and discuss the scene's events and character poses.
- Determine which students will play the characters.

Step 5: Describe the human slide show guidelines.
- Define the acting area.
- Explain the human slide show cues.

Step 6: Provide time to plan and rehearse the human slide shows.
- Emphasize concentration, stillness, and silence.

Conducting the Human Slide Show Presentation

Step 7: Present the human slide shows.
- Cue the student actors and the audience members to begin a human slide show.
- Cue the student actors to change poses from one slide to the next.
- Cue the student actors to end the human slide show.

Reflecting on the Human Slide Shows

Step 8: Discuss each human slide show.

Step 9: Provide time to revise each human slide show.

Step 10: Present each revised human slide show.

Step 11: Assess the students.
- observational assessments
- reflective discussions
- written assessments
- assessment checklists

FIGURE 8–1   *Steps for Effective Human Slide Shows*

- dream or nightmare sequences, or those that occur in a character's imagination

- scenes that involve magic or special effects

    Here are some text elements to avoid:

- descriptive text that is void of action or movement

- scenes in which there is much dialogue but little action

- love scenes

Because the most effective way to teach students how to create human slide shows is to model the entire process with them, choose one scene from your text to use as an introductory example. Use student volunteers to play the roles in the model human slide show. Involve the rest of the class in the learning experience by asking them for ideas and suggestions. Once you have guided students through the entire human slide show process, students will work in small groups and present their slide shows for the entire class.

The source for the model human slide show described in this chapter comes from a scene in Chapter 4 of *Freedom Train: The Story of Harriet Tubman*, by Dorothy Sterling (1987). Here's a summary of the background information, setting, characters, and events of the scene: In a barn on a plantation in Maryland in the 1800s, the overseer notices the absence of a slave named Jim. When the overseer heads off toward a store to find Jim, a female slave—Harriet Tubman—cuts across the fields and gets to the store ahead of him. Before she can warn Jim, the overseer arrives. He orders Jim back to the barn, but Jim does not obey and Harriet permits him to escape. The overseer throws a weight at Jim, but it strikes Harriet in the forehead instead and knocks her out.

The text from Chapter 4 reads:

While the overseer followed the road, she cut across the fields. Breathing hard, she reached the store before him. Jim was there, whispering to the man behind the counter. Before she had a chance to warn him of the danger, the overseer strode in.

"You there, Jim," he ordered. "Get back to the barn this instant. I'll whip you for this."

Cautiously, Jim circled away from the outstretched hands. As the overseer neared the counter, he sidestepped toward the door. Harriet, flattened against the wall and scarcely daring to breathe, touched his shoulder as he passed.

"Grab him, Harriet," the overseer bellowed. "Hold him for me while I tie him up."

In a flash, Harriet had moved to the doorway. Calmly, she stretched out her arms to block the overseer's pursuit. Outside, Jim was running for the sheltering woods.

Beside himself with rage, the overseer picked up a two-pound weight from the storekeeper's scales. He threw it after the retreating figure, but Jim was far out of range. The weight struck Harriet in the forehead. She fell to the ground with a moan. (45)

DETERMINE CAST SIZES

The number of characters in the scenes you choose to dramatize dictates the number of students involved in each human slide show. Consider the text scenes that you would like to dramatize, count the number of characters needed in each scene, and determine the number of students per group. Keep in mind that the same scene may be dramatized by two or more groups of students. You may also choose to have one student per group function as a director—someone who helps the student actors create each slide but does not play a role in the human slide show. Four student actors playing the roles of Harriet, Jim, the overseer, and the man behind the counter make up the cast for the model human slide show described in this chapter.

Step 2: Determine the Key Drama and Reading Comprehension Objectives

DRAMA OBJECTIVES

Every drama strategy in this book requires students to use most or all of the basic acting tools and skills. The following objectives, however, are the key drama objectives emphasized when planning, enacting, and reflecting on this chapter's model human slide show.

Body When they play roles, students will use aspects of body to communicate information about their characters and the drama's circumstances. While acting, students will:

- modify posture, poses, gestures, movements, and/or walk

- use facial expressions that communicate the thoughts and feelings of characters

Cooperation Because drama is a collaborative art form, students will work as members of an ensemble. When they plan, enact, observe, and reflect upon their work, students will:

- follow instructions
  - remain silent when cued
  - remain frozen when cued

Concentration When they play roles, students will use aspects of concentration to maintain the effectiveness of the drama experience. While acting, students will:

- focus intently on the given drama task

READING COMPREHENSION OBJECTIVES

Every drama strategy included in this book requires students to meet most or all of the reading comprehension objectives. When planning, enacting, and reflecting upon human slide shows, however, the students will work toward these key reading comprehension objectives.

Determining Importance To find the essentials in a text, students will distinguish between the main ideas and the details of what they read. Students will:

- demonstrate comprehension of the important elements of the text

Inferring To extend and enrich the meaning of a text, students will draw conclusions and make interpretations based on information provided, but not specifically stated, in the text. Students will:

- discover the implied information within the text—read between the lines

Synthesis To demonstrate their understanding of a text, students will take information from what they have read, combine it with prior knowledge, and create something new. Students will:

- extend and apply the information in the text to different contexts

The objectives listed above are the key drama and reading comprehension objectives for the model human slide show described in this chapter. Each time you use human slide shows, however, you may wish to vary the targeted objectives. (See pages 11 and 16.)

Student Preparation

Step 3: Identify the Key Drama and Reading Comprehension Objectives

Specify for students the targeted drama and reading comprehension objectives. For easy reference, you may wish to post both sets of objectives in the classroom. To ascertain that students comprehend the objectives, review and explain them. If necessary, clarify the objectives with examples.

DEFINE THE DRAMA STRATEGY

The tableau activities described in the previous chapter are the best preparation for student participation in human slide shows. Students who approach human slide shows with prior experience in creating one silent frozen picture with people who pose as characters are better prepared to extend this concept into the creation of several sequential tableaux. "Several tableaux" means that the number of slides may vary, but for newcomers to this drama strategy, limiting the number of slides to four or five simplifies planning, rehearsing, and presenting.

Explain to students that human slide shows are several silent frozen pictures—tableaux—that depict in sequence the events of a scene in a text. Posting this definition of human slide shows in the classroom is a helpful reminder for students.

You may also elaborate on the definition by explaining that the tableaux or slides, when presented in order, show a sequence of events—what happened first, second, third, fourth, and so on. (Note: *Slide show* is a familiar computer term for many students. Many computer programs and websites use slide shows to display a series of images.) When live actors vary their poses and facial expressions from one slide to the next, they create human slide shows.

As in the previous drama strategy chapters, you will find an assessment check-list at the end of this chapter (Figure 8–2). This checklist includes indicators that describe the strategy's key drama objectives and the additional acting tools and skills that contribute to high-quality human slide shows. Sharing this checklist with students prior to their participation in human slide shows clarifies the acting tools and skills that contribute to excellence in this drama strategy. You may photocopy and distribute the checklist, reproduce it as an overhead projection, or enlarge and post it.

By the time students participate in human slide shows, they should be somewhat proficient with the acting tools and skills. Before the students plan, rehearse, and present their human slide shows, review each checklist element so that they understand the assessment criteria. Later, during reflective discussions and written assessments, use the assessment checklist as a reference and as a tool for students to self-assess and set personal goals for their participation in the next human slide show experience.

CONDUCT PERTINENT WARM-UPS

Review the acting tools and skills with students. If you created a chart of these tools and skills, as suggested in Chapter 3, use that as a guide.

Lead the class in acting tool- and skill-building activities that correlate with the drama objectives for human slide shows. Show-Me Characters exercises (see page 36) give students practice in (1) modifying their posture, poses, gestures, and facial expressions and (2) freezing in silence. To practice the acting skill of concentration, lead students in Group Mirror and "Won't You Please Smile?" exercises (see pages 25 and 42–43).

Step 4: Describe the Human Slide Show Scenes and Characters

Review with students the scenes from the text they will be dramatizing as human slide shows. Identify where in the text the scenes appear. Either explain where in the text to look, or post or distribute a list of the scenes and their page numbers.

Sample Language: The model human slide show is from Chapter 4 in *Freedom Train: The Story of Harriet Tubman* by Dorothy Sterling. The scene begins with the discovery of a missing slave named Jim and ends with Harriet wounded by the force of a two-pound weight. The characters in the scene are Jim, Harriet, the overseer, and a man in the store.

REREAD, EXAMINE, AND DISCUSS PERTINENT SECTIONS OF THE TEXT

Students need to revisit the pages of the text that contain the scene to be dramatized. They need to think like actors and directors when they read—determining and visualizing the settings, characters, events, and any important details.

For the model human slide show, help students examine the text and discuss the following information:

- *Setting*—Where and when does the scene occur? (A store in Maryland in the 1800s)

- *Characters*—Who is involved? (Harriet Tubman, the plantation overseer, a slave named Jim, and a man behind the store counter)

- *Events*—What happens throughout the scene? (Jim, who has begun his escape, stops in the store. Harriet comes to warn him that the overseer knows he is missing and is coming to capture him. The overseer arrives and orders Jim to return. When Jim makes a run to leave, the overseer tells Harriet to stop Jim. Harriet does not cooperate, Jim escapes, and the infuriated overseer throws a weight at Jim that hits Harriet in the forehead and knocks her out.)

- *Details*—Are there any unfamiliar words, terms, or elements? (The two-pound weight was a piece of metal that would be placed on one side of a two-platform scale to balance two pounds of a customer's purchase—coffee, flour, sugar, and so on.)

BRAINSTORM POSSIBLE EVENTS OR MOMENTS TO DEPICT AS SLIDES

In any sequence of events there are a multitude of possible moments to freeze and present as tableaux. Encourage students to visualize the events described in the text and make a list of any potential slides. Create a short sentence that summarizes each event.

In the introductory lesson for human slide shows, you lead the students through this process. The list for the *Freedom Train* scene, therefore, might include the following:

- The overseer takes the road and Harriet cuts across the fields.

- Harriet reaches the store before the overseer.

- Jim is whispering to a man behind the counter.

- Harriet is about to warn Jim of the danger, but the overseer arrives at the store.

- The overseer orders Jim back to the barn.

- Jim moves away from the overseer.

- The overseer nears the counter and Jim moves closer to the door.

- Harriet flattens herself against the wall.

- Harriet touches Jim's shoulder as he passes.

- The overseer orders Harriet to grab Jim.

- Harriet moves to the doorway.

- Harriet reaches her arms out to stop the overseer.

- Jim runs to the woods.

- The overseer picks up a two-pound weight.

- The overseer throws the weight at Jim.

- The weight misses Jim but hits Harriet in the forehead.

- Harriet moans and falls to the ground.

DETERMINE THE FOUR OR FIVE MOST IMPORTANT MOMENTS TO DEPICT AS SLIDES

Because human slide shows limit the number of dramatized moments within the scene to four or five slides, students must determine the most important events or moments to depict as individual slides. Students' initial list may resemble the previous sample, with numerous potential slides. Their task then becomes to select the four or five most significant slides from that list—events that distill the essence of the scene. To simplify this process, have students consider whether (1) events can be omitted, (2) characters can be omitted, or (3) events can be combined into one slide.

(For examples of human slide show scenes from other pieces of literature, see pages 209–212.)

CREATE A SEQUENCE-OF-EVENTS CHART LISTING EACH SLIDE IN THE SLIDE SHOW

On a piece of chart paper, list, sequence, and number the events to enact as slides. A chart is preferable to a list on a chalkboard or overhead transparency because it can be positioned so that the student actors can see it while acting. It also serves as a reminder of the sequence events of the slides. Charts may also be stored and/or used with other students studying the same text, during this school year or in the future.

Describe each slide in a simple sentence or two. Model this process with students as you work together with the entire class to plan the model human slide show. Here is a list of the five slides for the *Freedom Train* text:

1. Breathing hard, Harriet reaches the store to warn fellow slave Jim about the overseer.
2. The overseer arrives and orders Jim to return home.
3. As Jim backs out of the store, the overseer orders Harriet to stop him.
4. Harriet refuses. Jim runs away. The overseer throws the two-pound weight.
5. The weight strikes Harriet in the forehead and she falls to the ground.

INVITE STUDENTS TO VISUALIZE AND DISCUSS THE SCENE'S EVENTS AND CHARACTER POSES

Before they create the poses and expressions for each individual slide, ask students to visualize how the characters in their human slide show scene might look, think, and feel. Encourage them to read the description of each slide and think like actors who use their bodies and faces to communicate information about the characters they play within the drama's circumstances.

For the model human slide show, ask all the students to visualize the character poses as you read the slide descriptions aloud.

Sample Language: Close your eyes and listen as I read aloud what happens in each slide. Visualize how the characters look. Think about how they might be feeling: "Breathing hard, Harriet reaches the store to warn fellow slave Jim about the overseer." Make a mental picture of this dramatic circumstance. "The overseer arrives and orders Jim to return home." Imagine what that scene looks like.

Continue in this manner, reading the remaining slide descriptions and encouraging students to visualize each one in silence. Then hold a brief discussion about the characters' possible thoughts and feelings throughout the episode. This discussion models what the students will do when they work in small groups to plan their own human slide shows.

Sample Language: How might the characters be feeling at the start of this scene? [*Jim—unaware of the danger, eager to make his escape; Harriet—nervous, frightened, exhausted; the overseer—angry, violent, hateful; the man behind the counter—worried, unsure, apprehensive*] What happens next? [*The overseer orders Jim back to the barn, but Jim moves away while Harriet watches in fright.*] What might the characters be thinking? [*The overseer might think he can intimidate Jim into obeying; Harriet might be wondering what she could do to help; Jim might be figuring out his escape route; the man behind the counter might be figuring out how to stay out of trouble.*]

Discuss each slide and consider the variety of choices available to the actors who will play the characters—poses, posture, gestures, facial expressions, and body positions in relation to one another. All of this reading, thinking, and planning mirrors in a small way what happens when actors and directors make choices as they develop scenes in a play.

Throughout all of this preparation, encourage students to return to the text for any information, clues, or verification it may provide. Remind them to make inferences that may inform the characters' poses and facial expressions.

DETERMINE WHICH STUDENTS WILL PLAY THE CHARACTERS

After identifying and discussing the events and the characters of the human slide show, determine which students will play each role. You may assign roles or ask for student volunteers to play characters. You may also choose to allow one student to work as a group's director, viewing each slide that the student actors create and offering ideas for improvement. During this model human slide show, you will work with four student actors while the rest of the students observe, offering suggestions as stage directors and responding as audience members.

Step 5: Describe the Human Slide Show Guidelines

DEFINE THE ACTING AREA

As with the acting area for tableaux, you will need a clear area of the classroom that can be easily seen by the students watching the human slide show as audience members. Having the audience view human slide shows head-on (rather than having an audience on three sides or completely surrounding the student actors) increases the visibility of student actors' poses and facial expressions. A space that is about four to six feet deep and at least eight feet wide can accommodate a small group of student actors.

Sample Language: Remember to keep your audience in mind when you choose the poses for each slide. Pose so that the audience can see your face and body. Try not to block the audience's view of another character.

In theatre, the *set* (short for *setting*) refers to the surroundings in which the events of the play occur. Some human slide show scenes require that participants establish locations of imaginary set elements like doorways, windows, furniture, or fences. If so, students need to determine where within the acting space these elements are located. Arrange classroom furniture to serve as set pieces such as benches, tables, sofas, and beds. Define other aspects of the set by sketching a diagram or a floor plan that the student actors can refer to or by identifying the features orally.

If you and your students wish to use theatrical stage terminology, explain that *stage right* and *stage left* refer to the acting areas from the actor's (not the audience's) perspective—the actor's right and left. *Downstage* is the acting area closest to the audience and *upstage* is the acting area farthest away from the audience.

Sample Language: In the model human slide show, the front door of the store is at stage right and the back door is at stage left. The counter is upstage left.

EXPLAIN THE HUMAN SLIDE SHOW CUES

Establish how you will signal student actors to strike each frozen pose ("blackout"), to remain in the pose ("lights up"), and to change poses for each subsequent slide ("blackout"). Explain that these are also cues for the audience to create the slide-show effect.

Sample Language: If this human slide show were to be performed in a theatre, the person who operates the lights could black out all stage lights. In the total darkness, the actors would take their positions and freeze. They would remain frozen when the stage lights came back on, or "up," and the audience would view the tableau until the next blackout. Again in darkness, the actors would take the positions of the second tableau, the lights would be brought up, remain bright for several seconds, and then black out, and so forth until the last tableau. If done well, the final effect would be that of a human slide show.

We cannot achieve this effect in the classroom. Even if we were to turn the lights off and on, we could not create total darkness. Therefore, when I cue you by saying, "Blackout," all audience members will close their eyes and keep them shut. The actors will assume their first poses. When I see that they are frozen and ready, I will say, "Lights up." The audience members will then open their eyes and view the frozen picture until I say, "Blackout." We'll continue in this manner until the last frozen picture, or slide, after which there will be one more blackout. The next "Lights up" is when the actors take a bow.

Step 6: Provide Time to Plan and Rehearse the Human Slide Shows

Give the student actors some time to collaborate on their poses for each slide. Using the chart with the list of four to five slides they created, the student actors must rehearse each set of poses. Remind them that choosing a point of concentration (see page 23) can help them maintain their focus during each slide.

During the model human slide show, lead this rehearsal with the four student actors and encourage the observing students to offer ideas for poses and facial expressions to the student actors. Explain to students that these ideas and suggestions are like those that a director gives to actors in rehearsal. Later, if each human slide show group has a director, that student will offer suggestions in the same way. A rehearsal period of ten to fifteen minutes is generally adequate to plan the poses in a human slide show.

Conducting the Human Slide Show Presentation

Step 7: Present the Human Slide Shows

CUE THE STUDENT ACTORS AND THE AUDIENCE MEMBERS TO BEGIN A HUMAN SLIDE SHOW

Assemble the student actors in the acting space and ask them to assume a neutral stance—facing the audience, hands at sides, faces expressionless. When you have everyone's full attention, call, "Blackout." The audience members will close their eyes and the student actors will assume the poses for their first slide. When you see that all student actors are frozen in their poses, call, "Lights up."

Pause for the audience members to view the slide for several seconds. The more characters there are to view, the longer you will need to pause for "lights up" (eyes open). Typically, the student actors will have to hold their frozen poses for no longer than ten seconds per slide.

CUE THE STUDENT ACTORS TO CHANGE POSES FROM ONE SLIDE TO THE NEXT

To view the next slide, call, "Blackout." The audience members will close their eyes and the student actors will assume their next poses. When you see that they are in their frozen positions, call, "Lights up."

CUE THE STUDENT ACTORS TO END THE HUMAN SLIDE SHOW

Continue in this manner, cueing the students with "blackout" and "lights up" until the final slide, in which the student actors signal the end of the human slide show by bowing together. The audience's typical signal of appreciation is a round of applause.

Once you reach this step with the model human slide show, your students should understand the process that they will follow when they work in small groups on different scenes. The reflection steps described in the next section, therefore, apply to the human slide shows that students plan, rehearse, and present in their small groups.

🎭 Dramatic Detail

You may choose to narrate a human slide show by reading aloud what will occur in each slide as the student audience's eyes are closed. Cue the blackout, read the words on the chart that describe the upcoming slide, and then cue, "Lights up."

Breathing hard, Harriet reaches the store to warn fellow slave Jim about the overseer.

The overseer arrives and orders Jim to return home.

As Jim backs out of the store, the overseer orders Harriet to stop him.

Harriet refuses. Jim runs away. The overseer throws the two-pound weight.

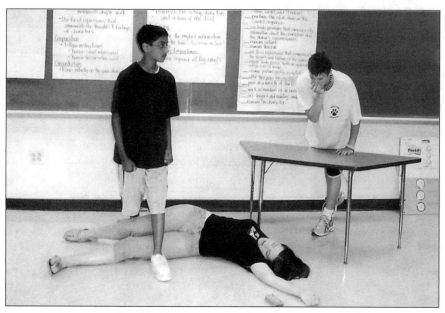

The weight strikes Harriet in the forehead and she falls to the ground.

Reflecting on the Human Slide Shows

Step 8: Discuss Each Human Slide Show

After each small group of student actors presents a human slide show, hold a discussion with all the students (audience and actors) to reflect on the presentation and offer ideas to improve the work. Refer to the dramatic coaching points explained under "Step 7: Revise the Tableau" on pages 162–63.

- energy and expression

- a variety of levels

- the audience's perspective

- upstaging

Step 9: Provide Time to Revise Each Human Slide Show

After discussing the ideas and coaching points in the previous section, give the student actors some time to revise the human slide shows. Encourage them to incorporate suggestions that they believe will strengthen their human slide shows and to disregard ideas that they do not agree with.

Step 10: Present Each Revised Human Slide Show

After the revising rehearsal time, present each human slide show again. Follow each presentation with a brief discussion on the changes and improvements that you and the observing students noticed.

Step 11: Assess the Students

OBSERVATIONAL ASSESSMENTS

During the planning, enacting, observing, and reflecting phases of human slide shows, students reveal much about their understandings. They discuss, ask questions, experiment with poses, make adjustments, offer ideas, and make and execute decisions. Observing and listening to students as they work give you insight into how well they have achieved the key drama and reading comprehension objectives. Use the following categories to focus your observations on the human slide show objectives, and refer to Chapter 4 for further information on observational assessment.

From a Drama Perspective

Body

- While the students rehearse the poses for the roles they'll play, note how they modify their posture and body positions. Note the changes they make in aspects of body and facial expressions to better communicate information about their characters and the drama's circumstances.

- Note whether students alter their posture, body positions, and facial expressions in each slide.

Cooperation

- When the students plan, enact, and observe a human slide show, notice examples of how they worked to help one another remember and follow instructions.

- Look for instances of students who work hard to remain silent and still during the rehearsal and presentation of the human slide shows.

Concentration

- Observe instances of students focusing intently on both the process and the presentation of the human slide show.

- While the students are presenting a human slide show, note the deliberate uses of concentration that enhance the effectiveness of the drama experience.

From a Reading Comprehension Perspective

Determining Importance

- Listen for the points students make as they discuss which events or moments from the text are significant enough to include as slides in their human slide shows.

- Note whether students' slides depict the scene's most important events or moments rather than its minor details.

Inferring

- As students plan their human slide shows, listen for discussions in which they draw conclusions and make interpretations based on information provided but not specifically stated in the text.

- During human slide show presentations, notice examples of students using their bodies or faces to express an action or emotion that indicates that they read between the lines of the text.

Synthesis

- Consider whether the students have accurately extended and applied information from the text to a human slide show.

REFLECTIVE DISCUSSIONS

As mentioned in all the previous drama strategy chapters and in Chapter 4, students' responses to reflective discussion questions give you insight into the depth of their understanding. Questions that focus on key drama and reading comprehension objectives prompt students to (1) recall and learn from the drama experience, (2) honor their classmates' work, (3) critique their own work, and (4) set goals for improvement. Following are some reflective discussion questions to pose after human slide show experiences.

Questions That Recall Elements of the Drama Experience

From a Drama Perspective

- What did you learn about the characters and the drama's circumstances by watching students strike a variety of poses with their bodies?

- How were facial expressions important in the human slide shows?

- How was concentration important in the human slide shows?

- How did the acting skill cooperation contribute to effective human slide shows?

- What other acting tools and skills did you use to create your human slide shows?

From a Reading Comprehension Perspective

- How did observing or participating in a human slide show help you understand important elements of the text?

- What inferences from the text did you try to communicate using your body?

- How did each human slide show serve as a synthesis of the text?

- What other reading comprehension strategies did you use in creating your human slide shows?

Questions That Encourage Praise

From a Drama Perspective

- What one facial expression by another student actor truly communicated the character's thoughts and feelings?

- Who posed in ways that were remarkably effective in communicating information about the characters and the drama's circumstances? Why were those poses effective?

- Which group of student actors was especially good at remaining still during the human slide show presentation?

- When you performed in a human slide show, how was your audience helpful? What audience behavior did you appreciate?

- Whose concentration during a human slide show presentation was particularly impressive?

From a Reading Comprehension Perspective

- What new information about a character did you learn by viewing the performance of one student actor?

- What student actors' poses or facial expressions were especially good at communicating inferences?

- What new thoughts occurred to you as you observed another group's human slide show presentation?

Questions That Encourage Change

From a Drama Perspective

- What ideas do you have for strengthening your use of the acting tool body the next time you participate in a human slide show?

- If you had trouble remaining still or silent when performing in a human slide show, what strategies might you use to improve in those areas?

- What aspects of concentration do you need to improve?

From a Reading Comprehension Perspective

- When you next read a text to prepare for a human slide show, how might you recognize the most important events in the scene—the best choices for your slides?

- How did the inferences you made while reading affect your human slide show? When preparing your next human slide show, how might you read more carefully so that you include deeper inferences?

- To make your human slide show the best possible synthesis of the scene in the text, what would you change or revise if you presented it again?

WRITTEN ASSESSMENTS

Student responses to writing prompts like the following are another way to assess understandings gained during human slide shows.

From a Drama Perspective

Brief Responses

- In your journal, draw each different pose you assumed in your human slide show (stick figures are perfectly acceptable). Underneath each drawing, identify what your character is doing.

- State three reasons why it is important for actors to remain still in the presentation of each slide in a human slide show.

- State three reasons why it is important for actors to remain silent in the presentation of each slide in a human slide show.

- Name two ways that actors can maintain concentration during a human slide show.

Extended Responses

- What are two pieces of advice you would give to an actor about striking effective poses in a human slide show? Explain the reasons behind your advice.

- There are a lot of instructions to remember when you plan and present a human slide show. Make a list of the five most important ones for you.

- Describe three examples of how your classmates' use of concentration when acting improved the human slide show for you as an audience member.

- Imagine that you are the man behind the counter in the model *Freedom Train* human slide show. In your journal, write an eyewitness account of what happened, why it happened, who was at fault, and what you did immediately after Harriet was struck in the head.

From a Reading Comprehension Perspective

Brief Responses

- Think about all the different human slide shows you saw your classmates perform. Based on those human slide shows, make a list of four of the most important events from the book that was the source for those slide shows.

- Explain three ways in which the reading comprehension skill inferring helped you make decisions about how to pose in the human slide show.

- Look at the chart with the list of the four or five slides for your human slide show. Rewrite each short description to add more details; include a variety of interesting adjectives and verbs.

Extended Responses

- Choose one human slide show you observed or participated in. Write a newspaper article in which you describe the events of the scene depicted in the human slide show. Use more than ninety but fewer than one hundred words.

- Think about the final slide in the *Freedom Train* human slide show. Recall the body pose and facial expression of the student actor who played the overseer. What might you infer about that character's thoughts and feelings as he stood over Harriet's body? Compose a paragraph of his thoughts at that moment. Make it at least five sentences long.

- Pretend that the character you played in the human slide show writes a letter to a friend to explain the scene's events and his or her feelings about what happened. Using three to five paragraphs, write this letter in character.

Assessment Checklists

The Human Slide Show Assessment Checklist in Figure 8–2 provides an additional written assessment for students. You may complete the checklist and provide the students with your appraisal of their human slide show, or students may use the checklist to assess peers and/or themselves. Remind students to fill in the space at the bottom of the checklist with personal goals for their participation in the next human slide show experience.

For a reading comprehension strategy assessment checklist that can be used with any of the drama strategies in this text, refer to Figure 4–6.

Additional Assessment Idea: Digital Photography

Digital photos of each slide in a human slide show allow both teachers and students an immediate way to review and assess the use of the acting tools and skills. Students can examine the photos for evidence of how well they modified their posture and poses, posed with energy, used effective facial expressions, reacted to imaginary sights, sounds, smells, tastes, and textures, and maintained concentration.

Viewed on a computer programmed to display the photos as a slide show, the digital images can provide the student actors with the opportunity to observe themselves in action. This computer slide show can help students assess how effectively they varied levels, posed with an audience's perspective in mind, and altered their poses from one slide to the next.

Time Allotments

The introduction to the human slide show drama strategy, including the identification of objectives and text section, the planning and conducting of the model human slide show, and the reflecting upon, revising, and re-creating it should take about an hour.

The time needed for planning, rehearsing, conducting, discussing, revising, and re-creating each small group's human slide show varies according to the number of slide shows. Allowing about 20 minutes per group should result in enough class time to complete the steps involved. The amount of time required for assessment will vary according to the types of assessment you use.

Sample Human Slide Show Scenes from Literature

Liang and the Magic Paintbrush, by Demi (1980)

1. Because whatever Liang paints with his magic paintbrush becomes a real object, the greedy emperor orders Liang to paint a sea full of fish.
2. The emperor orders Liang to paint a boat. The emperor calls his family to join him on the boat.
3. Then he tells Liang to paint wind and then more wind.
4. Liang does, and soon wind is blowing and waves are crashing.
5. The boat breaks into a million pieces and the emperor and his family sink to the bottom of the sea.

HUMAN SLIDE SHOW ASSESSMENT CHECKLIST

Student Actor's Name _____

DURING THE HUMAN SLIDE SHOW, THE ACTOR . . .	CONSISTENTLY 3	USUALLY 2	RARELY 1	NEVER 0
Imagination/Mind				
. . . agrees to pretend.				
. . . reacts to imaginary sights, sounds, smells, tastes, and textures.				
. . . retells the predetermined story in the correct sequence.				
Body				
. . . modifies posture, poses, gestures, movements, and/or walk, including: ■ varies levels. ■ poses with an audience's perspective in mind. ■ alters poses from one slide to the next.				
. . . uses energy when modifying or adjusting body.				
. . . uses facial expressions that communicate the thoughts and feelings of the character.				
Cooperation				
. . . works as a member of an ensemble/team, including: ■ changes positions quickly, quietly, and efficiently.				
. . . remains silent when cued.				
. . . remains frozen when cued.				
Concentration				
. . . focuses intently on the given drama task.				
. . . remains in character.				

Total _____

29–33   Standing Ovation
24–28   Round of Applause
19–23   Polite Clapping
0–18   Back to Rehearsal

Personal Goal: _____
_____

FIGURE 8–2   *Human Slide Show Assessment Checklist*

From the Mixed-Up Files of Mrs. Basil E. Frankweiler, by E. L. Konigsburg (1967)

1. Jamie spots a candy bar on the ground.
2. He picks it up and Claudia warns him not to eat it because it could contain drugs.
3. He takes a bite while Claudia looks at him in disgust.
4. Jamie feigns passing out after eating the bite. Claudia stands stunned with her mouth wide open.
5. She is ready to scream for help when Jamie opens his eyes and smiles.

The Sign of the Beaver, by Elizabeth Speare (1983)

1. Matt climbs a tree to take honey from a hive.
2. He is attacked by a swarm of bees so he runs to a pond and dives in.
3. He tries to swim, but his feet are tangled in weeds and he loses consciousness.
4. An Indian lifts Matt out of the water.
5. He awakes on dry ground to find two Indians bending over him.

Bridge to Terabithia, by Katherine Paterson (1977)

1. Jess and Leslie and several other boys prepare to run a race at recess. Jess is confident that he will win.
2. At the signal, the race begins. Jess is in the lead. The crowd of kids is cheering.
3. Suddenly, Leslie catches up with Jess and pulls ahead.
4. She crosses the finish line three feet ahead of Jess.
5. She turns and smiles at him as he walks away. The other boys and the crowd of kids are stunned. There is no cheering.

The Outsiders, by S. E. Hinton (1997)

1. The Socs approach Ponyboy.
2. The Socs jump Ponyboy, pulling him to the ground.
3. Ponyboy screams.
4. The greasers chase the Socs away while Darry helps Ponyboy to his feet.

Maniac Magee, by Jerry Spinelli (1992)

1. McNab amuses himself by pitching a frog for Jeffrey Magee to bat.
2. Magee bunts the frog and runs for first base.
3. McNab chases the frog, but it hops over his foot and continues toward third base. Magee runs the bases.
4. McNab lurches, lunges, and throws his hat and glove at the frog, who is hopping toward second base.
5. The crowd cheers as Magee makes a home run and jogs out of the park while McNab shouts at him.

Tuck Everlasting, by Natalie Babbitt (1975)

1. The Tuck family—Mae, Miles, Jesse, and Tuck—are confronted by the man in the yellow suit. He has come to return young Winnie to her family.
2. The man begins to drag the protesting child away. Mae grabs a shotgun, holds it like a club, and tells him to stop.
3. The man refuses. Mae lifts the shotgun. Miles gasps, "Ma! No!"
4. Ma swings the shotgun around her head and smashes the man in the back of the skull.
5. The man drops to the ground with his eyes wide open.

Roll of Thunder, Hear My Cry, by Mildred D. Taylor (1991)

1. Cassie and her brothers (Stacey, Christopher-John, and Little Man) and their friend T. J. are walking along a dusty country road on their first day of school.
2. Stacey, spotting the school bus that transports the white kids to school, shouts, "Quick! Off the road!"
3. Everyone but Little Man scrambles up the steep bank into the forest. "But I'll get my clothes dirty!" protests Little Man as he keeps walking.
4. The bus comes roaring and Little Man struggles onto the bank, but not before the bus sprays dirt and dust all over him.
5. Little Man shakes a threatening fist at the bus and then looks down at himself dismally.

Harry Potter and the Sorcerer's Stone, by J. K. Rowling (1999)

1. Harry opens his last Christmas present. His friend Ron recognizes it as a rare and valuable invisibility cloak and he tells Harry to try it on.
2. Harry picks up the shining, mysterious cloth and throws it around his shoulders.
3. Harry's body disappears and Ron gives a yell.
4. Harry looks in a mirror and sees only his head.
5. Then he pulls the cloak over his head and his reflection vanishes completely.
6. Harry removes the invisibility cloak and reads a note that fell out of it: "Your father left this in my possession before he died. It's time it was returned to you. Use it well."

WORKS CITED

BOLTON, GAVIN. 1985. "Changes in Thinking About Drama in Education." *Theory into Practice* 24: 151–57.

BUMGARNER, CONSTANCE GEE. 2001. "I Can See Clearly Now: Possible Sequelae of the Reviewing Education and the Arts Project (REAP)." In *Beyond the Soundbite: Arts Education and Academic Outcomes*, edited by Ellen Winner and Lois Hetland. Los Angeles: Getty Center.

BURNAFORD, GAIL, ARNOLD APRILL, AND CYNTHIA WEISS, eds. 2001. *Renaissance in the Classroom: Arts Integration and Meaningful Learning*. Mahwah, NJ: Lawrence Erlbaum.

CATTERALL, JAMES. 2002. "Research on Drama and Theater in Education." In *Critical Links: Learning in the Arts and Student Academic and Social Development*, edited by Richard J. Deasy. Washington, DC: Arts Education Partnership.

CATTERALL, JAMES S., RICHARD CHAPLEAU, AND JOHN IWANAGA. 2000. "Involvement in the Arts and Human Development: General Involvement and Intensive Involvement in Music and Theater Arts." In *Champions of Change: The Impact of the Arts on Learning*, edited by Edward B. Fiske. Washington, DC: Arts Education Partnership.

CATTERALL, JAMES, AND BETTY JANE WAGNER. 2002. Commentary on "The Flight of Reading: Shifts in Instruction, Orchestration, and Attitudes Through Classroom Theatre" by Shelby A. Wolf. In *Critical Links: Learning in the Arts and Student Academic and Social Development*, edited by Richard J. Deasy. Washington, DC: Arts Education Partnership.

Champions of Change: The Impact of the Arts on Learning. 2002. Washington, DC: Arts Education Partnership. aep-arts.org.

DEASY, RICHARD J., ed. 2002. *Critical Links: Learning in the Arts and Student Academic and Social Development*. Washington, DC: Arts Education Partnership.

DUPONT, SHERRY. 1992. "The Effectiveness of Creative Drama as an Instructional Strategy to Enhance the Reading Comprehension Skills of Fifth-Grade Remedial Readers." *Reading Research and Instruction* 31 (3): 41–52.

FLYNN, ROSALIND M. 2002. "Shakespearean Slide Shows." *English Journal* 92 (1): 62–68.

HARVEY, STEPHANIE, AND ANNE GOUDVIS. 2000. *Strategies That Work: Teaching Comprehension to Enhance Understanding.* Portland, ME: Stenhouse.

HEINIG, RUTH B. 1992. *Improvisation with Favorite Tales: Integrating Drama into the Reading/Writing Classroom.* Portsmouth, NH: Heinemann.

JABLON, JUDY R., AMY LAURA DOMBRO, MARGO L. DICHTELMILLER. 1999. *The Power of Observation.* Washington, DC: Teaching Strategies.

JOHNSON, LIZ, AND CECILY O'NEILL. 1984. *Dorothy Heathcote: Collected Writings on Education and Drama.* London: Hutchinson.

KEENE, ELLIN OLIVER, AND SUSAN ZIMMERMAN. 1997. *Mosaic of Thought: Teaching Comprehension in a Reader's Workshop.* Portsmouth, NH: Heinemann.

KELNER, LENORE B. 1993. *The Creative Classroom: A Guide for Using Creative Drama in the Classroom, Pre-K–6.* Portsmouth, NH: Heinemann.

MACY, LEONORA. 2004. "A Novel Study Through Drama." *The Reading Teacher* 58 (3): 240–48.

MANTIONE, ROBERTA D., AND SABINE SMEAD. 2003. *Weaving Through Words: Using the Arts to Teach Reading Comprehension Strategies.* Newark, DE: International Reading Association.

MCCASLIN, NELLIE. 1996. *Creative Drama in the Classroom and Beyond.* White Plains, NY: Longman.

MCMASTER, JENNIFER CATNEY. 1998. "'Doing' Literature: Using Drama to Build Literacy." *The Reading Teacher* 51 (7): 574–84.

MCTIGHE, JAY, AND GRANT WIGGINS. 1999. *The Understanding by Design Handbook.* Alexandria, VA: Association for Curriculum Development.

MOBLEY, JONNIE PATRICIA. 1995. *NTC's Dictionary of Theatre and Drama Terms.* Lincoln-wood, IL: National Textbook.

MORGAN, NORAH, AND JULIANA SAXTON. 1987. *Teaching Drama: A Mind of Many Wonders.* Portsmouth, NH: Heinemann.

O'NEILL, CECILY, AND ALAN LAMBERT. 1987. *Drama Structures.* London: Hutchinson.

PERKINS, DAVID. 2001. "Embracing Babel: The Prospects of Instrumental Uses of the Arts for Education." In *Beyond the Soundbite: Arts Education and Academic Outcomes,* edited by Ellen Winner and Lois Hetland. Los Angeles: Getty Center.

PODLOZNY, ANN. 2001. "Strengthening Verbal Skills Through the Use of Classroom Drama: A Clear Link. A Summary of a Meta-Analytic Study." In *Beyond the Soundbite: Arts Education and Academic Outcomes,* edited by Ellen Winner and Lois Hetland. Los Angeles: Getty Center.

ROSE, DALE S., MICHAELA PARKS, KARL ANDROES, AND SUSAN MCMAHON. 2000. "Imagery-Based Learning: Improving Elementary Students' Reading Comprehension with Drama Techniques." *The Journal of Educational Research* 94 (1): 55–63.

SIKS, GERALDINE BRAIN. 1958. *Creative Dramatics: An Art for Children.* New York: Harper and Row.

SOMERS, JOHN. 2001. "Learning in Drama." In *Beyond the Soundbite: Arts Education and Academic Outcomes*, edited by Ellen Winner and Lois Hetland. Los Angeles: Getty Center.

SPOLIN, VIOLA. 1986. *Theater Games for the Classroom*. Evanston, IL: Northwestern University Press.

———. 1999. *Improvisation for the Theater*. Evanston, IL: Northwestern University Press.

STEIN, DANIELLE R. 2004. "Wearing Two Hats: The Case of Visiting Artists in the Classroom." GoodWork Project Report Series 29. Cambridge, MA: Harvard Graduate School of Education GoodWork Project.

SUN, PING-YUN. 2003. "Using Drama and Theatre to Promote Literacy Development." ED477613. Bloomington, IN: ERIC Clearinghouse on Reading and English Communication.

TARLINGTON, CAROLE. 1985. "'Dear Mr. Piper . . .': Using Drama to Create Context for Children's Writing." *Theory into Practice* 24: 199–204.

TARLINGTON, CAROLE, AND PATRICK VERRIOUR. 1991. *Role Drama*. Portsmouth, NH: Heinemann.

WAGNER, BETTY JANE. 1976. *Dorothy Heathcote: Drama as a Learning Medium*. Washington, DC: National Education Association.

WARD, WINIFRED. 1930. *Creative Dramatics*. New York: D. Appleton-Century.

WAY, BRIAN. 1967. *Development Through Drama*. Atlantic Highlands, NJ: Humanities.

WILHELM, JEFFREY D. 2002. *Action Strategies for Deepening Comprehension*. New York: Scholastic Professional.

WILSON, G. PATRICIA. 2003. "Supporting Young Children's Thinking Through Tableau." *Language Arts* 80 (5): 375–83.

WRIGHT, L. 1985. "Preparing Teachers to Put Drama in the Classroom." *Theory into Practice* 24: 205–10.

Literature Cited

ALIKI. 1998. *Marianthe's Story: Spoken Memories*. New York: Greenwillow.

BABBITT, NATALIE. 1975. *Tuck Everlasting*. New York: Scholastic.

BLUME, JUDY. 1986. *Freckle Juice*. New York: Yearling.

BRETT, JAN. 1989. *The Mitten*. New York: Putnam.

CHERRY, LYNNE. 1993. *The Great Kapok Tree*. New York: Scholastic.

COHEN, BARBARA. 1990. *Molly's Pilgrim*. New York: Bantam Skylark.

CRONIN, DOREEN. 2000. *Click, Clack, Moo: Cows That Type*. New York: Scholastic.

DEMI. 1980. *Liang and the Magic Paintbrush*. New York: Henry Holt.

DEPAOLA, TOMIE. 1983. *The Legend of the Bluebonnet*. New York: Putnam.

DORRIS, MICHAEL. 1992. *Morning Girl*. New York: Hyperion.

HINTON, S. E. 1997. *The Outsiders*. New York: Puffin.

KIMMEL, ERIC A. 1988. *Anansi and the Moss-Covered Rock*. New York: Holiday House.

KONIGSBURG, E. L. 1967. *From the Mixed-Up Files of Mrs. Basil E. Frankweiler*. New York: Bantam Doubleday Dell.

LEE, HARPER. 1960. *To Kill a Mockingbird*. New York: Time Warner.

L'ENGLE, MADELEINE. 1962. *A Wrinkle in Time*. New York: Dell.

LEVINE, GAIL CARSON. 1997. *Ella Enchanted*. New York: Harper Trophy.

LOWRY, LOIS. 1993. *The Giver*. Boston: Houghton Mifflin.

LUENN, NANCY. 1990. *Nessa's Fish*. New York: Scholastic.

MACLACHLAN, PATRICIA. 1985. *Sarah, Plain and Tall*. New York: Harper Trophy.

MATAS, CAROL. 1993. *Daniel's Story*. New York: Scholastic.

MCCULLY, EMILY ARNOLD. 1993. *Mirette on the High Wire*. New York: Scholastic.

MCKISSACK, PATRICIA C. 2000. *Color Me Dark*. New York: Scholastic.

MYERS, WALTER DEAN. 1988. *Scorpions*. New York: Harper Collins.

NOBLE, TRINKA HAKES. 1980. *The Day Jimmy's Boa Ate the Wash*. New York: E. P. Dutton.

ORWELL, GEORGE. 1946. *Animal Farm*. New York: Harcourt Brace.

PATERSON, KATHERINE. 1977. *Bridge to Terabithia*. New York: HarperTrophy.

PERRAULT, CHARLES. 1965. "Cinderella." In *The Blue Fairy Book*, edited by Andrew Lang, 64–71. New York: Dover.

ROWLING, J. K. 1999. *Harry Potter and the Sorcerer's Stone*. New York: Scholastic.

SAN SOUCI, ROBERT D. 1989. *Talking Eggs*. New York: Scholastic.

SHARMAT, MITCHELL. 1980. *Gregory, the Terrible Eater*. New York: Scholastic.

SLOBODKINA, ESPHYR. 1968. *Caps for Sale*. New York: Harper Collins.

SPEARE, ELIZABETH. 1983. *The Sign of the Beaver*. Boston: Houghton Mifflin.

SPINELLI, JERRY. 1992. *Maniac Magee*. New York: HarperTrophy.

———. 1997. *Wringer*. New York: Harper Trophy.

———. 2000. *Stargirl*. New York: Scholastic.

STEPTOE, JOHN. 1987. *Mufaro's Beautiful Daughters*. New York: Scholastic.

STERLING, DOROTHY. 1987. *Freedom Train: The Story of Harriet Tubman*. New York: Scholastic.

TAYLOR, MILDRED D. 1991. *Roll of Thunder, Hear My Cry*. New York: Puffin.

TRESSELT, ALVIN. 1964. *The Mitten*. New York: Lothrop, Lee and Shepard.

TURNER, ANN. 1987. *Nettie's Trip South*. New York: Simon and Schuster.

———. 1992. *Katie's Trunk*. New York: Aladdin.

TWAIN, MARK. 1994. *The Adventures of Tom Sawyer*. New York: Puffin.

WILDER, LAURA INGALLS. 1971. *Little House on the Prairie*. New York: HarperTrophy.

WISNIEWSKI, DAVID. 1992. *Sundiata, Lion King of Mali*. New York: Clarion.

YOLEN, JANE. 1992. *Encounter*. Orlando, FL: Harcourt Brace.

SELECTED BIBLIOGRAPHY

Recommended Reading

CORNETT, CLAUDIA E. 1999. *The Arts as Meaning Makers: Integrating Literature and the Arts Throughout the Curriculum.* Upper Saddle River, NJ: Prentice-Hall.

DAVIES, GEOFF. 1988. *Practical Primary Drama.* London: Heinemann.

ERICKSON, KAREN. 2003. *181 Favorite Level I Ideas for Drama.* Evanston, IL: Creative Directions.

HEINIG, RUTH B. 1992. *Improvisation with Favorite Tales: Integrating Drama into the Reading/Writing Classroom.* Portsmouth, NH: Heinemann.

HEINIG, RUTH BEALL, AND LYDA STILLWELL. 1974. *Creative Dramatics for the Classroom Teacher.* Englewood Cliffs, NJ: Prentice-Hall.

JABLON, JUDY R., AMY LAURA DOMBRO, AND MARGO L. DICHTELMILLER. 1999. *The Power of Observation.* Washington, DC.: Teaching Strategies.

KELNER, LENORE B. 1993. *The Creative Classroom: A Guide for Using Creative Drama in the Classroom, Pre-K–6.* Portsmouth, NH: Heinemann.

MCCASLIN, NELLIE. 1996. *Creative Drama in the Classroom and Beyond.* White Plains, NY: Longman.

MILLER, CAROLE, AND JULIANA SAXTON. 2004. *Into the Story: Language in Action Through Drama.* Portsmouth, NH: Heinemann.

O'NEILL, CECILY, ALAN LAMBERT, ROSEMARY LINNELL, AND JANET WARR-WOOD. 1987. *Drama Guidelines.* London: Heinemann.

ROSENBERG, HELANE S. 1987. *Creative Drama and Imagination: Transforming Ideas into Action.* New York: Holt, Rinehart, and Winston.

SALAZAR, LAURA GARDNER. 1995. *Teaching Dramatically, Learning Thematically.* Charlottesville, VA: New Plays.

SALDANA, JOHNNY. 1995. *Drama of Color: Improvisation with Multiethnic Folklore.* Portsmouth, NH: Heinemann.

SIKS, GERALDINE BRAIN. 1958. *Creative Dramatics: An Art for Children*. New York: Harper and Row.

SPOLIN, VIOLA. 1986. *Theater Games for the Classroom*. Evanston, IL: Northwestern University Press.

SWARTZ, LARRY. 1995. *Drama Themes: A Practical Guide for Teaching Drama*. Portsmouth, NH: Heinemann.

VERRIOUR, PATRICK. 1994. *In Role: Teaching and Learning Dramatically*. Markham, Ontario: Pippin.

WAGNER, BETTY JANE. 1976. *Drama as a Learning Medium*. Washington, DC: National Education Association.

WILHELM, JEFFREY D., AND BRIAN EDMISTON. 1998. *Imagining to Learn: Inquiry, Ethics, and Integration Through Drama*. Portsmouth, NH: Heinemann.

Suggested Books for Story Dramatization and Character Interviews

The books listed here work well with the drama strategies of story dramatization and character interviews. For additional texts, see Figures 6–2, 7–2, 7–4, and pages 209–211. The code (P) indicates a primary-level text. The code (I) indicates an intermediate-level text. The code (M) indicates a middle school–level text.

AARDEMA, VERNA. 1969. *Who's in Rabbit's House?* New York: E. P. Dutton. (P and I)
———. 1975. *Why Mosquitoes Buzz in People's Ears*. New York: Dial. (P and I)
ALEXANDER, LLOYD. 1992. *The Fortune Tellers*. New York: Puffin. (P and I)
BOYCE, FRANK COTTRELL. 2004. *Millions*. New York: HarperCollins. (I and M)
CARLE, ERIC. 1977. *The Grouchy Ladybug*. New York: Scholastic. (P)
———. 1995. *Walter the Baker*. New York: Scholastic. (P)
CLIMO, SHIRLEY. 1995. *The Little Red Ant and the Great Big Crumb: A Mexican Fable*. New York: Clarion. (P)
CURTIS, CHRISTOPHER PAUL. 1999. *Bud, Not Buddy*. New York: Scholastic. (I and M)
dePAOLA, TOMIE. 1975. *Strega Nona*. New York: Simon and Schuster. (P)
———. 1992. *Jamie O'Rourke and the Big Potato*. New York: Putnam. (P and I)
FLEISCHMAN, SID. 1986. *The Whipping Boy*. New York: William Morrow. (I and M)
GEORGE, JEAN CRAIGHEAD. 1972. *Julie of the Wolves*. New York: HarperCollins. (I and M)
GIPSON, FRED. 1945. *Old Yeller*. Harper Collins. (I and M)
HESSE, KAREN. 1997. *Out of the Dust*. New York: Scholastic. (M)
KIMMEL, ERIC A. 1988. *The Chanukkah Guest*. New York: Holiday House. (P and I)
———. 1994. *The Three Princes: A Tale from the Middle East*. New York: Holiday House. (P and I)
LEAF, MUNRO. 1936. *The Story of Ferdinand*. New York: Scholastic. (P and I)
LIONNI, LEO. 1963. *Swimmy*. New York: Scholastic. (P)
———. 1967. *Frederick*. New York: Scholastic. (P)
LOWRY, LOIS. 1989. *Number the Stars*. Boston: Houghton Mifflin. (I and M)

MacDonald, Amy. 2003. *Little Beaver and the Echo*. London: Candlewick. (P)

McDermott, Gerald. 1972. *Anansi the Spider*. New York: Holt, Rinehart and Winston. (P)

Moreton, Dan. 1997. *La Cucaracha Martina: A Caribbean Folktale*. New York: Turtle. (P)

Paterson, Katherine. 1990. *The Tale of the Mandarin Ducks*. New York: Penguin. (I and M)

————. 1999. *Katherine Paterson Treasury*. New York: Barnes and Noble. (I and M)

Sachar, Louis. 1998. *Holes*. New York: Random House. (I and M)

Scieszka, Jon. 1989. *The True Story of the 3 Little Pigs!* New York: Puffin. (P and I)

Shusterman, Neal. 2003. *Full Tilt*. New York: Simon and Shuster. (M)

Twain, Mark. 1881. *The Prince and the Pauper*. London: Penguin. (I and M)

White, E. B. 1945. *Stuart Little*. New York: Harper and Row. (I)

————. 1952. *Charlotte's Web*. New York: Harper Collins. (I)

Wisniewski, David. 1991. *Rain Player*. New York: Clarion. (I and M)

Yagawa, Sumiko. 1979. *The Crane Wife*. New York: Mulberry. (I and M)

Zemach, Margot. 1990. *It Could Always Be Worse: A Yiddish Folktale*. New York: Farrar, Straus and Giroux. (P and I)

THE NATIONAL STANDARDS
FOR THEATRE★

Grades K–4 and 5–8

Developed by the Consortium of National Arts Education Associations (under the guidance of the National Committee for Standards in the Arts), the National Standards for Arts Education is a document which outlines basic arts learning outcomes integral to the comprehensive K–12 education of every American student. The Consortium published the National Standards in 1994 through a grant administered by MENC, the National Association for Music Education.

Theatre (K–4)

Theatre, the imagined and enacted world of human beings, is one of the primary ways children learn about life—about actions and consequences, about customs and beliefs, about others and themselves. They learn through their social pretend play and from hours of viewing television and film. For instance, children use pretend play as a means of making sense of the world; they create situations to play and assume roles; they interact with peers and arrange environments to bring their stories to life; they direct one another to bring order to their drama; and they respond to one another's dramas. In other words, children arrive at school with rudimentary skills as playwrights, actors, designers, directors, and audience members; theatre education should build on this solid foundation. These standards assume that theatre

★From National Standards for Arts Education. Copyright © 1994 by Music Educators National Conference (MENC). Used by permission. The complete National Arts Standards and additional materials relating to the standards are available from MENC—The National Association for Music Education, 1806 Robert Fulton Drive, Reston, VA 20191.

education will start with and have a strong emphasis on improvisation, which is the basis of social pretend play.

In an effort to create a seamless transition from the natural skills of pretend play to the study of theatre, the standards call for instruction that integrates the several aspects of the art form: script writing, acting, designing, directing, researching, comparing art forms, analyzing and critiquing, and understanding contexts. In kindergarten through the fourth grade, the teacher will be actively involved in the students' planning, playing, and evaluating, but students will be guided to develop group skills so that more independence is possible. The content of the drama will develop the students' abilities to express their understanding of their immediate world and broaden their knowledge of other cultures.

CONTENT STANDARD #1

Script writing by planning and recording improvisations based on personal experience and heritage, imagination, literature, and history

ACHIEVEMENT STANDARD

- Students collaborate to select interrelated characters, environments, and situations for classroom dramatizations.

- Students improvise dialogue to tell stories, and formalize improvisations by writing or recording the dialogue.

CONTENT STANDARD #2

Acting by assuming roles and interacting in improvisations

ACHIEVEMENT STANDARD

- Students imagine and clearly describe characters, their relationships, and their environments.

- Students use variations of locomotor and nonlocomotor movement and vocal pitch, tempo, and tone for different characters.

- Students assume roles that exhibit concentration and contribute to the action of classroom dramatizations based on personal experience and heritage, imagination, literature, and history.

CONTENT STANDARD #3

Designing by visualizing and arranging environments for classroom dramatizations

ACHIEVEMENT STANDARD

- Students visualize environments and construct designs to communicate locale and mood using visual elements (such as space, color, line, shape, texture) and aural aspects using a variety of sound sources.

- Students collaborate to establish playing spaces for classroom dramatizations and to select and safely organize available materials that suggest scenery, properties, lighting, sound, costumes, and makeup.

CONTENT STANDARD #4

Directing by planning classroom dramatizations

ACHIEVEMENT STANDARD

- Students collaboratively plan and prepare improvisations and demonstrate various ways of staging classroom dramatizations.

CONTENT STANDARD #5

Researching by finding information to support classroom dramatizations

ACHIEVEMENT STANDARD

- Students communicate information to peers about people, events, time, and place related to classroom dramatizations.

CONTENT STANDARD #6

Comparing and connecting art forms by describing theatre, dramatic media (such as film, television, and electronic media), and other art forms

ACHIEVEMENT STANDARD

- Students describe visual, aural, oral, and kinetic elements in theatre, dramatic media, dance, music, and visual arts.

- Students compare how ideas and emotions are expressed in theatre, dramatic media, dance, music, and visual arts.

- Students select movement, music, or visual elements to enhance the mood of a classroom dramatization.

CONTENT STANDARD #7

Analyzing and explaining personal preferences and constructing meanings from classroom dramatizations and from theatre, film, television, and electronic media productions

ACHIEVEMENT STANDARD

- Students identify and describe the visual, aural, oral, and kinetic elements of classroom dramatizations and dramatic performances.

- Students explain how the wants and needs of characters are similar to and different from their own.

- Students articulate emotional responses to and explain personal preferences about the whole as well as the parts of dramatic performances.

- Students analyze classroom dramatizations and, using appropriate terminology, constructively suggest alternative ideas for dramatizing roles, arranging environments, and developing situations along with means of improving the collaborative processes of planning, playing, responding, and evaluating.

CONTENT STANDARD #8
Understanding context by recognizing the role of theatre, film, television, and electronic media in daily life

ACHIEVEMENT STANDARD

- Students identify and compare similar characters and situations in stories and dramas from and about various cultures, illustrate with classroom dramatizations, and discuss how theatre reflects life.

- Students identify and compare the various settings and reasons for creating dramas and attending theatre, film, television, and electronic media productions.

Theatre (5–8)

In theatre, the artists create an imagined world about human beings; it is the role of the actor to lead the audience into this visual, aural, and oral world. To help students in grades 5–8 develop theatre literacy, it is important that they learn to see the created world of theatre through the eyes of the playwright, actor, designer, and director. Through active creation of theatre, students learn to understand artistic choices and to critique dramatic works. Students should, at this point, play a larger role in the planning and evaluation of their work. They should continue to use drama as a means of confidently expressing their world view, thus developing their "personal voice." The drama should also introduce students to plays that reach beyond their communities to national, international, and historically representative themes.

CONTENT STANDARD #1
Script writing by the creation of improvisations and scripted scenes based on personal experience and heritage, imagination, literature, and history

ACHIEVEMENT STANDARD

- Students, individually and in groups, create characters, environments, and actions that create tension and suspense.

- Students refine and record dialogue and action.

CONTENT STANDARD #2
Acting by developing basic acting skills to portray characters who interact in improvised and scripted scenes

ACHIEVEMENT STANDARD

- Students analyze descriptions, dialogue, and actions to discover, articulate, and justify character motivation and invent character behaviors based on the observation of interactions, ethical choices, and emotional responses of people.

- Students demonstrate acting skills (such as sensory recall, concentration, breath control, diction, body alignment, control of isolated body parts) to develop characterizations that suggest artistic choices.

- Students, in an ensemble, interact as the invented characters.

CONTENT STANDARD #3
Designing by developing environments for improvised and scripted scenes

ACHIEVEMENT STANDARD

- Students explain the functions and interrelated nature of scenery, properties, lighting, sound, costumes, and makeup in creating an environment appropriate for the drama.

- Students analyze improvised and scripted scenes for technical requirements.

- Students develop focused ideas for the environment using visual elements (line, texture, color, space), visual principles (repetition, balance, emphasis, contrast, unity), and aural qualities (pitch, rhythm, dynamics, tempo, expression) from traditional and nontraditional sources.

- Students work collaboratively and safely to select and create elements of scenery, properties, lighting, and sound to signify environments, and costumes and makeup to suggest character.

CONTENT STANDARD #4
Directing by organizing rehearsals for improvised and scripted scenes

ACHIEVEMENT STANDARD

- Students lead small groups in planning visual and aural elements and in rehearsing improvised and scripted scenes, demonstrating social, group, and consensus skills.

CONTENT STANDARD #5

Researching by using cultural and historical information to support improvised and scripted scenes

ACHIEVEMENT STANDARD

- Students apply research from print and nonprint sources to script writing, acting, design, and directing choices.

CONTENT STANDARD #6

Comparing and incorporating art forms by analyzing methods of presentation and audience response for theatre, dramatic media (such as film, television, and electronic media), and other art forms

ACHIEVEMENT STANDARD

- Students describe characteristics and compare the presentation of characters, environments, and actions in theatre, musical theatre, dramatic media, dance, and visual arts.

- Students incorporate elements of dance, music, and visual arts to express ideas and emotions in improvised and scripted scenes.

- Students express and compare personal reactions to several art forms.

- Students describe and compare the functions and interaction of performing and visual artists and audience members in theatre, dramatic media, musical theatre, dance, music, and visual arts.

CONTENT STANDARD #7

Analyzing, evaluating, and constructing meanings from improvised and scripted scenes and from theatre, film, television, and electronic media productions

ACHIEVEMENT STANDARD

- Students describe and analyze the effect of publicity, study guides, programs, and physical environments on audience response and appreciation of dramatic performances.

- Students articulate and support the meanings constructed from their and others' dramatic performances.

- Students use articulated criteria to describe, analyze, and constructively evaluate the perceived effectiveness of artistic choices found in dramatic performances.

- Students describe and evaluate the perceived effectiveness of students' contributions to the collaborative process of developing improvised and scripted scenes.

CONTENT STANDARD #8

Understanding context by analyzing the role of theatre, film, television, and electronic media in the community and in other cultures

ACHIEVEMENT STANDARD

- Students describe and compare universal characters and situations in dramas from and about various cultures and historical periods, illustrate in improvised and scripted scenes, and discuss how theatre reflects a culture.

- Students explain the knowledge, skills, and discipline needed to pursue careers and avocational opportunities in theatre, film, television, and electronic media.

- Students analyze the emotional and social impact of dramatic events in their lives, in the community, and in other cultures.

- Students explain how culture affects the content and production values of dramatic performances.

- Students explain how social concepts such as cooperation, communication, collaboration, consensus, self-esteem, risk taking, sympathy, and empathy apply in theatre and daily life.

GLOSSARY OF BASIC DRAMA AND THEATRE TERMS

acting area—the space in which the dramatic activity occurs

action—the events that happen in a play or story

"action"—a spoken cue that signals actors to begin acting

actor—a person who plays a role or character in any dramatic activity

articulate—speak clearly enough to be understood

audience—persons who observe and react to a dramatic activity

audience's perspective—the dramatic activity as viewed by observers

believability—portrayal of a role in a manner that is credible and convincing

"blackout"—a lighting cue that calls for the stage to be totally darkened in a split second

blocking—the basic movements and positions of the actors on stage

cast—all the actors who play characters in a dramatic activity

characters—the people or animals (and also inanimate objects that move and talk) in a story or play

communication—the verbal and nonverbal exchange of ideas and meanings among people

concentration—an acting skill; the actor's focused attention on what's happening at each moment during the drama

conflict—the problem, struggle, or tension in a play or story

cue—any word, sound, or action that signals the beginning of another word, sound, or action

"curtain"—a spoken cue (generally used in rehearsals) that indicates that the dramatic action is about to start; it may also be said to indicate the completion of a scene

dialogue—the words spoken by actors playing characters in a drama

director—the person who interprets a play, rehearses the actors, and makes artistic decisions about a dramatic production

downstage—the part of the stage or acting area closest to the audience

energy—vitality and intensity of expression, movement, poses, and other acting choices

ensemble—the cooperation of all the people who work as a team with others while participating in drama

focus—the words, actions, or images intended to receive the audience's attention

"freeze"—a spoken cue that signals actors to stop whatever they are doing and remain perfectly still and silent

improvisation—the spontaneous, unscripted creation of a scene or dialogue by actors

in character—describes acting choices that accurately communicate information about the character and the drama's circumstances

levels—the relative positions (high, medium, low) of actors in relationship to one another on stage to heighten visual interest

lines—words that actors speak in the dramatic activity

mime/pantomime—the silent use of body, hand, and face movements to show imaginary objects or experiences

monologue—a speech by one person

motivation—the reasons behind a character's actions and words

"places"—a spoken signal for actors to get ready to begin acting and for observers to give their attention to the actors

playwright—the person who writes a play

plot—the beginning, middle, and end of a play or story

point of concentration—a specific spot or small object upon which actors focus their eyes and energy

portray—to play a role

project—to speak loudly enough to be heard easily by observers and participants in the drama activity

props—objects that actors hold or use while on stage

rehearsal—a practice session for actors

role—a character in any dramatic activity

role drama/role play—an improvisational drama strategy guided by an idea or objective in which the actor pretends to be someone or something else

scene—a portion of a play or story that has a beginning, middle, and end

script—a play in written format

sense memory—recall of personal feelings, sensations, and experiences by actors to help them portray characters in drama activities

setting—the place and time of a play or story

side coaching—when the teacher or director comments to the actors while they are acting

slow motion—movement that is deliberately exaggerated and much slower than the same movement performed at a normal pace

stage left—the playing area to the actor's left

stage picture—the overall look of the actors and visual elements on the stage as seen from the audience's perspective

stage right—the playing area to the actor's right

subtext—the underlying meanings of a character's words and actions

suspension of disbelief—an implicit agreement among actors and audience to pretend that the dramatic action is real and happening for the first time

tableau—a silent frozen picture made by people holding poses to create a visual image of a moment in a story

teacher-in-role—a drama technique in which the teacher plays a role and interacts with the students who are playing roles

tempo—speed of speech

text—the written form of a story or play

upstage—the part of the stage or acting area farthest away from the audience

upstaging—any noise or action that takes attention away from the focus of the drama activity